THE BROKEN COMPASS

THE
BROKEN COMPASS

A STUDY OF THE MAJOR COMEDIES
OF BEN JONSON

Edward B. Partridge

GREENWOOD PRESS, PUBLISHERS
WESTPORT, CONNECTICUT

Library of Congress Cataloging in Publication Data

Partridge, Edward Bellamy, 1916-
    The broken compass.

    Reprint of the 1958 ed. published by Columbia Uni-
versity Press, New York.
    Bibliography: p.
    Includes index.
    1.   Jonson, Ben, 1573?-1637--Criticism and interpre-
tation. 2. Figures of speech. 3.   Jonson, Ben,
1573?-1637--Style. I. Title.
[PR2638.P3 1976]   822'.3   75-38386
ISBN 0-8371-8662-5

Originally published in 1958 by Columbia University Press,
New York

Reprinted with the permission of Edward B. Partridge

Reprinted in 1976 by Greenwood Press,
a division of Williamhouse-Regency Inc.

Library of Congress Catalog Card Number 75-38386

ISBN 0-8371-8662-5

Printed in the United States of America

Contents

PREFACE

PREFACES at best warn; at worst, justify. This one does both. In it I should like to make clear, first, what I conceive to be the province of studies of imagery, and, second, what I have tried to do in this study of Jonson's imagery.

If a dramatist is any good, he is usually taken over by readers, who waft him away to that impossible country, dramatic literature, and there study his plays as though they were literary works. Breathing that rarefied air, they transform dialogue meant to be spoken into sentences written to be read. The play is likely to become a novel or a narrative poem or a case study rather than to remain what it was originally meant to be—a series of speeches for actors to deliver in order to produce an aesthetic experience in anyone who listens. Now, of course, standards used in literary analysis can be applied to plays—indeed, and this is part of the point I am going to make, *must* be applied to plays because plays use words just as fundamentally as poems or novels do. But these standards must be applied in a way that never once forgets that the play is a play, that the characters are primarily dramatic devices, and that the words require non-literary interpreters that no literary form requires. In other words, as Susanne Langer put it, drama is 'poetry', but not literature. It is poetry because it creates its imaginative experience partly, and in some cases primarily, by means of words: a good dramatist like Shakespeare or Shaw may talk his play alive without setting or costumes or lighting— just several good actors. But it is not 'literature', not even when it is printed in magnificent folios, because it was not originally put down on paper in order to be read and because, properly speaking, it never can be simply read.

Still, though drama is not literary, it is verbal. All drama uses words, and the greatest drama uses words to create its finest effects. Neo-Aristotelians such as Elder Olson claim that diction is the least important element in drama. That, I think, is wrong. To begin with, not much is gained by ranking the elements of drama as critics since Aristotle have been prone to do. Spectacle—in the bare sense of something seen—is inevitable if a play is produced, just as rhetoric or *dianoia* is present, so long as dialogue is spoken; but is anything momentous gained by thinking *dianoia* more important than spectacle or either less important than *ethos*? Better thar this meaningless ranking is a recognition that the play involves a fusion of several elements, none self-existing, each requiring some or all the others for its final expression. This recognition leads to my second point: where would plot be without diction? Imagine *Macbeth* dependent on dancing and pantomime, without the words that Shakespeare wrote. Contrast the dumb show in *Hamlet* with even the weakest scene in the rest of the play. To put it positively: plot needs diction in order to operate most fully; physical action, music, scenes and machines, helpful as they can be, are not enough to express the intricacies and the depths of a good play. The diction of many plays can be— and in Renaissance plays frequently is—a central way by which the audience knows men in action. Man speaking was apparently to Shakespeare man at his most characteristic activity. '*Speech*', as Jonson said, 'is the only benefit man hath to expresse his excellencie of mind above other creatures. It is the Instrument of *Society*.'[1]

Diction is worth analysing, then, because it is one way of creating the dramatic effect. But it is not the only way, and any study of it must recognize its limitations. Since imagery (that is, metaphorical language) is only one aspect

---

[1] C. H. Herford and Percy and Evelyn Simpson, eds., *Ben Jonson* (Oxford, 1925-1952), VIII, 620-621. From now on, this edition will be referred to as 'Herford and Simpson'.

of diction, studies of imagery are even more severely limited, as the following paragraphs attempt to show.

Linguistic critics are sometimes like those torturers who, according to Ben Jonson, bring all wit to the rack. Anxious to make a certain point, such a critic may torture words out of all countenance, finding all their meanings, but stressing only the meanings which agree with his thesis. He twists, stretches, shortens, racks, and betrays words. He reads sentences for their least obvious interpretation and emphasizes ambiguities more than direct meanings. Ambiguities have become the seven deadly virtues of many modern critics. They are virtues because literature, by its nature, tends to be oblique and ambiguous, though there are, as Tillyard put it, degrees of obliquity. But ambiguities can be deadly if the critic is enticed into pursuing them with no more than an occasional glance at the obvious meanings of the poem or play. This is not to deny that, in some works, especially in lyric poems, the total effect may be achieved by what is called, rather pretentiously, 'a contrapuntal interplay of various ambiguities'. The point is that the surface meanings of a work should never be lightly dismissed in an intense pursuit of the subtle meanings. All special approaches to a piece of literature have weaknesses inherent in them, and this kind of word-torturing seems to be one weakness of the linguistic approach.

Of course, linguistic critics are not the only ones who rack words. Actually, like many crimes, such painful interpretation has had a most respectable history. Think of how much torturing a Greek professor's private lecture notes on poetics and rhetoric have suffered at the hands of all critics within the last twenty-five hundred years! How many other teachers would want their own lecture notes subjected to so close a scrutiny? But a crime, unfortunately, does not become less reprehensible as it becomes more frequent. There is no justification for such witlessness except to point out that a poem, even a long dramatic poem such as an Elizabethan play, almost demands this kind of criticism because words take on specialized meanings in specialized contexts. Like the names of characters in plays, the meanings of words tend to be concentrated by their use within two hours, by a few speakers, in a special universe of discourse. But this is an explanation of how a critic is seduced, and not a justification for his seduction. It is still an error, no matter how fashionable it has now become, to flee from the obvious and the rational as though they were contaminated. The solution is not to ignore the implications of a work, but to understand the relation between them and the total effect.

Any study of a play which concentrates on its diction is open to a more serious error than the search for ambiguities —more serious because less easily detected. It is this: an analysis of the diction or of one part of the diction such as the imagery throws the whole work out of focus because it puts undue emphasis on a single element in the total artistic effect. Such an error, bad enough in a lyric or narrative poem, is even worse in a play which is heard without necessarily being closely examined. Semanticists or Gestaltists might point out that the error begins when an artistic whole is thought of in terms of 'elements'. They may be right, but how else can one criticize anything as complex as a play without provisionally concentrating on separate aspects such as the metrical pattern, the tone, the *mise en scène*, or those dramatic devices called 'characters'? Indeed, the same charge brought against imagery can be brought against any one of these elements: attention to it distorts, to some degree, the total effect. The cure for this distortion is certainly not the one with which most teachers are familiar: 'Don't analyse this poem, please; just read it. Why tear it to pieces? I've never liked *Macbeth* since high school, when . . .' The cure will come, if it comes at all, both from the critic and from the common reader, the man whom critics sometimes forget. One function of the critic should be to show the relation between the special aspect he is concerned with and the total meaning of the work. The common reader also has an active critical function. By the 'common reader' I mean anyone who reads a literary work for pleasure (sometimes even a teacher) or for necessity (students, teachers, scholars), but who is not writing an essay on the work. His sense and sensitivity will readjust the focus so that the work can be seen in its totality. Part of his active function as a reader is to relate the part to the whole and to evaluate what special studies contribute to an understanding of the whole experience.

A study of imagery, then, can be objected to on at least two grounds: frequently it tortures words, and always it distorts the total effect of a play. These can be serious limitations to the usefulness of such studies. And there are others. A third limitation, closely allied to the distortion already mentioned, comes from the misuse of the word 'pattern' (or, more recently, 'structure'). Maud Bodkin applied Jung's theory of 'primordial images' to poetry and found what she called 'archetypal patterns'. Later Muriel Bradbrook observed that, reacting from the nineteenth century concern with characters, modern critics sometimes referred to a play 'as though "the pattern of the imagery" or some other kindred abstraction were the axis of it'.[1] To her this is as absurd as the concern with characters, and her criticism is certainly justified if 'pattern' is thought of as an 'abstraction' from the play. So long as one does not take either 'pattern' or 'structure' too seriously, there is no harm done. Either term may even be justifiably used if it is apparent that in speaking of the pattern or structure of images one is really trying to analyse the effect of the whole play. Cecil Day Lewis evidently uses 'pattern' in this sense

[1] M. C. Bradbrook, *Themes and Conventions of Elizabethan Tragedy* (Cambridge: University Press, 1935), 29.

in the third chapter of *The Poetic Image*. But if either 'pattern' or 'structure' leads one to assume that there is a structure of images which has an independent existence when abstracted from the total work, one may be led to the further assumption that the pattern of imagery is a kind of key which, to those who have it, unlocks the inmost secrets of the play—secrets barred from the infidels outside. There are no keys to a complex work of art and no short-cuts to understanding it. Besides, the imagery is not something laid on a play after the plot is thought out. If it is meaningful at all, it is unified with the plot, the characters, and the verse, all of which help to create the play. Properly, a study of imagery is only one more way of getting inside a literary work. It is not the only way and, for some works, may not be the best way.

This suggests a fourth limitation: an analysis of imagery is not uniformly useful. Some plays of Jonson, such as *Poetaster* and *Catiline*, are not much illuminated by a study of their metaphorical language. The relative bareness of the diction of such plays is not, in itself, a proof of lack of artistic merit. Their direct diction may be as good for Jonson's aesthetic purpose as the highly metaphorical language of *Volpone*.

A fifth limitation is that imagery cannot be safely used to settle questions about the canon of an author. So perceptive a critic as Kenneth Burke claims that imagery in what he calls 'associated clusters' is the most obvious clue to the symbolic action in a writer's work. These clusters can reveal to us what kinds of images and situations go with a writer's notions of heroism, villainy, and despair. So far, so good: most writers probably tend to repeat psychic correlatives in their metaphors and symbols. Keats was charmed by casements; and Blake by children. But writers also repeat each other or take their imagery from a common stock. Massinger borrowed Jonson's imagery extensively, and

Congreve apparently was content to sharpen the duller wit and polish the cruder metaphors of other writers. This kind of imitation was so prominent in the Renaissance that one would have a hard time tracking down the first user of a certain image. Hence, to formulate valid criteria, based on imagery, for discovering Jonson's contribution to *Eastward Ho!* seems to me quite impossible.

Nor can imagery be used—by itself—to prove anything about the life or the character or the personality of the writer. Lillian H. Hornstein has demonstrated incisively that Caroline Spurgeon's attempt to picture Shakespeare the man by analysing the imagery of his plays is highly questionable.[1] Jonson, perhaps more than any other Elizabethan, would seem to lend himself to such a method because so many of his plays have a subjective element (as well as a great objective element) and because there is so much external evidence to guide one. But even with him there is more risk involved than there would be value received. An essay on Jonson by Edmund Wilson shows how risky such biographical inferences are. Though Wilson does not rest his whole argument on the imagery, he makes enough use of it to warrant considering his essay here. According to Wilson, Jonson is an obvious example of the 'anal erotic' because his personality illustrates the usual triad of such maladjusted people—orderliness, parsimony, and obstinacy —and because he displays their 'hoarding and withholding instinct' to a high degree.[2] To prove this interesting theory Wilson interprets not merely the external evidence of the conversations with Drummond and his life, but also the internal evidence of his writings. For example, when Jonson praises Shakespeare for being of an 'open and free nature'

[1] Hornstein, 'Analysis of Imagery: a Critique of Literary Method', *PMLA*, LVII (1942), 638-653. See also Mario Praz's review of Miss Spurgeon's book in *English Studies*, XVIII (1936), 177-181.
[2] Wilson, *The Triple Thinkers* (New York: Oxford University Press, 1948), 218. The essay on Jonson was not in earlier editions of this work.

and for flowing 'with that facility, that sometime it was
necessary he should be stopped', the diction, according to
Wilson, reveals Jonson's constipated nature. This is
evidently another example of Wilson's wound-and-bow
theory of interpreting literature: the kind of literary work
an artist creates is inseparable from the disease or disability
he has.

Wilson is, of course, right in assuming that there is a
relation between a poet's personality and his artistic works,
but the crucial questions are—what kind of relation, and to
what extent does the diction reveal the writer? Simply on the
basis of Wilson's method, one could discover many worse
things about Jonson than anal eroticism. Why, the man was
at least a latent cannibal or a suppressed werewolf. What else
can all the symbolic eating in his plays mean? Furthermore,
his contemporaries sometimes referred to him as the 'Man-
Eater'. The first answer one is tempted to give such
criticism is, simply, 'Who cares?' There are passages enough
to support any of several sensational interpretations, but
who cares how obscene Ben Jonson might have been as a
man? To read his plays in order to discover what he was like
as a person is, aside from the probability that the discovery
would be unpleasant, scarcely rewarding as an aesthetic
experience. Surely there are better reasons for reading
literature than to find out what Jonson or Shakespeare was
really like. Yet such an answer does not meet Wilson's
criticism on its own ground. As a matter of fact, we
frequently do care what kind of man the author was, and
our conception of him does play a part in the total response
to his work. A better answer to Wilson, then, is this: his
criticism may be right by chance, but his method is dubious,
because he assumes that what a man writes in an artistic
work completely and infallibly reveals his inner nature and
that, from the distance of three hundred years, one can
label a man by means of his diction. Both these assumptions

seem to me wrong because they over-simplify the complex relations between art and character.

Underlying all of these limitations is, of course, the special nature of drama. It is curious that much of the work in imagery has been done by those primarily interested in Shakespeare's dramatic poetry. Drama, the most direct of the mimetic arts using language, as well as the art most dependent on interpreters—that is, actors, musicians, and stage technicians—would seem to be the least adaptable of all forms of 'literature' to studies of imagery. The imitation of men in action—so immediate, so public, so forward-moving—makes it inevitable that imagery is but one of the means by which the dramatist can create the total dramatic effect—and sometimes the least important means, rather than, as in lyric poetry, often the most vivid of means. Since imagery can never swallow the plot, studies of imagery must never swallow the play. Hence, they must always co-operate with studies of other elements in the play—plot ethos, rhetoric, verse, spectacle, and other kinds of diction.

Imagery, thus studied, rarely, if ever, reveals a new insight into the theme of a play or into the general effect of its scenes. Generally, a study of imagery reveals the theme of a play, its tone and the impact of its scenes to be what everything else in the play has suggested it to be. Thus, most of what is new in studies of Shakespearean imagery is bad. Robert Heilman's study of *King Lear* is most convincing where it is most conventional. Wilson Knight ceases to be illuminating precisely when he stops listening to the rest of the play and begins to construct his own system of metaphor on and around and sometimes under Shakespeare's. Mind you, I am not saying that studies of imagery are useless: they have a real usefulness in showing how the imagination of an artist works. Frankly, such a revelation is more important than the highly involved philosophical romances that studies of imagery usually offer. Anyone with sufficient ingenuity can come up with a perfectly horrendous system of ideas in a Shakespearean play; but to reveal how the diction of the play, into which the emotions as well as the ideas of the characters have irradiated, fuses with the dramatic structure, the development of characterization, and the use of rhetoric—to pick only three elements—takes tact, humility, and a willingness to say the obvious. To reveal some of the shapes that imagination can take is not a little thing, though it may not be the great thing some analysts want it to be. With the limitations marked out above, then, studies of imagery normally will say what oft was thought (and, one is tempted to add, sometimes better expressed).

This study of Jonson's imagery tries to reveal how his imagination works in his major comedies. The first three chapters define the nature and the functions of metaphorical language and show Jonson's awareness of decorum in the use of metaphor. Chapters four through eight analyse how metaphorical language helps to create the comic effect in *Volpone, The Alchemist, Epicoene* and the last plays. The final chapters attempt to draw the conclusions concerning Jonson's language and the effect of his comedies which (I hope) most sensibly follow from the previous analyses.

I should like to thank the following people who have been kind enough to read all or some of these chapters: O. J. Campbell, Alfred Harbage, Henry W. Wells, W. R. Keast, and Gerrit Y. Lansing. I am also indebted to the editors of *ELH, a Journal of English Literary History* and *The Journal of English and Germanic Philology* for granting me permission to use, in Chapters VII and VIII, material that they had previously published.

CHAPTER I

DEFINITIONS

I

HARDIN CRAIG recently observed that 'late in the twenties of this century a somewhat ancient form of study again came in fashion. Scholars began to study figures of speech under the name of "imagery".'[1] Craig is right in pointing out that frequently *imagery* is a new name for a group of rhetorical devices at least as old as Quintilian. New imagery is but old rhetoric writ large— sometimes too large. Like rhetoric, *imagery* sometimes is used so vaguely that it refers to any aspect of language that the critic wants to bring into his discussion. One excuse for this vague use is that in literary analysis we are always concerned with complex verbal organization; as F. R. Leavis has said, images are 'worth examining—they are there to examine—because they are foci of a complex life, and some-times the context from which they cannot be even pro-visionally separated, if the examination is to be worth any-thing, is a wide one'.[2] To sharpen the focus of this study, I have used the term *imagery* only when at least two (and often more than two) concepts from different areas of experience meet in a single word or sentence or passage. In short, *imagery* here means metaphorical language.

But *imagery* is a confusing term, semantically, because it has referred and still refers to other things than metaphorical language. Originally, *image* pointed to sensory experience with no implication of analogy. But now, in literary criticism,

---

[1] Craig, 'Recent Scholarship of the English Renaissance: a Brief Survey', *Studies in Language and Literature*, ed. G. R. Coffman (Chapel Hill, North Carolina, 1945), 148.
[2] Leavis, 'Imagery and Movement', *Scrutiny*, XIII (September 1945), 119.

as I. A. Richards has observed, *image* may have at least these meanings:

1. 'a copy of a sensation': 'Tis bitter cold.'
2. 'an idea, any event in the mind which represents something': 'The readiness is all.'
3. 'a figure of speech, a double unit involving a comparison': 'This fell sergeant, Death, / Is strict in his arrest.'[1]

Image can, of course, have other meanings which further complicate its use in criticism, as any reader of English literature since the Renaissance is aware. The confusion comes in when critics from Dryden, Johnson, and Coleridge down to G. Wilson Knight and Caroline Spurgeon use *image* to mean all of these, often in the same passage and often without making clear which meaning they are using. To try to show how, historically, the sensory, the ideal, and the analogical meanings of *image* and *imagery* have become entangled is happily beyond my intention here. I might give one warning: the *OED*, good as it is in giving the various meanings of these terms, fails to show how they have come together in literary criticism. For instance, it gives this definition of *imagery*, after the usual ones of 'images collectively', 'a material representation of something', and 'the formation of mental images': '8. The use of rhetorical images, or such images collectively; descriptive representation of ideas; figurative illustration, esp. of an ornate character.' Here the confusion would seem to be recorded without being clarified. I am not sure what 'rhetorical images' are, but the rest of the definition seems to point toward the ideal and the analogical meanings. The passage cited with this definition is from Puttenham's *Arte of English Poesie* (1589?), where he explains '*Icon* or Resemblance by imagerie': 'But when we liken an humane person to another

---

[1] Richards, *Coleridge on Imagination* (New York, 1935), 32-33. The definitions are Richards's; the examples are mine.

in countenaunce, stature, speach, or other qualitie, it is not called bare resemblance, but resemblaunce by imagerie or pourtrait, alluding to the painters terme, who yeldeth to th' eye a visible representatiō of the thing he describes and painteth in his table.'[1] To cite this passage as an example of 'figurative illustration' is somewhat deceptive, because Puttenham used 'imagerie' to apply simply to one figure (out of over a hundred) and not to all of his figures or even to all of his figures of Resemblance. Still, it is an early—perhaps the earliest—instance of the use of *imagery* for any aspect of figurative language. Puttenham possibly applied *imagery* to Icon because the Latin equivalent of Icon was *Imago*, a figure which compared two things with certain resemblances.[2] More important is the connection that Puttenham makes between figurative language and painting. Since *imagery* could also refer in the sixteenth century to the art of statuary and even of painting, Puttenham may have appropriated it for the figure which most resembles portraiture. That imagery possibly came into literary criticism with a prior reference to the graphic arts may help to explain why images, until recently, were thought of as primarily visual. The Renaissance dictum that 'Painting is silent Poetry and Poetry is Painting that speaks' obviously justified and emphasized this tendency to consider images in poetry as visual.[3] By the time of the neo-classic critics this emphasis on visual images had hardened into a devastating test by which one could judge metaphors: can they be visualized and do they seem sensible when visualized? Such a test, which considerably narrowed the understanding of metaphorical language, only began to be seriously challenged in

---

[1] George Puttenham, *The Arte of English Poesie*, ed. Gladys Willcock and Alice Walker (Cambridge, 1936), 243.

[2] [Cicero?] *Rhetorica ad C. Herennium:* see *similitudo* and *imago*.

[3] In *The Virtues Reconciled: an Iconographical Study* (Toronto, 1947), Samuel C. Chew examines the relationship between verbal and visual imagery in the English Renaissance.

twentieth century criticism, chiefly by I. A. Richards. Richards has frequently pointed out that to try to visualize all metaphors is to mangle many of them and may make one ignore other kinds of images, such as olfactory or auditory.[1]

Disentangling the present meanings of *image* and *imagery* is more important than showing how these meanings have become entangled. *Imagery* in modern literary criticism can refer to three kinds of images (which are not identical with the three meanings of *image* noted by Richards). First, *imagery* can refer to sensory images—that is, the concrete details by which the poet's imagination is realized. Imagery of this kind is not the same as a mere description of an object, as Elder Olson has pointed out, though such images can be used to describe objects as well as bodily feelings.[2] Italian Renaissance critics, such as Mazzoni and Tasso, apparently had this kind of imagery in mind when they called the poet a maker of images: his function is to body forth his vision as vividly as possible. In his analysis of various kinds of sensory images—visual, olfactory, auditory —Richards acutely observes that the efficacy of such images comes not from their vividness as sensations but from their being mental events peculiarly connected with sensation.[3] Second, *imagery* can refer to images which, though not structurally metaphorical, take on symbolic significance because of their context. Such latently symbolic images might seem, if isolated, only concrete details or copies of sensations, but, in the context created by the poet, they can symbolize, there and there only, a complex of emotions and ideas. 'We have heard the chimes at midnight, Master Shallow.' Here the concrete detail, which would be suggestive in isolation, becomes symbolic when spoken by an old Falstaff to an old Shallow concerning their wonderfully mis-

[1] Richards, *The Principles of Literary Criticism* (London, 1924), 121.
[2] Olson, 'William Empson, Contemporary Criticism, and Poetic Diction', *Critics and Criticism: Ancient and Modern*, ed. R. S. Crane (Chicago, 1952), 79-80.
[3] Richards, *The Principles of Literary Criticism*, 119-120.

spent youth. By combining the sad and lonely sound of bells at night with the contextual references to roistering, night-wandering, and amorous dallying, the spectator loads the concrete image of' chimes at midnight with symbolic meaning, so that Falstaff's remark suggests the pathos of growing old, the ironic pleasure of remembering past pleasure, and the curious satisfaction of having had his life in his time. This miraculous transformation of image into symbol has been described in many different ways. When Coleridge analyses the shaping power of the imagination, he is referring, I think, to this kind of imagery and not, as is sometimes thought, primarily to metaphorical language. Eliot's 'objective correlative' is, among other things, a modern way of describing this imagery. Robert Frost may also be alluding to this movement of image toward symbol when he says, 'Imagery and after-imagery are about all there is to poetry. Synecdoche and synecdoche.'[1] R. P. Blackmur's fourth category in criticism deals with the way an image 'provisionally, and for once only' is made into a symbol. His example is especially good: the doctor in *Madame Bovary* wants to marry Emma when he sees her tip her head back and insert her tongue into a cordial glass. 'She is given as nubile, ripe, romantic, and ready. In this image—this touch of the actual—are present, by authority, the institutions, conventions, and fictional formulas that have to do with marriage.'[2] A recent writer on the aesthetic use of language, M. Hope Parker, uses *imagery* exclusively for this kind of image, avoiding any use of the term for the first kind or for the third.[3] This third kind of *imagery* is, of course, metaphorical language.

[1] Quoted by Gorham B. Munson in *Robert Frost: a Study of Sensibility and Good Sense* (New York, 1927), 97.
[2] Blackmur, 'Notes on Four Categories in Criticism', *Sewanee Review*, LIV (Autumn, 1946), 587.
[3] Parker, *Language and Reality: a Course in Contemporary Criticism* (London, 1949), 1-40.

Dealing with imagery in literature is so difficult because these three kinds of images work together and shade off into each other. The second kind is obviously transitional between the non-metaphorical concrete image and the metaphorical image; psychologically, it is a sensory image, but it is lifted to the level of symbol when, in interaction with its context, it attracts to itself or draws up out of itself, by its very suggestiveness as a sensory image, meanings and emotions not otherwise expressible. These three kinds of images can be distinct: analogies need not be concrete or sensory any more than sensory references need be analogical —or even latently symbolic. But, normally, in literary works, metaphorical language is sensory so that the analogy becomes concrete, and, often, the concrete image, under the pressure of its context, takes on symbolic meaning.

To show how profound this involvement of the three images is and how confusing the use of one term for several distinct poetic processes can be, let us look at an essay by Dryden—'The Author's Apology for Heroic Poetry and Poetic License'. One remark in this essay—'Imaging is, in itself, the very height and life of Poetry'—is used and, I think, misused by two recent writers on imagery.[1] Both Father Stephen J. Brown[2] and C. Day Lewis[3] interpret 'imaging' to mean metaphorical language. But does it refer to the creation of analogies or to concrete realization by sensory reference? The rest of the paragraph from which this is taken makes one pause. 'Imaging is, in itself, the very height and life of Poetry. It is, as Longinus describes it, a discourse, which, by a kind of enthusiasm, or extraordinary emotion of soul, makes it seem to us that we behold those things which the poet paints, so as to be pleased with them, and to admire them. If poetry be imitation, that part of it

[1] 'The Author's Apology for Heroic Poetry and Poetic Licence', *The Essays of John Dryden*, ed. W. P. Ker (Oxford, 1900), I, 186.
[2] Brown, *The World of Imagery* (London, 1927), 98.
[3] C. Day Lewis, *The Poetic Image* (London, 1947), 17-18.

must needs be best which describes most lively our actions and passions; our virtues and vices; our follies and our humours. . . .'[1] The passage of Longinus to which Dryden probably is alluding deals with imaginative visualization or bodying forth rather than with metaphorical language. Images (φαντασίαι), according to Longinus, contribute greatly to rhetorical power: 'In this sense some call them mental representations. In a general way the name of *image* or *imagination* is applied to every idea of the mind, in whatever form it presents itself, which gives birth to speech. But at the present day the word is predominantly used in cases where, carried away by enthusiasm and passion, you think you see what you describe, and you place it before the eyes of your hearers.'[2] Furthermore, Longinus makes a fundamental distinction between images, which belong to the first source of sublimity, and tropes, such as metaphors, similes, and hyperboles, which belong to the fourth source. If Dryden had this passage and these distinctions in mind—as he probably did—the imaging which is the very life of poetry must refer to representation so concrete that it becomes intensely visualized, and not simply to metaphorical language.

But the rest of Dryden's essay does not let us off quite so easily. Both before and after the passage on 'imaging' Dryden deals with metaphorical language, sometimes using *image* where he might have used *hyperbole* or *metaphor*. To illustrate poetic licence, he argues that even the severest writers such as Virgil and Horace made frequent use of the 'hardest metaphors' and the 'strongest hyperboles'. After illustrating his point with passages containing catachreses, he makes this comment: 'In both of these, you see, he fears not to give voice and thought to things inanimate.'[3] This sounds like 'imaging', but it is applied to metaphorical

[1] *Essays of John Dryden*, ed. Ker, I, 186.
[2] [Longinus] *On the Sublime*, ed. W. Rhys Roberts (Cambridge, 1935), 82-85.
[3] *Essays of John Dryden*, ed. Ker, I, 184.

language. Shortly afterwards, he quotes another passage from Virgil containing a hyperbole and concludes that 'you are pleased with the image, without being cozened by the fiction'.[1] Cowley's strong 'images' (his conceits?) are defended in the sentence immediately before the passage on imaging. Immediately after, Dryden quotes a passage from Lucretius to substantiate the point that poetical fictions such as centaurs can be imaged by joining two natures, each of which has a real separate being. Lucretius, according to Dryden, uses *image* oftener than any of the poets—as he certainly does in his Fourth Book, but he never uses it for metaphor or hyperbole. Generally, Lucretius uses *imago* to mean the representation or the *simulacrum* which, according to Epicurean philosophy, comes off things.[2] At any rate, the Epicurean use of *imago* seems to have little connection with Dryden's previous use of *image*. Finally, when he produces an example of 'excellent imaging' from his opera, *The State of Innocence*, it turns out to be a metaphor.

This failure to distinguish concrete image from trope seems confusing to us, but Dryden probably kept the distinctions sharp in his own mind. He does suggest, near the end, a relation between the two that clarifies their separate functions. To express his imaginative fiction (in other words, to 'image'), a poet may admit tropes and figures. This licence, according to Dryden, is the poet's birthright. Metaphorical and figurative language, then, is a vivid means of expressing—that is, of *imaging*—his thought, but it is not the only way of imaging and it may not be the best. If this interpretation be correct, the very height and life of poetry is not metaphorical language *per se* (though metaphors may help to image); the life, the height, is, to use other words of Dryden, 'lively and apt description, dressed in

---

[1] *Ibid.*, 185.

[2] See *De Rerum Natura*, ed. Cyril Bailey (Oxford, 1941), I, 400-1, and III, Commentary.

such colours of speech, that it sets before your eyes the absent object, as perfectly, and more delightfully than nature'.[1] Since the poet is a maker of images, imaging is the direct agent of *mimesis*; imagery (as metaphorical language) is one of the means of imaging.

II

Because these three images—the concrete, the concrete which is potentially symbolic, and the metaphorical—interpenetrate so closely in poetry, they can be separated only provisionally in criticism. But focus is necessary, and the focus here is on metaphorical language. I use *metaphorical language* comprehensively to embrace metaphor, simile, metonymy, synecdoche, symbol, hyperbole, irony, allusion, and allegory. Aristotle was the first to use *metaphorical* in this wider sense when he divided metaphors into four classes: a word transferred from genus to species, species to genus, one species to another, and analogy. A number of commentators on the *Poetics* since then have pointed out that only the last is metaphor proper, and that the first two are really examples of synecdoche and the third of metonymy. The justification for this extended use is that metaphor seems to be the archetypal trope, which is latent in the shyest of allusions as well as in the most permanent of symbols. In metaphor, as in all of these kinds of *metaphorical language*, two things, not necessarily concrete, are '*seen to be in a parallel predicament*'.[2] Though Aristotle did not use the Aristotelian predicaments in defining metaphor, he would have agreed that in metaphor diverse concepts are thrown into a parallel engagement. So would most critics of metaphor since Aristotle. When Dante explained to Can Grande della Scala the 'double' sense in which the *Commedia* is to be

[1] *The Works of John Dryden*, ed. Scott and Saintsbury (Edinburgh, 1884), IX, 96.
[2] Rosemond Tuve, 'Imagery and Logic', *Journal of the History of Ideas*, III (1942), 377.

understood or when Puttenham described how figures draw the mind from plainness to a 'certain doublenesse' or when Johnson told Boswell how metaphorical expression gives you two ideas for one, each phrased for his own age its characteristic view of the parallel predicament of metaphorical discourse. According to this definition, then, the following works in whole or in part would be studies of imagery: the first chapter of the Second Treatise of Dante's *Convivio* (as well as the letter to Can Grande della Scala); Puttenham's *Arte of English Poesie*; Addison's essays on wit; C. S. Lewis's *The Allegory of Love*. Each is a classic study of some phase of imagery in that each analyses the parallel predicament of concepts or images.

In order to understand how imagery works aesthetically, we can concentrate on this archetypal trope, metaphor. Allen Tate has said that metaphor is 'the *pons asinorum* of literary criticism' because any study of metaphor soon involves one in the most radical of psychological and metaphysical problems—problems which literary critics are usually unsuited to solve.[1] That is true, and disheartening. Metaphor looks at first like a mode of discourse, but, as it unfolds, it turns into a problem in metaphysics. For example: allegorizing was the means by which medieval writers expressed the multiple meanings which were thought to be latent in all material objects and in all of man's life. Can one then say that the architecture of metaphors in their allegorical works reflected their stratified feudal society and their dualistic world view? Or could this allegorical technique be the poetic counterpart of that polyphonic composition in which musical phrases are fitted in side by side, with each part being of equal melodic importance? Would it then follow that homophonic music and metaphysical imagery, both of which developed at the end of the

[1] Tate, '*Longinus*', *Lectures in Criticism*. Bollingen Series, XVI (Pantheon Books, 1949), 68-70.

sixteenth century, are related? Or again: can one say that in the age of the Enlightenment metaphor was thought to have a simpler function because metaphysical inquiry had narrowed down largely to those things that everybody knows? This interplay between the metaphorical and the metaphysical is frightening, of course; but, if it is any comfort, one ought to remember that any literary analysis turns one into an unwilling and usually inexpert metaphysician because every poem or play marries the image and the concept in the same impossible way that metaphor does.

A metaphor involves a complex interaction of thoughts and emotions. In order to speak analytically about this interaction, we must have critical terms such as those invented by I. A. Richards (*tenor* and *vehicle*) or those more recently invented by Elder Olson (*referent, analogue*, and *continuum*).[1] Olson's terms seem more useful, but since they are not well known, I have used Richards's. In a simple metaphor such as 'This fell sergeant, Death / Is strict in his arrest', the tenor is 'Death', and the vehicle is 'This fell sergeant [who] Is strict in his arrest'. Without these terms even such thorough treatments of metaphor as Hedwig Konrad's *Étude sur la métaphore* or Gustaf Stern's remarks in *Meaning and Change of Meaning* are crippled.

Critics of figurative language in the past have spent much of their time attempting to classify metaphors, but few of these attempts are now useful aesthetically. Some of them, though helpful to rhetoricians, are otherwise harmless. Only one of Aristotle's several classifications has endured. Rhetoricians generally abandoned the classification given in the *Poetics* and preferred that suggested in the *Rhetoric* and imitated by Quintilian in the *Institutes*: the animate is equated with the inanimate, the inanimate with the animate, the inanimate with the inanimate, and the animate with the

[1] See Richards, *The Philosophy of Rhetoric* (New York, 1936), 97 ff., and Olson, 'William Empson', *Critics and Criticism*, 81.

animate. Much is made of Aristotle's animizing metaphor (the inanimate is equated with the animate) by Hermann Pongs, who builds a whole metaphysic on it in *Das Bild in der Dichtung*. Vico had anticipated this use of the metaphor which 'gives sense and passion to insensate things' when he claimed that 'every metaphor so formed is a fable in brief'.[1] But, though this classification lingers in other works on metaphor, such as Friedrich Brinkmann's *Die Metaphern* (1878), it seems to me to leave the ordinary reader with no sharper awareness of the way metaphor works.

Philologists such as Max Müller and his followers tried to distinguish 'radical' from 'poetical' metaphors—'radical' being those which were the source of new words during the primitive stage of language, and 'poetical' those which are created by poets.[2] But, again, this distinction seems of little help in literary analysis.

A third kind of classification concentrates on either the tenor or the vehicle alone. Some rhetoricians in the eighteenth century thought that the vehicle could be detached and that the tenor—'the plain meaning'—wa sall that finally mattered. Such ignoring of the vehicles obviously results in an impoverishment of the poetic experience. But in some modern studies of imagery there is the reverse practice of thinking that the only thing that really matters is the vehicle and that the tenor can be detached. Thus, in the least convincing part of her study, Caroline Spurgeon made graphs and coloured charts to show how many images (that is, vehicles) of town life or law or hunting Shakespeare used.[3] The most extraordinary of such attempts to classify

---

[1] Giambattista Vico, *The New Science*, trans. T. G. Bergin and M. H. Fisch (Ithaca, N.Y., 1948), 116.

[2] Max Müller, *Lectures on the Science of Language, Second Series* (New York, 1875), 370 ff.

[3] Spurgeon, *Shakespeare's Imagery and What It Tells Us* (Cambridge, 1935). Even a sophisticated critic like Stanley Edgar Hyman can overrate the usefulness of such graphs: he calls them 'invaluable'. Hyman, *The Armed Vision* (New York, 1948), 215-216.

metaphors is that of Edmond Huguet in *Le Langage Figuré au Seizième Siècle* (1933). In the first part of this work Huguet classifies metaphors according to the fields from which they are borrowed, such as religion, customs, commerce; in the second part he classifies them according to the objects which, in the sixteenth century, had been most often described by the aid of metaphors. In other words, there is an exact division between the two elements: the first part being exclusively concerned with vehicles; the second with tenors. The trouble is that this concern with either tenor or vehicle alone is artistically irrelevant. A statistical listing of either tenor or vehicle which neglects the use of a metaphor in a certain situation by a certain person ignores the only relationships which matter: that is, the interaction between tenor and vehicle, and the relation between the metaphor and its context.

Classifications which are concerned with these relationships are aesthetically more relevant. I. A. Richards tried to distinguish a 'sense' metaphor from an 'emotive' metaphor. In the former the metaphoric shift is occasioned and justified by a similarity between the object the word is usually applied to and the new object. In the 'emotive' metaphor the shift occurs through some similarity between the feelings aroused by the new situation and those aroused by the normal situation.[1] Later, in his *Philosophy of Rhetoric* Richards held to this same distinction: 'A very broad division may be made between metaphors which work through some direct resemblance between the two things, the tenor and the vehicle, and those which work through some common attitude which we may . . . take up toward them both.'[2] This division does not really divide. Almost all 'sense' metaphors are 'emotive' in Richards's meaning of the word, just as most 'emotive' metaphors involve some resemblance

[1] Richards, *Practical Criticism* (New York, 1939), 221.
[2] Richards, *The Philosophy of Rhetoric*, 117-118.

31

between the tenor and the vehicle. Besides, this classification implies that a human being is split, too simply, into intellect and emotion, though Richards does insist in *Practical Criticism* that the total meaning of a passage is always a blend of several contributory meanings—sense, feeling, tone. The same split is implied in Henry Wells's *Poetic Imagery* where we are told to distinguish poetic metaphor from analogy, which is a logical figure, and from exemplification, which is a literary figure. Poetic metaphor is sympathetic, prejudicial, and 'emotive'. If Wells means by 'poetic metaphor' a metaphor that appears in a poem, there can be no fault to find, but he recognizes a poetic metaphor by the presence of a 'subjective element'. His examples show the weakness of this position. According to him, 'the sky is as grey as lead' is not a poetic simile, but 'If a sportsman likens a drooping flag to the corpse of a brilliant bird', the comparison is poetic.[1] Yet neither one by itself seems to me poetic, and either one, in a poem, could be used poetically. The context cannot be ignored in deciding whether a metaphor is poetic or not, good or bad, decorative or functional. Wells worked out a more meaningful classification when he concentrated on the relationship between the tenor and the vehicle and marked out seven types of imagery in Elizabethan literature, which he called the decorative, the sunken, the violent (or fustian), the radical, the intensive, the expansive, and the exuberant. But these, like all meaningful classifications ultimately, are really different uses that metaphors can be put to.

Both the Spurgeon method and the Richards method of classifying imagery have recently been criticized by Rosemond Tuve in *Elizabethan and Metaphysical Imagery*. The basis for classifying images used by the Spurgeon school—that is, the area from which comparisons are drawn —seems to Miss Tuve 'unfirm'. Instead, she thinks that

[1] Henry W. Wells, *Poetic Imagery* (New York, 1924), 21-23.

images ought to be defined and classified according to their logical bases in the Aristotelian predicaments, such as substance, quality, and manner of doing. Such a classification is particularly valuable, according to her, in analysing Elizabethan or seventeenth century imagery because Renaissance writers, schooled in logic, were acutely conscious of the structural and logical nature of images. For instance, the close relation between defining and the creation of poetry appears when one tries to define the true nature of any subject or to divide the whole into its parts or the substance from its accidents: all produce images. Furthermore, many images are produced by thinking from such 'places of invention' as *similitude*, *adjuncts*, and *cause*.[1]

Miss Tuve's criticism brings us to the heart of this whole problem of classification. To begin with, she is certainly right in criticizing the method used by Miss Spurgeon, whose choice of a class for some of the complex images in *Hamlet* and *King Lear* seems arbitrary. Simply as a method, Miss Tuve's classification is probably the most sensible one yet advanced because it involves less disputable criteria. In the second place, her emphasis on the logical bases of imagery is valuable as a corrective to the tendency of such critics as Richards, Wells, and Cleanth Brooks to distinguish too simply a logical image from an emotive image. This whole argument about logic and emotion in imagery may come from a confusion of the two relationships of a metaphor—first, the tenor-vehicle relationship and, second, the relationship between the whole metaphor (that is, the tenor plus the vehicle) and the context in which it appears. If Richards and Brooks confine their statements to the first relationship, they may be right in claiming that the effect of few metaphors can be traced to the logical connection

---

[1] Tuve, *Elizabethan and Metaphysical Imagery: Renaissance Poetic and Twentieth Century Critics* (Chicago, 1947), 254, 287, 299, 300-323.

between a tenor like a Grecian urn and a vehicle like a 'still unravished bride of quietness'. Just so, Miss Tuve may be right if she refers to the second relationship, because even the least logical metaphor may have a logical function in its context: it may serve to define the true nature of something or to describe its manner of acting.

To emphasize unduly either the emotional power or the logical function of metaphors may keep one from perceiving the delicate mingling of feeling and thought in artistic works. In all good literature (and not merely, as Eliot once thought, in metaphysical poetry) there is a fusion of thought with feeling or a perception of thought in terms of emotion or of emotion in terms of thought. Perhaps Coleridge was trying to express this interpenetration of emotion and intellect when he observed that figures of speech were 'originally the offspring of passion, but now the adopted children of power'.[1] Certainly anyone who looks back to Coleridge as much as Richards and Brooks claim to should remember that it was Coleridge who wrote that the imagination was 'first put in action by the will and understanding, and retained under their irremissive, though gentle and un-noticed, control'; 'understanding' was Coleridge's term for the mental faculty by which we arrange and generalize on our sense perceptions.[2] The fate of Richards may be instructive: once one makes a radical distinction between scientific and emotive language, one may end with either a predominantly emotive language, like that of Surrealist poets, or a predominantly scientific language like Basic English (C. K. Ogden has called Basic English a 'universal scientific language'); both are unconvincing except for the lowest level of communication.

There should never have been a quarrel over the presence

[1] Coleridge, *Biographia Literaria*, ed. J. Shawcross (New York, 1907), II, 50. For a recent discussion on this point see Philip Wheelwright, *The Burning Fountain* (Bloomington, 1954), pp. 33-40, 45-50.
[2] *Ibid.*, II, 12.

of logic even in poetic language. Of course, language has an inner logic, imposed partly by its symbolic nature and partly by the syntactical structure of phrases and sentences. Being an element in language, images are necessarily involved in such logic. The recognition that the function of an image may be logical need not deny the emotional power of imagery. Emotion, which gathers around even primarily logical symbols such as numbers (3 or 7, for example), suffuses dramatic speech in poems and plays. Images pick up emotion from their context—from the rhythm of the speech, the sound of the words, the tempo of the scene, the tone, and the plot. The important fact about images in literary work is this contextual relationship (of which their logical base is one element) rather than any undue emphasis on either the logical function or the emotional attitude.

But the fundamental question which few of the classifiers answer remains: why classify at all? Miss Tuve's answer appears when she is searching for the basic element by which the nature of an image may be defined: '. . . we have otherwise no basis on which all readers are bound to agree, for comparing one image with another—in another poem by the same poet, in another poet, or in another literary period'.[1] But how much value is there in comparing one image with another? There may be a little value in comparing an image Jonson used in *Volpone* with a similar one he used in *The Alchemist*. But is there more than a detective interest in comparing an image that Jonson used in *The Alchemist* with an image Yeats used in 'Among School Children'? The value in any study of imagery comes not from such comparisons but from the added light that is thrown on specific literary works. One should study images, as Richards, Wells, Spurgeon, Tuve, and others have shown at times, in order to discover what images do in a certain

[1] Tuve, *Elizabethan and Metaphysical Imagery*, 253.

context. This action within the context or the interaction between tenor and vehicle may suggest a tentative classification for that poem or play, but this classification would have no validity outside the universe of discourse of that particular work.

CHAPTER II

THE FUNCTIONS OF
METAPHORICAL LANGUAGE

T HE twentieth century may be the heir of all the ages, but so far as literary criticism goes it has preferred not to use all of its inheritance. The 'ornamental' metaphor of ancient rhetoric, which reappeared in the Renaissance and in neo-classical criticism, appears rarely in modern rhetoric, though it may enter, disguised, into those criticisms of imagery which claim that its chief function is to give elevation and distinction to style. But only a brave man (like Elder Olson) actually uses *ornamental* in speaking of images. Gilbert Murray's statement that Sappho's love poetry is 'too serious to allow room for metaphor or imaginative ornament' is almost unparalleled except among classical scholars, rhetoricians, and others similarly insulated from fashionable modern criticism.[1] Medieval allegorizing, which detected a number of senses, usually four, in Scripture and in secular poetry, has been transformed into 'levels of significance' or 'layers of meaning'. I. A. Richards has observed that a characteristic of plays during the Elizabethan age was the 'possibility of being enjoyed at many levels'.[2] T. S. Eliot is more explicit about such 'levels of significance' when he explains that, in a mature play, 'For the simplest auditors there is the plot, for the more thoughtful the character and conflict of character, for the more literary the words and phrasing, for the more musically sensitive the rhythm, and for auditors of greater sensitiveness and understanding a meaning which reveals itself gradually.'[3] The chief contemporary allegorists—the followers of G. Wilson

---

[1] Murray, *A History of Ancient Greek Literature* (New York, 1912), 93.
[2] Richards, *Principles of Literary Criticism*, 211.
[3] Eliot, *The Use of Poetry and the Use of Criticism* (Cambridge, Mass., 1933), 146.

Knight and Marxist critics like Christopher Caudwell—secularize and narrow, though rarely isolate so sharply as Eliot does, the possible senses in which writing can be interpreted. But, except for the avoidance of 'ornament' as a term and the curious transformation of medieval allegorizing, most past theories of the functions of metaphor are operative in modern criticism. Metaphysical imagery has been resurrected by the criticism and exemplified in the poetry of T. S. Eliot and his followers. The eighteenth century distrust of metaphorical language and its habit of getting at the plain text after the metaphors have been cut away confront teachers often in classes of literature. Perhaps most prominent of all in modern criticism is Coleridge's 'shaping spirit of Imagination' whose imagery can unify works of art emotionally and intellectually.

But the problem of metaphorical language, like the whole larger problem of literature, has become more complicated than ever before because, though the old theories of metaphor are available, the old audience is not. If it is true, as R. P. Blackmur claims, that the modern audience badly needs instruction in the 'lost skill of symbolic thinking'—and it seems true—then one crucial problem for modern criticism will continue to be what it has been since Coleridge's time: to re-educate modern readers in the ways metaphor works.[1] Thus far, the larger audience has gained little of its lost skill, and an interest in metaphorical language has been confined to coteries of scholars, critics, and other unacknowledged legislators. Since the Romantic period discussions of metaphor generally have tried to answer several questions: what is the relation between myth and metaphor? how has metaphor operated in the growth of language? what is the function of metaphor in literature? Though these questions are inter-related, only the final question can concern us here.

[1] Blackmur, 'A Burden for Critics', *Lectures in Criticism*, 199.

Metaphor, we have said, involves a complex interaction of thoughts and emotions. It works with what is commonly accepted about two concepts or emotions in order to suggest a third new concept or emotion or several new concepts or emotions out of the interaction of the two. Two kinds of relationships can provisionally be distinguished in meta-phorical language. One kind is the relationship between the tenor and the vehicle. The other kind is the relationship between the whole metaphor (the tenor plus the vehicle) and its context. Cecil Day Lewis may have this distinction in mind when he points out that the component parts of images (that is, the tenor and the vehicle) 'have been brought into an association from which each of them profits and to which (the complete image) each contributes, just as each complete image contributes to and profits from the poem as a whole'.[1] Ultimately, these two relationships cannot be separated because both the tenor and the vehicle, considered separately or together, belong to the context. Metaphor, as Richards correctly says, is fundamentally 'a transaction between con-texts'.[2] For this reason, neither the tenor nor the vehicle can be understood except contextually, and the context may be the sentence or the speech or the scene or, finally, the play. For example, the lines of Claudius in *Hamlet* after he hears Ophelia sing her mad songs:

> O, this is the poison of deep grief; it springs
> All from her father's death. O Gertrude, Gertrude,
> When sorrows come, they come not single spies,
> But in battalions. IV. v. 76-79

Any comment on these metaphors must depend on what we already know from the preceding action of the play. The man who speaks of madness as 'the poison of deep grief' and of sorrows as battalions rather than spies is a king who has used poison once and will use it again and who commands spies rather than, as Fortinbras does, battalions.

[1] Day Lewis, *The Poetic Image*, 35.   [2] Richards, *The Philosophy of Rhetoric*, 94.

Poison and spies are so completely a part of his life that they unconsciously enter his speech as vehicles for his metaphors. Only the whole context of the speech can make us aware of the irony of a poisoner's thinking that poison springs from death or of the pity that one feels for a king, even a murdering king, who is invaded by sorrows. In short, only the rest of the play can tell us what either the tenor or the vehicle means in any single metaphor.

But, for the sake of analysis, we can make a provisional distinction between the tenor-vehicle relationship and the relationship between the whole metaphor and its context. Let us first note some of the interactions between tenor and vehicle. Several kinds of mental and emotional actions occur when a tenor such as Ophelia's madness is said to be 'the poison of deep grief'. For one thing, the similarity suggested between the effects of deep grief and madness tend to make us identify the tenor and the vehicle and suppose that deep grief necessarily poisons Ophelia's sanity with madness. But, at the same time that there is a tendency to identify the two, there is a contrary tendency to resist the identification and to recognize ways in which deep grief need not have poisoned her sanity as it did not poison Hamlet's. This antithetical pull creates the tension which gives life to metaphor. The likenesses observed between tenor and vehicle attract them to each other; the disparities repel them from each other. At the same time we admit that madness or grief's poison springs from death, we know that it does nothing of the kind; nothing springs from death, not even worms. Still, no matter how much of a lie the identification of tenor and vehicle involves, the human mind tends to make the identification, particularly in religious metaphors. Gibbon maliciously quoted Selden's remark that transubstantiation was 'only rhetoric turned into logic'.[1] (Hobbes

---

[1] E. Gibbon, *The History of the Decline and Fall of the Roman Empire*, ed. J. B. Bury (London, 1902), V, 244 n. 1. For the following quotation see VI, 355.

evidently considered it even less than rhetoric because he said that '*transubstantiate*' was one of those words that signify nothing.) Selden observed (and Gibbon, who considered transubstantiation one of the 'most signal triumphs over sense and humanity', enjoyed his observation) that often religious metaphors are misinterpreted by being taken for fact. The Bread to sceptics is only rhetorically, not logically, the Body of Christ, though wars have been fought over the belief that it is literally the Body. Ernst Cassirer may be referring to such identifications when he says that for 'mythic thinking' there is much more in metaphor than a substitution; it is 'mythically conceived as a genuine and direct identification'.[1] Perhaps Richards's belief that a 'command of metaphor' might order life is relevant here. Could a realization that the metaphors of religion were really metaphors and not literal facts have prevented the religious wars of the Reformation?

Though we rarely accept the identifications in poetic imagery as unquestioningly as we accept them in religious imagery (there is a difference between 'belief' in poetry and faith in religion), the brief and intense life of a play or poem forces us toward a provisional acceptance of the lie. Longinus thought that, in metaphor as well as hyperbole, strength of feeling makes us accept the unbelievable as true.[2] The aim of the poetical image, according to him, is 'enthrallment'. We accept the metaphors of a play in the same way that we accept the play itself: we know that it is all an illusion, but so long as we remember that it is an illusion, believing it can be a joy, precisely because we do not have to believe it.

This tendency to identify tenor and vehicle sometimes results in a reverse movement. The mind supposes that identical things are convertible. Aristotle evidently had such convertibility in mind when he wrote that the proportional

---

[1] Cassirer, *Language and Myth*, trans. Susanne Langer (New York, 1946), 94.
[2] [Longinus] *On the Sublime*, ed. W. Rhys Roberts, 139-141.

metaphor should always be transferable reciprocally: 'if the goblet is the shield of Dionysus, then the shield may be properly called the goblet of Ares'.[1] As soon as we are confronted with the metaphor that sorrows come as spies or battalions, we tend to turn it around and ask ourselves what sense it would make to say that spies or battalions come as sorrows—that is, bring sorrows. For example, Polonius spying behind the arras or Fortinbras with his thousands of soldiers. The closer the tenor and vehicle are, the more interaction there is likely to be. When Dol Common in *The Alchemist* is compared to a great lady, there is a tendency to reverse the movement and ask ourselves how a great lady might be like Dol Common. But there is less likelihood of such reverse action when Dol is compared to the Queen of Faery, and still less when she is compared to a castle or Dover pier. There is sometimes this kind of interaction in both the erotic imagery used in mystical works and the religious imagery used in love poems, frequently with the startling if interesting result that religion becomes a form of love, and love a form of religion. Such inversion is suggested so often throughout *The Beggar's Opera* that, near the end, in the explicit fashion of the early eighteenth century, the Beggar openly says, 'Through the whole piece you may observe such a similitude of manners in high and low life, that it is difficult to determine whether (in the fashionable vices) the fine gentlemen imitate the gentlemen of the road, or the gentlemen of the road the fine gentlemen.'[2] If the manners of high and low life are so similar and the highwaymen have so many of the fashionable vices of fine gentlemen, the pressure of the play makes us conclude that the fine gentlemen are no better than highwaymen.

Yet in many metaphors there is so much disparity

---

[1] Aristotle, *Rhetoric*, ed. J. E. C. Welldon (New York, 1886), 240-241.
[2] John Gay, *The Poetical Works of John Gay*, ed. G. C. Faber (London, 1926), 531.

between tenor and vehicle that the interaction is of a different kind from an identification or reversal. The more remote the tenor and vehicle are, the greater is the tension between them. This tension can be used for purposes of wit as Marvell used it in 'The Garden' where the soul

> into the boughs does glide;
> There like a bird it sits and sings,
> Then whets, then combs its silver wings.

Or it can be used for extravagant humour as Jonson used it in *Bartholomew Fair* when Knockem, the horse-courser, refers to women as though they were horses with the gait, the habits, and the diseases of horses. Or it can be used for a gentler kind of humour as Shakespeare used it in *The Winter's Tale* when Florizel tells Perdita that

> This your sheep-shearing
> Is as a meeting of the petty gods
> And you the queen on't.

In all of these examples we are more interested in the disparities between the unlike things which have been brought together than in the similarities. The ways in which birds preening in gardens are not like souls and cannot be thought like souls, or in which women are not like horses, or in which a sheep-shearing is not like a meeting of the gods contrast comically with the likenesses found between the tenor and the vehicle. Richards calls this 'disparity action' and describes it thus: 'In general, there are very few metaphors in which disparities between tenor and vehicle are not as much operative as the similarities. Some similarity will commonly be the ostensive ground of the shift, but the peculiar modification of the tenor which the vehicle brings about is even more the work of their unlikenesses than of their likenesses.'[1] Addison is getting at this same 'disparity

[1] Richards, *The Philosophy of Rhetoric*, 127.

43

action' when he analyses the opposition of ideas in true wit. Such action also takes place in tragic passages. When Lear tells Cordelia to come away to prison where they will 'sing like birds i' the cage' and take upon themselves 'the mystery of things / As if we were God's spies', the fact that they are a deposed king and a captive queen who are about to be murdered, not birds at all, and scarcely their own spies, much less God's, emphasizes the pathos, the irony, and the exaltation of the scene.

All of these kinds of transaction between tenor and vehicle have involved the second kind of relationship—that between the whole metaphor and the context in which it appears. Only the context makes clear both in what sense Lear and Cordelia can be said to 'sing like birds i' the cage', and in what sense there are great disparities between them and caged birds. Only the rest of the play, then, shows how the full meaning of the metaphor—the illusory identification and the immense disparity—emphasizes the tragic stature of Lear and Cordelia who are caught yet never truly caged.

Too much emphasis has been given here, as in most discussions of metaphor, to its mental and cognitive actions. Even Richards, who has pointed out the flaw in attending simply to the conceptual side of the image, seems to intellectualize metaphors when he sets down four possible modes of interpreting them: '1. Extract the tenor and believe that as a statement. 2. Extract the vehicle. 3. Taking tenor and vehicle together, contemplate for acceptance or rejection some statement about their relations. 4. Or accept or refuse the direction which together they would give to our living.'[1] Only the third of these seems to allow much room for feeling or sense experience. As we have already seen, at least part of metaphorical interaction is emotional, though 'emotional' and 'mental' are scarcely adequate to describe the peculiar life of an image. Unfortunately, literary criticism has not

[1] *Ibid.*, 135.

been able to come up with any term for the primary datum of the aesthetic act: its unique fusion of the sensuous, the intuitive, the conceptual, and the emotional. This fusion is not an 'idea' as such, though it may involve ideas or one can talk about it as though it involved ideas; nor is it simply an emotion, though it may arouse in us reactions that depend on our having, or once having had, emotions. Fundamental to this fusion may be some representation of sense experience, but what is 're-presented' to us is not of the same quality as the sense experience outside the aesthetic act. This fusion may involve the intuitive, but no one except Croceans would reduce it to intuition. Just so, metaphor cannot be reduced to any one of the elements—intuitive, ideal, sensuous, emotional—that constitute it. For example, in the analysis of the imagery of Elizabethan plays (which has been disproportionately popular) too much attention is usually paid to the intellectual relationship between tenor and vehicle or to the 'ideas' which the vehicles bring into the play, as though the philosophical pattern of the imagery was all that mattered. But this is wrong. Fundamentally, in plays where an experience is being rendered, rather than a philosophy formulated, the action within the imagery is never simply or even largely conceptual. It may even be quite the opposite—largely emotional and sensuous—especially in the imagery of comedies. One of the favourite manœuvres of a comic dramatist is to violate the decorous or expected relationship between tenor and vehicle: 'Kisse, like a scallop, close', Face advises Dol Common. Such violation arouses surprise and laughter in the listener who is prepared for one set of emotions and, by means of the metaphorical action, given another. Of course, all metaphorical language requires some mental activity, and some requires much mental activity, but normally, in a comedy, the metaphorical language acts primarily to control the tone of the play rather than to enrich its thought.

Such comic indecorum is at the heart of the chief mode of interpreting metaphors in this study. In his *Principles of Literary Criticism* Richards points out that metaphors may bring into the poem what is needed for the wholeness of the aesthetic experience.[1] What is needed in a play may be an order of values against which the characters and their actions can be measured. In the scene from *The Winter's Tale* already referred to, there are numerous allusions to classical mythology. Just before Florizel's reference to the sheep-shearing, Autolycus (whose name itself suggests Odysseus and Mercury) says that he was 'littered under Mercury'. In the following scene Florizel alludes to Flora, Jupiter, Neptune, Apollo; and Perdita, to Jove, Prosperina, Dis, Juno, Cytherea, and Phoebus. Such references shadow forth the world of the Greek gods which stands, dimly and hugely, around the Shepherd's cottage in Bohemia. Only gradually, after Florizel calls Perdita the queen of the meeting of the petty gods, do we sense how comic the juxtaposition of petty gods and sheep-shearing is. Perdita herself chides Florizel for his 'extremes'—that is, his hyperboles of speech and conduct—and finds it inappropriate that she, a 'poor lowly maid', should be 'most goddess-like prank'd up'. When Camillo remarks that Perdita is 'the queen of curds and cream', he brings together the two worlds of the minor Greek gods and of the Bohemian cottage. And, after Polixenes throws off his disguise and denounces his son, Perdita decisively separates the two worlds when she says that

> this dream of mine—
> Being now awake, I'll queen it no inch farther,
> But milk my ewes and weep.

When the tenor-vehicle (Perdita is the queen of the petty gods) is measured against the mythological world of Greece which the vehicles had brought into the context, we see

[1] Richards, *The Principles of Literary Criticism*, 240.

Perdita and the sheep-shearing against a background that makes them at once charming and comic. To refer to Perdita as a queen of gods enhances her, and all that we hear and see of her makes the hyperbole understandable: she is gentle and fine-spirited, a princess in action as well as in birth. But to call any woman, however royal, a queen of a meeting of the petty gods is comic because it involves an indecorous exaltation of a human being.

Imagery, then, may help suggest the standards by which the words and actions of characters are to be judged. The allusions made and the metaphors chosen may refer to the standards implicit in the culture for which the play was written or they may suggest another order of values—a past but still powerful order or an ideal and eternal order. Each successive generation of readers has its own interpretation of a play because each has its own understanding and acceptance of the standards suggested by the play. The better the play, the more often will different ages find it meaningful, though perhaps for different reasons. Even the finest comedies are barren in some ages: Pepys thought *Twelfth Night* one of the weakest plays he had ever seen on the stage. And the mutilation which *King Lear* suffered at the hands of Nahum Tate illustrates how much the standards justifying the tragic can change. But, generally, there has been and will continue to be an agreement about the standards which a civilized society establishes and which its literary works embody or criticize. Murder has usually been recognized as murder whatever the euphemistic names it has been dressed in—sacrificial offering, blood revenge, defence of one's country, capital punishment, saving the souls of sinners. Treachery has usually been recognized as treachery however it may have been justified as an act of party discipline or as the expedient of fighting fire with fire. This is not to say that each society in turn may not need—or may not think it needs—to commit murder and treachery in order to perpetuate itself: that is its original sin. But no matter how sinful its practice may be, any civilization worthy of the name keeps its allegiance to its ideals. And it evaluates its literature on standards sanctioned by its ideals. One function of metaphorical language may be to bring the relevant standards to the attention of readers.

A metaphor, then, is like a marriage: once united, neither partner is quite the same again (sometimes fortunately), and, if the union is fruitful, new life emerges. Each robs the other of freedom; each gives the other a meaning neither had before. But we can be more specific than this about the contributions of metaphor.

1. Metaphor can juxtapose, meaningfully, things which are in an obscure but true relationship. Aristotle first described this function when he remarked that a command of metaphor is a mark of genius because it implies an eye for resemblances. I. A. Richards, Middleton Murry, C. Day Lewis, E. M. W. Tillyard, and Wallace Stevens deal in different ways with this function, but all at least agree that metaphor, as the chief agent for revealing resemblances, helps us to discover and compose our world. In this function, too, metaphor and wit come together. Both are ways of giving that special pleasure which comes from suddenly seeing resemblances between hitherto unconnected things. In the eighteenth century, when metaphor proper was restrained, wit became the principal—almost the sole—means of giving this pleasure. The essays on wit by Addison and Corbyn Morris show how wit became a kind of metaphorical language in the neo-classic age.

2. Metaphor can keep in a state of tension discordant concepts or images. Johnson's description of the 'discordia concors' of metaphysical imagery, Coleridge's secondary imagination, and Cleanth Brooks's paradox are different analyses of this function.

3. Metaphor can suggest, with great economy, the

multiplicity of experience. The centrifugal impulse at the heart of images directs the mind outward beyond the confines of the thought at hand and brings the contradictory, the apparently irrelevant, and even the inexplicable within the aesthetic structure. Modern analyses of metaphysical imagery emphasize this function of metaphor. In particular, Cleanth Brooks has this function in mind in his various remarks on paradox and irony. Una Ellis-Fermor has emphasized how imagery can be a powerful way of deepening the imaginative significance of a play without increasing its length or destroying its concentration and immediacy.

4. Metaphor can give sensuous particularity to the abstract. This, the 'imaging' function of metaphor, was first described in classical rhetoric. Aristotle's animizing metaphor, Quintilian's 'necessary' metaphor, and Longinus's fourth source of sublimity emphasize this function.

5. Metaphor can help unify a poem emotionally. The metaphors created by Coleridge's secondary imagination would carry out this function by establishing and maintaining a unified tone. In the most valuable part of her study of Shakespeare, Caroline Spurgeon shows how the plays are unified emotionally by recurrent imagery.

6. Metaphor can give aesthetic distance to the poem or the play by marking the dialogue as different from normal speech. When classical rhetoricians describe how 'ornamental' metaphors raise language above the commonplace and the mean and give elevation and distinction to style, they may be suggesting a way to 'distance' the work of art rather than, as is often thought now, justifying merely decorative figures.

7. Metaphor can suggest the standards by which the words and actions of characters are to be judged.

Metaphor can theoretically have any of these functions in literary works. Actually, some functions are characteristic of lyric poetry (such as 1, 2, and 3); some characteristic of satiric poetry (such as 5 and 7); some characteristic of the drama (such as 3, 5, 6, and 7). Studies of metaphorical language can be valuable if they analyse the contribution that any of these various functions of metaphor make to the total aesthetic experience.[1]

[1] Some of the discussions of metaphor which are referred to in this summary have already been documented in previous footnotes. See also: J. M. Murry, 'Metaphor', *Countries of the Mind, Second Series* (London, 1931); E. M. W. Tillyard, *Poetry, Direct and Oblique* (London, 1934); Wallace Stevens, 'Resemblance', *Three Academic Pieces* (Cummington, Mass., 1947); Joseph Addison, *The Spectator*, Nos. 62, 160, 595; Corbyn Morris, *An Essay towards Fixing the True Standards of Wit, Humour, Raillery, Satire, and Ridicule* (1744); S. T. Coleridge, *Biographia Literaria*, ed. J. Shawcross (New York, 1907), I, 60-62, 202, II, 5-20, 43-49, 124; Cleanth Brooks, *Modern Poetry and the Tradition* (Chapel Hill, N.C., 1939) and 'The Language of Paradox', *The Language of Poetry*, ed. Allen Tate (Princeton, 1942); Una Ellis-Fermor, 'The Functions of Imagery in Drama', *The Frontiers of Drama* (London, 1946), 77-95; Quintilian, *Institutio Oratoria*, trans. H. E. Butler (New York, 1921), esp. Book VIII; Norman Friedman, 'Imagery: From Sensation to Symbol', *Journal of Aesthetics and Art Criticism*, XII (September 1953), 25-37; William Empson, *The Structure of Complex Words* (London, 1951); Northrop Frye, *Anatomy of Criticism: Four Essays* (Princeton, 1957).

CHAPTER III

JONSON ON METAPHOR

I

DURING the Renaissance critics analysed the functions of metaphorical language in great detail, but in terms different from those used in the preceding chapter—terms which Rosemond Tuve has illuminated in her *Elizabethan and Metaphysical Imagery*. Since she has covered the whole field of Renaissance imagery definitively, going over her ground would be both superfluous and presumptuous. I shall confine myself here to considering how Jonson's theories of metaphorical language reveal his sensitivity to decorum, the crucial standard for a comic dramatist. This sensitivity follows so naturally from his fundamental principles of language and style that we might begin by summarizing these principles.

We should take care, he stated in a passage which characteristically emphasizes judgment and decorum, that our style 'be neither dry, nor empty: wee should looke againe it be not winding, or wanton with far-fetcht descriptions; Either is a vice. But that is worse which proceeds out of want, then that which riots out of plenty. The remedy of fruitfulnesse is easie, but no labour will helpe the contrary.'[1] Jonson anticipates the age of Dryden by recognizing that both bareness and superfluity are vices; but he still belongs to the age of Shakespeare by realizing that it is better to err on the side of plenty than on the side of want. Jonson's metaphors—dry, empty, winding, wanton, fruitfulness—imply that style has a kind of life. Style to Jonson was not so much a 'garment' as the body of thought which has 'blood, and juyce, when the words are proper and apt, their

---

[1] Herford and Simpson, VIII, 617.

sound sweet, and the *Phrase* neat and pick'd. . . . But where there is Redundancy, both the blood and juyce are faulty, and vitious.' When juice is wanting, 'the Language is thinne, flagging, poore, starv'd, scarce covering the bone; and shewes like stones in a sack'.[1]

The assumption that style is the body of thought is only part of an extended comparison of language and men. Words in language are what 'features and composition' are to men. 'Some men are tall, and bigge, so some Language is high and great . . . all grave, sinnewye and strong. Some are little, and Dwarfes: so of speech it is humble, and low, the words poore and flat. . . . The middle are of a just stature. There the Language is plaine, and pleasing: even without stopping, round without swelling; all well-torn'd, compos'd, elegant, and accurate. The vitious Language is vast, and gaping, swelling and irregular.'[2] This recognition of different kinds of language—high, low, middle, and vicious —brings us back again to the question of propriety. Styles vary according to their subjects. 'For that which is high and lofty, declaring excellent matter, becomes vast and tumorous, speaking of petty and inferiour things.'[3] Here, in this awareness of indecorum, is the basis for the comic speech of *Volpone* and *The Alchemist*, where lofty language is used for petty things.

There is a Golden Mean in language as in men and conduct—a Mean to which Jonson constantly referred his own language. 'Pure and neat Language I love, yet plaine and customary. A barbarous Phrase hath often made mee out of love with a good sense; and doubtfull writing hath wrackt mee beyond my patience.'[4] Jonson might not have completely agreed with Puttenham's claim that 'The foulest vice in language is to speake barbarously', but he certainly felt that incorrectness was vicious because it denies good sense

---

[1] *Ibid.*, 626-627.
[2] *Ibid.*, 625.
[3] *Ibid.*, 626.
[4] *Ibid.*, 620.

its decent form.[1] 'The foulest vice in language' might instead be applied to 'doubtfull writing' because it violated the need for perspicuity. The emphasis on perspicuity also explains the descriptive words—'plaine' and 'customary'. The middle language, which is praised, as we have seen, for being 'accurate', is called 'plaine and pleasing'. And the criterion of custom is established in one of the best known passages in the *Discoveries*.

> *Custome* is the most certaine Mistresse of Language, as the publicke stampe makes the current money. But wee must not be too frequent with the mint, every day coyning. Nor fetch words from the extreme and utmost ages; since the chiefe vertue of a style is perspicuitie, and nothing so vitious in it, as to need an Interpreter. . . . But the eldest of the present, and newest of the past Language is the best. . . . Yet when I name Custome, I understand not the vulgar Custome: For that were a precept no lesse dangerous to Language, then life, if wee should speake or live after the manners of the vulgar: But that I call Custome of speech, which is the consent of the Learned. . . . [2]

The very structure of this passage vividly expresses Jonson's attitude toward language. Even in the shortened form given here, one can feel Jonson moving out to the limits of his standard, then drawing back to the central criteria again. Custom, like the public stamp, gives currency to words, but don't coin every day. Antique words have the authority of years, but . . . ; custom is not vulgar speech, but . . . ; Jonson returns always to the two central criteria—perspicuity, the chief virtue of a style, and propriety. His insistence that the proper custom of speech is the 'consent of the Learned' is the positive side of his sense of decorum in language. By the 'Learned' he apparently meant educated gentlemen,

[1] Puttenham, *The Arte of English Poesie*, ed. Alice Walker and Gladys Willcock (Cambridge, 1936), 250.
[2] Herford and Simpson, VIII, 622.

whose colloquial speech should be the norm of social discourse. Jonson's 'Learned' seem appreciably far from the courtly speakers of Puttenham, who defined the standard language of his time as 'the vsuall speach of the Court, and that of London and the shires lying about London within LX myles, and not much aboue'.[1] But, in reality, the standards were probably close together. At the very heart of the 'language, such as men doe vse' is this customary speech of the 'Learned'. Departures from it—such as the jargon of an alchemist or the affected phrase-making of a gull like Stephen or Matthew—are comic.

In general, then, Jonson's attitude toward language is that of a man steering a controlled course between the extremes of wantonness and dryness, extravagance and poverty. The use of language must be self-conscious and artful, because the kinds of words used have to be adapted to the particular ends of style. There is an organic connection between the fable or fiction which is 'the forme and Soule of any Poeticall worke' and the style which is its body. And that body should be alive (that is, have blood and juice); it should be neat and proper, and neither thin nor swollen. Jonson's emphasis on perspicuity, custom, and propriety in language is exactly what one might expect from a critic who, much as he was influenced by Sidney and the Italian critics, never spoke of the freedom of the imagination or even of the power of genius alone, but who felt that a poet ought to be brought down through 'the disciplines of *Grammar*, *Logicke*, *Rhetoricke*, and the *Ethicks*, adding somewhat, out of all, peculiar to himselfe . . .'[2]

II

Among the many strange remarks that Drummond recorded is one which, let us hope, was said as carelessly as

---

[1] Puttenham, 145. [2] Herford and Simpson, VIII, 636.

most of the others: 'That Verses stood by sense without either Colour's or accent, which yett other tymes he denied.'[1] What could Jonson have meant? If 'Colour's' (that is, 'ornament' or figures of speech) and accent are taken away from verse, what remains? Prose. Perhaps there is some connection between this statement and the statement immediately preceding it in the *Conversations* in which Jonson said he wrote all his verses first in prose as his master, Camden, had instructed him. If a poet really did write poetry that way, he might easily be tempted to think that the sense is all that matters, though even such a prosy poet might have seen that what was achieved after versifying was much more than the prose statement with which he began. It is easier to explain Jonson's remark than to explain it away. His dismissal of accent may be another indication of his difficulty with the creation of poetry. Verse came hard for him, as everyone knew. Rhyme to him was 'the rack of finest wits', and he finally came to like only one metrical pattern—the couplet. As for 'Colour's', a distrust of the rhetorical figures might have been a healthy thing at the end of the sixteenth century. Perhaps Jonson overstated his case as a corrective to the contemporary emphasis on figures auricular, figures sensable, and figures sententious. Of course, this remark may only show Jonson, the dialectician, spoiling for a fight. Here, as I suspect elsewhere, he may be trying to arouse the somewhat humourless Drummond to argument or shock his host into copying down his remarks. Other times he denied it because he never meant it in the first place.

In the *Discoveries* (the critical statements of which are to be trusted more completely than the *Conversations with Drummond*) this questioning of metre and style is not apparent. To be sure, he seems to question the imaginative use of figurative language in several of these discoveries on men and matter. One such is a puzzling passage that was

[1] *Ibid.*, I, 143.

translated almost literally from Marcus Seneca's *Contro-versiae*: 'Hee never forc'd his language, nor went out of the high-way of *speaking*; but for some great necessity, or apparent profit. For hee denied *Figures* to be invented for ornament, but for ayde; and still thought it an extreme madnesse to bend, or wrest that which ought to be right.'[1] Part of the puzzle (a part I shall not try to solve) is the meaning of 'Hee' in this context. I assume that Jonson is praising the figurative language of a man who has proper ease and grace.

More puzzling still are the lines in themselves. Three distinct ideas seem to be fused. Chronologically the first is that which denies '*Figures* to be invented for ornament, but for ayde'. This statement refers, I think, not to each poet's invention, but to the original invention of figurative language. When figures first appeared in the language, they appeared to help the speaker communicate, not to embellish his speech. The second idea brings one up to modern times. 'Still'—at this later day as at that earlier—Jonson thought it madness to bend or wrest language that, for the point one is making, ought to be direct. This insistence on not forcing direct discourse unnecessarily into figurative obliqueness carries one back to the opening statement. The easy, graceful speaker or writer, the man who has *sprezzatura* ('his subtilty did not shew it selfe'), would leave the common way of speaking only when he could not express himself at all or so vividly without the circuitous language of figures. Jonson might well be accused here of not knowing what is now commonly accepted about the primitive stage of any language: that it is characteristically metaphorical and, to that extent, 'figurative'. No language was ever purely direct at some pristine moment in its history, and then bent into figures for rhetorical or poetic reasons. It was from its foundation metaphorical; if it was bent at all, it was bent

[1] *Ibid.*, VIII, 589.

into directness (though this seems a silly way of dealing with these dubious terms). But, though on quicksand historically, Jonson is on solid ground linguistically in claiming that figures were invented for aid, not adornment. ('Adornment' was not the only meaning of this complex word, 'ornament', in the seventeenth century, but it seems to be the primary meaning in this passage.)

Jonson deals with this same problem of ornament and aid in his final words on figures in the *Discoveries*: 'But why doe men depart at all from the right, and naturall wayes of speaking? Sometimes for necessity, when wee are driven, or thinke it fitter to speake that in obscure words, or by circumstance, which utter'd plainely would offend the hearers. Or to avoid obscenenesse, or sometimes for pleasure, and variety; as Travailers turne out of the high way, drawne, either by the commodity of a foot-path, or the delicacy, or freshnesse of the fields. And all this is called ἐσχηματισμένη, or figur'd Language.'[1] Since this passage is one of the few that Percy Simpson has not turned up a source for, it might have been Jonson's considered summation of his own views. Here, dealing with the general question of why anyone *now* uses figurative language, he considerably extends its functions. Pleasure, variety, the avoiding of indelicacy and obscenity—these are apparently kinds of 'profit' that one could gain by leaving the highway of speaking. 'The delicacy, or freshnesse of the fields' is a metaphorical way of picturing ornament, as an earlier passage makes clear: 'Some words are to be cull'd out for ornament and colour, as wee gather flowers to straw houses, or make Garlands; but they are better when they grow to our style; as in a Meadow, where though the meere grasse and greenesse delights, yet the variety of flowers doth heighten and beautifie. Marry, we must not play, or riot too much with them, as in *Paranomasies*.'[2] Characteristically, even when

[1] *Ibid.*, 625. [2] *Ibid.*, 622-623.

working in the ancient *flores* tradition (which tended to emphasize the ornamental function of figures), Jonson threw his weight on the side of aid and naturalness. The best of all the 'colours' are those which grow naturally out of the object represented. The crucial test must always be: is it useful in carrying out the purpose at hand? To riot with colours is to violate decorum, that most exacting of mistresses. The earlier Jonson would probably have agreed with the remark of the later Johnson that Shakespeare was fatally fascinated with quibbles.

To return to Jonson's final passage on figures: just as the imagery of flowers points toward ornament, so 'the commodity of a foot-path' points toward necessity, because commodity is a kind of necessity. 'But in this Translation wee must only serve necessity (*Nam temerè nihil transfertur à prudenti*) or commodity, which is a kind of necessity; that is, when wee either absolutely want a word to expresse by, and that is necessity; or when wee have not so fit a word, and that is commodity. As when wee avoid losse by it, and escape obscenenesse, and gaine in the grace and property, which helpes significance.'[1] This definition may show how Jonson would ideally resolve the troublesome question of ornament or aid. The principal emphasis is, as always with Jonson, on serving necessity. The parenthetical quotation from Quintilian—'a wise man never uses metaphors at random'—was probably one of his favourite rules of thumb. (The sixth, seventh, and eighth books of Quintilian, he told Drummond, 'were not only to be read but altogither digested'.)[2] But when he explains how a metaphor serving commodity can help significance by gaining grace and propriety, he invades the very camp of 'ornament' to carry off a prominent general. At least this kind of ornamental metaphor (that which gains grace and propriety) could be as essential to the effect desired as those necessary metaphors

---

[1] *Ibid.*, 621.   [2] *Ibid.*, I, 136.

which say what could not otherwise be said.

The close rein which Jonson kept on language—or which he said ought to be kept—appears most clearly in his critical approach to specific figures. '*Brevity* is attained in matter', he writes at one point, 'by avoiding . . . superfluous circuit of figures.'[1] Whenever he mentions a figure, he emphasizes how it ought not be used. '*Metaphors* farfet hinder to be understood, and affected, lose their grace.'[2] Stated more positively (and less powerfully), this prescription would read: metaphors ought to be perspicuous and decorous. Or, concerning allegory, he states that 'Neither must wee draw out our *Allegory* too long, lest either wee make our selves obscure, or fall into affectation, which is childish'.[3] Once again, the fundamental criteria of perspicuity and propriety appear. Jonson, the master of hyperbole, saw that 'there are *Hyperboles*, which will become one Language, that will by no meanes admit another. As *Eos esse* P. R. *exercitus, qui coelum possint perrumpere*: who would say this with us, but a mad man? Therefore wee must consider in every tongue what is us'd, what receiv'd.'[4] Here propriety and custom join to dictate Jonson's attitude. One final example of this emphasis on the faults of figurative language is Jonson's diatribe in 'The Epistle' to *Volpone* against '*the present trade of the stage*', '*where nothing but the filth of the time is vtter'd, and that with such impropriety of phrase, such plenty of* soloecismes, *such dearth of sense, so bold* prolepse's, *so rackt* metaphor's, *with brothelry, able to violate the eare of a pagan, and blasphemy, to turne the bloud of a christian to water*'. This quotation may indicate one reason for Jonson's—and his age's—emphasis on the faults rather than the powers of figures. The contemporary stage furnished so many examples of bad uses of figurative language—and examples that too few saw to be bad—that what was needed, according to

---

[1] *Ibid.*, VIII, 631.
[3] *Ibid.*, 625.
[2] *Ibid.*, 621.
[4] *Ibid.*, 624.

Jonson, was judicious criticism and emphasis on the latent errors in the use of metaphors and other common figures.

But Jonson was too judicious (in matters of language, at any rate) to see only the faults of a stylistic device. Even when he says that '*Metaphors* are thus many times deform'd', we soon find him adding that 'All attempts that are new in this kind, are dangerous, and somewhat hard, before they be softned with use. A man coynes not a new word without some perill, and lesse fruit; for if it happen to be received, the praise is but moderate; if refus'd, the scorne is assur'd. Yet wee must adventure, for things, at first hard and rough, are by use made tender and gentle. It is an honest errour that is committed, following great *Chiefes*.'[1] 'Yet wee must adventure.' The whole paragraph wheels on that statement, which redresses the balance. Custom may be the most certain mistress of language, but she becomes a shrewish wife if language is married indissolubly to her. Much as one ought to avoid excessive innovation and the affected use of obsolete expressions (such as Spenser's archaisms), still fear of innovation or affectation could drain the blood and juice out of one's style. Besides—and this is characteristic of Jonson—if you err in coining metaphors, you err in great company.

Yet Jonson, though an influential leader, was not the great adventurer in language that some of his contemporaries were. His attitude toward mixed metaphors shows most clearly the difference between his kind of adventuring and the adventuring of Shakespeare or Webster. '*Quintilian* warnes us, that in no kind of Translation, or *Metaphore*, or *Allegory*, wee make a turne from what wee began; As if wee fetch the originall of our *Metaphore* from the sea, and billowes; wee end not in flames and ashes; It is a most fowle inconsequence.'[2] Jonson himself was not rigid on this point of mixing metaphors. One has to look no further than a

[1] *Ibid.*, 622.   [2] *Ibid.*, 624-625.

few pages in the *Discoveries* to find the vehicles turning from the body to clothes to carpentry. Besides, there is his famous statement—'*Custome* is the most certaine Mistresse of Language, as the publicke stamp makes the current money.' Jonson's answer to an accusation that his practice belied his theory could have been—'Yet wee must adventure.'

The last point to be made about figurative language concerns the fundamental question of propriety. As we have already seen, propriety was one of Jonson's central critical dogmas by which a good style could be measured. For a dramatic poet it was of fundamental importance because words 'are to be chose according to the persons wee make speake, or the things wee speake of. Some are of the Campe, some of the Councell-board, some of the Shop, some of the Sheepe-coat, some of the Pulpit, some of the Barre, &c. And herein is seene their Elegance, and Propriety, when wee use them fitly, and draw them forth to their just strength and nature, by way of Translation or *Metaphore*.' Here the emphasis is on choice according to 'the things wee speake of'. But shortly after, he deals with choice 'according to the persons wee make speake': '*Metaphors* farfet hinder to be understood, and affected, lose their grace. Or when the person fetcheth his translations from a wrong place. As if a Privie-Counsellor should at the Table take his *Metaphore* from a Dicing-house, or Ordinary, or a Vintners Vault; or a Justice of Peace draw his similitudes from the *Mathematicks*; or a *Divine* from a Bawdy-house, or Tavernes.'[1] Impropriety appears along with obscurity and affectation (which is a kind of impropriety) as a possible defect of figurative language. Both of these passages on propriety rest solidly on Jonson's thorough knowledge of dialects, professional jargon, grammar, and cant terms which Henry W. Wells has investigated.[2] Jonson had such a sharp sense of decorum in

[1] *Ibid.*, 621.
[2] Wells, 'Ben Jonson: Patriarch of Speech Study', *Shakespeare Association Bulletin*, XIII (January 1938), 54 ff.

language partly because he knew the low as well as the high words, the vicious as well as the middle language and could use each kind with precision. When he is speaking of his love for 'Pure and neat Language' and his hatred for barbarous phrase and doubtful writing, he notes that a poet 'ought to have all knowledges' so that 'hee should not be ignorant of the most, especially of those hee will handle'.[1]

Neither in his reconciling of ornament and aid nor in his emphasis on the decorum of figures was Jonson unusual in his age. Like all of the rhetoricians, he quoted Quintilian and the continental Aristotelians, with the result that his theories of figures are not radically different from the theories of Wilson or Puttenham. Like Wilson and Puttenham, he recognized various levels of language and kinds of style that ought to be used. Like them, he was chiefly concerned with the decorous use of figures.

His constant search for a balanced critical position resulted in a delicately adjusted attitude toward language, in which he held himself suspended between antitheses. Thus: be perspicuous, but not bare; be vigorous, but not riotous; be brief, but do not write riddles; adventure, but do not be foolhardy; coin metaphors, but do not bankrupt your language. Jonson's insistence on art and judgment was, in part, his admission of how hard it is to achieve such a balance and of how vigilant the poet must be who has to reconcile so many opposites. And decorum, especially decorum in dramatic language, received so extraordinary an emphasis in Jonson's critical writings because it was, for him, the desired synthesis of all of these antithetical forces. It was also the basis of his comic diction, as the following chapters attempt to show.

[1] Herford and Simpson, VIII, 620.

CHAPTER IV

TRANSCHANGED WORLD

JONSON, like all comic poets, explored the gap which always opens between what men say and what they do, between their occasional profession of piety, morality, and reason and their usual practice of selfishness and folly. In order to dramatize this discrepancy, Jonson inverted the values which are commonly accepted and made those inverted values the real values of the world which he dramatically created. For instance, most people say that they worship God, but live as though they worship money or worldly power. To ridicule such folly and to arouse the scorn that such impiety ought to call forth, Jonson created an imaginative world in which money or food or sensual experience is regarded as divine; thus, Volpone, Mammon, and Peniboy Senior worship gold, sacrifice to it, and live for it. All things within the Volpone or Mammon world are measured by such inverted values. 'All this *Nether-world*', as Peniboy Senior tells Pecunia,

> Is yours, you command it, and doe sway it,
> The honour of it, and the honesty,
> The reputation, I, and the religion,
> (I was about to say, and had not err'd)
> Is Queene *Pecunia's*.   II. i. 38-43

That is the speech of a usurer in *The Staple of Newes*, but he is only voicing a conviction that everyone else in the play, except the Canter, is too busy acting on to speak about.

The most explicit statement showing Jonson's awareness of this inversion of values comes in his Epistle to the universities prefacing *Volpone*. There he claims that *'the writers of these dayes are other things; that, not only their manners, but their natures are inuerted; and nothing remayning with them of the dignitie of Poet, but the abused name, which euery Scribe vsurps: that now, especially in* dramatick, *or (as they terme it) stage-poetrie, nothing but ribaldry, profanation, blasphemy, all license of offence to god, and man, is practis'd'.*[1] There is an extraordinarily high function for poets assumed in this condemnation of '*the writers of these days*' who are ribald, profane, blasphemous, and impious. That this assumption is not one which Jonson in time lost can be seen from a passage in the *Discoveries,* which was presumably written fairly late in life. 'I could never thinke the study of *Wisdome* confin'd only to the Philosopher: or of *Piety* to the *Divine*: or of *State* to the *Politicke*. But that he which can faine a *Common-wealth* (which is the *Poet*) can governe it with *Counsels,* strengthen it with *Lawes,* correct it with *Iudgements,* informe it with *Religion,* and *Morals*; is all these.'[2] The true poet not only creates a world, but also becomes its law-giver, judge, philosopher, and priest. Since the poet must be the wisest, best, and completest man alive, the precious name of poet must not be lightly bestowed. Something of this high ideal of poetry apparently prompted Jonson to make those remarks to Drummond which cause wincing even to those disposed to think the best of Jonson. If one were to isolate a remark like—'that Sharpham, Day, Dicker were all Rogues and that Minshew was one'—one might justifiably conclude that the man who so cavalierly calls a writer like Thomas Dekker a rogue is himself one.[3] But place that remark next to a somewhat similar one, and observe the assumption made by Jonson: 'that Markham (who added his English Arcadia) was not of the number of the Faithfull .j. Poets and but a base fellow that such were Day and Midleton.'[4] Dekker, Day, Middleton, and the others were base fellows and rogues because they were not 'of the Faithfull', that is, poets who were at the same time

---

[1] Herford and Simpson, V, 18.
[3] *Ibid.,* I, 133.
[2] *Ibid.,* VIII, 595.
[4] *Ibid.,* I, 137.

priest, politician, and philosopher. Such writers were poetasters because they lacked, in Jonson's opinion at least, the true vision of the religious, moral, political, and philosophical functions of poetry. They were infidels who were embarked, as he says in the Epistle for *Volpone*, on '*this bold aduenture for hell*'.[1] Uncharitable and offensively proud as these judgments now seem, they should not blind us to the realization that Jonson was acutely aware of what values a poet ought to have and of the way most poets of his own day had degraded those values by their inverted manners and natures.

But this awareness of inversion was not confined simply to the writers of his day. Ultimately, it encompassed the moral life of the age.

> How many have I knowne, that would not have their vices hid? Nay, and to bee noted, live like *Antipodes* to others in the same *Citie*; never see the Sunne rise, or set, in so many yeares; but be as they were watching a Corps by Torch-light; would not sinne the common way; but held that a kind of *Rusticity*; they would doe it new, or contrary, for the infamy? They were ambitious of living backward; and at last arrived at that, as they would love nothing but the vices; not the vitious customes . . . they are a little angry with their follies, now and then; marry they come into grace with them againe quickly.[2]

Here Jonson depends on a geographical reference ('like *Antipodes*') and an allusion to the fashionable world ('a kind of *Rusticity*'), as well as direct diction, to convey his contempt for those who are 'ambitious of living backward'. But most often, both in his non-dramatic poetry and in his plays, he used religious imagery in order to arouse the greatest scorn for those who have so lost their sense of the right true way of living that they love what normally they should hate. Even in the passage just quoted, there is probably some use

[1] *Ibid.*, V, 18.   [2] *Ibid.*, VIII, 580-581.

of the religious meaning of 'grace'—a use which Jonson exploited in many of his plays. In his occasional verse Jonson used religious terms more systematically to dramatize the worship of false values which he detected in this upside-down world. Observe how allusions to religion increase the bite and bitterness of the passage in '*An Epistle to Sir* Edward Sacvile' where he speaks of the 'trembling zeale' and the 'superstition' which is paid to those who 'make tribute, what was gift'.

> I only am alow'd
> My wonder, why the taking a Clownes purse,
> Or robbing the poore Market-folkes should nurse
> Such a religious horrour in the brests
> Of our Towne Gallantry! or why there rests
> Such worship due to kicking of a Punck!
> Or swaggering with the Watch, or Drawer, drunke;
> Or feats of darknesse acted in Mid-Sun,
> And told of with more Licence then th' were done!
> Sure there is Misterie in it, I not know,
> That men such reverence to such actions show!
> And almost deifie the Authors! make
> Lowd sacrifice of drinke, for their health-sake!
> Reare-Suppers in their Names! and spend whole
>   nights
> Unto their praise, in certaine swearing rites!
> Cannot a man be reck'ned in the State
> Of Valour, but at this Idolatrous rate?[1]

As we shall discover by analysing *Volpone* and *The Alchemist*, the technique used here is typical of Jonson: the emotions appropriate for religious worship are metaphorically applied to the worship of worldly goods—with an effect of ironic shock. Usually in the plays, he applied it to the impious worship of gold—a worship which appears as early as *The Case is Altered* and as late as *The Magnetick Lady*. But, at times in the non-dramatic poetry, he used it in reference to

[1] *Ibid.*, VIII, 155-156.

gambling,[1] the practice of lawyers,[2] and the scenery of Inigo
Jones whom he caustically asked who can

> (w[t]h miracle) see
> Thy twice conceyud, thrice payd for Imagery?
> And not fall downe before it? and confess
> Allmighty Architecture? who noe less
> A Goddess is, then paynted Cloth, Deal-Boards,
> Vermilion, Lake, or Cinnopar affoards
> Expression for! w[t]h that vnbounded lyne
> Aymed at in thy omnipotent Designe![3]

In none of the poems cited did Jonson rely simply on
religious allusions to create his inverted world—that would
have been monotonous and finally deadening—but he used
them as one of the effective ways of dramatizing his theme.

In Jonson's plays, imagery is one means by which this
inversion of the commonly accepted values of humanity is
accomplished. It is not the only means, of course, and its
function can be studied only in the context of the whole
play where it works together with all that the characters say
and do. But the use of terms taken from religion or love or
classical mythology as either the tenor or the vehicle of
images is an imaginative and economical way of showing
how vicious or foolish or comic certain actions are. A simple
example is Pug's reaction to the morality he finds on earth
in *The Divell is an Asse*. One of the themes of this play,
which does not entirely live up to its comic idea, is impiety.
When Pug, listening to the open viciousness of the ladies,
says, 'You talke of a *Vniuersity*! why, *Hell* is / A Grammar-
schoole to this!' (IV. iv. 170-171), he is suggesting a contrast
between the vice of hell and the vice of earth, in which the
former is found less learned. This contrast is thrown into a

---

[1] *An Epistle to a Friend, to perswade him to the Warres*, ll. 145-150. Note also
ll. 57-58, 163. *Ibid.*, VIII, 167.
[2] *An Epigram to the Councellour that pleaded, and carried the Cause*, ll. 15-16,
Ibid., VIII, 187.
[3] 'An Expostulacon w[t]h Inigo Jones', *Ibid.*, VIII, 405-406.

religious context when Pug, in his 'torment' (l. 195), admits that 'My daies in *Hell*, were holy-daies to this!' (l. 223). The play on 'holy' days emphasizes the whole point of *The Divell is an Asse*: earth is so devilish that a devil would be an ass if he tried to compete in villainy with the fashionable people of earth. As the astonished Pug later admits, 'There is no hell / To a *Lady* of fashion' (V. ii. 14-15). The implication of the whole play is that the human mind, so adept at concealment and hypocrisy, can outwit a devil who is committed wholly to vice, perhaps because some alloy of good only makes men more proficient at evil or gives them more opportunities to sin. Pug's references to education and to religion not only emphasize the comic contrast between an inept devil and clever human beings, but also suggest the very standards by which he and the clever human beings ought to be judged. The mention of grammar school and holy days reminds us of the high ideals of learning and religion and ironically emphasizes how thoroughly these ideals have been perverted in a world where a devil is only an ass.

In the final scene of the Quarto *Every Man in his Humour*, just after a parody of Daniel's *Delia* has been read and before Clement had it burned, there is the following dialogue, which was cut out in the revision for the Folio.

> GIU. [lliano] Call you this poetry?
> LO. [renzo] *iu.* [nior] Poetry? nay then call blasphemie, religion;
> Call Diuels, Angels; and Sinne, pietie:
> Let all things be preposterously transchanged.[1]

'Preposterously' here probably carries its Latin meaning of inverting the natural order by putting the last first. This is an earlier and shorter statement of the charge made in the Epistle prefacing *Volpone*: not only the manners, but also the natures of the writers of the day are inverted, so that they

[1] *Ibid.*, III, 284-285.

write only parodies of true poetry. If such parody is called poetry, then everything else must be 'preposterously trans-changd' in order that the bad will appear to be the best in society as well as in literature. In such a 'transchangd' world sin becomes piety, devils appear as angels, and blasphemy is the true religion. This sense of inversion or perversion appears in some form or other in most of Jonson's plays, but most clearly in *Volpone* and *The Alchemist*. In part, Jonson hoped that, if his plays could show men how preposterous their manners and natures had come to be, they would go and sin no more. In part, too, he apparently found that this particular vision of a distorted and dislocated life satisfied him aesthetically in a way that the clearer and sunnier mood of romantic comedy could not. At any rate, consistently in two of his best plays and sporadically in his last plays, there is an attempt to create a world which is governed with counsels, strengthened with laws, corrected with judgments and informed with religion and morals, but a world so 'preposterously transchangd' in religion and morals that it appears ridiculous. Like all masters of irony, Jonson celebrated the good obliquely: he made the foul ludicrous.

CHAPTER V

'VOLPONE'

I

THE special quality of *Volpone* is not easy to define. Is it a comedy? Jonson in his prologue refers to it as 'quick *comoedie*, refined', and critics normally follow this lead because no other category seems satisfactory. But comic masks are not entirely appropriate for a play which creates such a profound sense of evil that the tone seems closer to tragedy than comedy. The question has even been raised by F. S. Boas as to whether such an exposure of villainy ought not to have had a tragic end.[1] But not even a scholar pressing a thesis would be bold enough to try to prove that *Volpone* ought to have been a tragedy or is a tragedy that never quite came off. Is it satire, burlesque, farce, comedy of humours, melodrama? Even one who is unwilling to accept T. S. Eliot's position on most questions probably would agree with him that none of these terms is satisfactory in dealing with Jonson's best plays, especially *Volpone*. According to Eliot, Jonson's type of personality 'found its relief in something falling under the category of burlesque or farce'— terms which, according to Eliot, are manifestly inadequate when dealing with the unique world created in *Volpone*.[2] Even satire, which may be the least unsatisfactory term (as well as a conveniently vague one), seems more like a term describing Jonson's method than any description of the aesthetic result. In short, all of these critical terms have some validity, but none is wholly justifiable. This suggests that, in *Volpone*, Jonson either failed to create anything aesthetically pleasing or created a drama too complex in nature and unique

[1] Boas, *An Introduction to Stuart Drama* (New York, 1946), 110.
[2] T. S. Eliot, *Selected Essays, 1917-1932* (New York, 1932), 137-138.

in effect to be encompassed by the traditional categories.

How else can one explain the peculiar judgments of the play? For example, Coleridge thought *Volpone* a good proof of 'how impossible it is to keep up any pleasurable interest in a tale, in which there is no goodness of heart in any of the prominent characters'. According to him, 'After the third act, this play becomes not a dead, but a painful weight on the feelings. . . .'[1] Such a sentimental judgment sounds strange coming from the critic who did not find *Timon of Athens* equally painful. *Timon*, another play in which a poet sees the world as a place in which men have become beasts, is ranked by Coleridge a little below *Lear*: 'It is a *Lear* of domestic or ordinary life. . . .'[2] Coleridge's solution of what he apparently considers to be the unsatisfactory nature of *Volpone* seems even stranger: 'If it were possible to lessen the paramountcy of Volpone himself, a most delightful comedy might be produced, by making Celia the ward or niece of Corvino, instead of his wife, and Bonario her lover.'[3] His change of Celia from wife to ward suggests that Corvino's sacrifice of his own wife and Volpone's attempted seduction of her especially bother him. Nor is he alone in this opinion. A. W. Ward agrees with him that it is impossible to enjoy a play whose prominent characters lack goodness of heart, though Ward does not go so far as to say that the play becomes a 'painful weight on the feelings'.[4]

This confusion about the kind of drama that *Volpone* is cannot be entirely cleared up by a study of its imagery. But a study of how the imagery helps create the total effect may reveal the tone of the play. And the tone may suggest a category to anyone who feels one necessary.

[1] *The Literary Remains of Samuel Taylor Coleridge*, ed. H. N. Coleridge (London, 1837), II, 276.
[2] *Coleridge's Shakespearean Criticism*, ed. Thomas Raysor (Cambridge, 1930), I, 108.
[3] Coleridge, *Literary Remains*, II, 276.
[4] A. W. Ward, *A History of English Dramatic Literature* (New York, 1899), II, 364.

II

Volpone's opening speech wastes no time in dramatizing an attitude and exposing a world.

> Good morning to the day; and, next, my gold:
> Open the shrine, that I may see my *saint*.

Two lines are spoken, and the listener is thrown suddenly into a world where gold is blessed, sainted, enshrined. Volpone's morning prayer—for this speech is apparently meant to be a parody of a prayer—moves on. 'Haile the worlds soule, and mine.' This equation is brutally direct: gold is his saint, his soul, and the world's soul. The shock of this whole soliloquy is all but lost on an age, like the present one, whose saint seems to be money or whose attitude is closer to Volpone's than to the one which Jonson, by implication, proposes. But to an age which, like the Elizabethan, at least knew the normal Christian attitude, this perversion of religious imagery must have been shocking. To realize how blasphemous this speech is, one has only to contrast the attitude expressed here with that of the *Benedicte* in the Matins, or Psalm 148, or even, if one can ignore chronology, the morning prayer of Adam and Eve in *Paradise Lost*, V. 153 ff.

Jonson is not merely glancing at religious imagery here, but insisting on it in detail.

> More glad then is
> The teeming earth, to see the long'd-for sunne
> Peepe through the hornes of the celestiall *ram*,
> Am I, to view thy splendor, darkening his:
> That, lying here, amongst my other hoords,
> Shew'st like a flame, by night; or like the day
> Strooke out of *chaos*, when all darkenesse fled
> Vnto the center.   I. i. 3-10

The traditional religious implications in 'sunne', 'celestiall', 'splendor', and '*chaos*' are wrenched around by Volpone's impious statement that he is 'more glad' to see his gold than the earth is to see the sun and by his claim that the gold's splendour darkens the sun's. The sudden change from the metaphor of the previous lines to the similes in 'Shew'st like a flame, by night; or like the day / Strooke out of *chaos*', momentarily slows up the rapid movement of Volpone's speech and, by making it more deliberate, makes it more shocking. These are large figures, as they should be, and extraordinarily simple and vivid. There is violence in 'Strooke out of *chaos*' and 'all darkenesse fled / Vnto the center'. The light imagery suggested before in sun and day is made more explicit in the apostrophe which follows.

> O, thou sonne of Sol,
> (But brighter then thy father) let me kisse,
> With adoration, thee, and euery relique
> Of sacred treasure, in this blessed roome.   I. i. 10-13

The reversal of normal values is re-emphasized: gold is brighter than the sun. The religious terms crowd thick on the listener here: adoration, relic, sacred, blessed.

The use of 'Sol' sets into motion another kind of imagery —that taken from alchemy. According to the alchemists, the sun is the father of gold, and the moon, which receives the seeds of the sun, is the mother of gold.[1] Latent in this speech, then, may be the gross, worldly, anti-Christian implications of alchemy.

In the rest of his morning hymn Volpone lays his motives bare with a frankness worthy of a Richard III.

> Thou being the best of things: and far transcending
> All stile of ioy, in children, parents, friends,
> Or any other waking dreame on earth.
> Thy lookes, when they to Venvs did ascribe,

---

[1] See Edgar Duncan, 'Jonson's *Alchemist* and the Literature of Alchemy', *PMLA*, LXI, 709.

> They should haue giu'n her twentie thousand
>   CVPIDS;
> Such are thy beauties, and our loues! Deare *saint*,
> Riches, the dumbe god, that giu'st all men tongues:
> That canst doe nought, and yet mak'st men doe all
>   things;
> The price of soules;   I. i. 16-24

The barrenness and the monolithic fanaticism of Volpone's life appear when he says that gold transcends the joy found in children, parents, or friends. Such emotional relationships are trances, then, from which one could be awakened by 'Riches, the dumbe god'. The solitariness of Volpone, which he apparently does not find so barren as a normal person would find it, is emphasized later in this first scene when he says that he has 'no wife, no parent, child, allie' to give his substance to. His life is dedicated as completely as that of any monk to his saint.

The paradox at the heart of this distorted religion is suggested in the lines about 'Riches, the dumbe god'. Here is the central mystery of Volpone's 'faith': a god which, though inarticulate, makes all men verbal, and though powerless, is the motive for all action. 'Riches' becomes almost a parody of Aristotle's Unmoved Mover. But a vicious parody, for it is 'the price of soules'. This Mephisto-phelian note is developed when Volpone states with a shameless directness the logical end of his perverted piety:

>   euen hell, with thee to boot,
> Is made worth heauen! Thou art vertue, fame,
> Honour, and all things else!   I. i. 24-26

Once grant his major premise, and the conclusion follows that in this Satanic world it is better to enjoy riches in hell than be poor in spirit in heaven.

Balancing Christian humility is Volpone's arrogance and muscular worldliness.

> Yet, I glory
> More in the cunning purchase of my wealth,
> Then in the glad possession; since I gaine
> No common way: I. i. 30-33

We sense here the ethical side of this religion. There are some things Volpone will not do to serve his saint: trade, speculation, farming, cattle raising, milling, shipping, banking, usury. Nor, as Mosca says, will he 'deuoure / Soft prodigalls', or 'fathers of poore families' or 'widdowes'. What, then, does he glory in? Neither he nor Mosca states in so many words what it is, but we see before long that his aristocratic villainy is exercised only on the strongest—a miser, a lawyer, a merchant—all birds of prey, and all practised in serving Mammon themselves. The aristocratic tenor of Volpone is implied in the similes Mosca chooses when saying that his master knows how to use riches.

> You are not like the thresher, that doth stand
> With a huge flaile, . . .
> Nor like the merchant, who hath fill'd his vaults
> With *Romagnía*, and rich *Candian* wines,
> Yet drinkes the lees of *Lombards* vineger:
> You will not lie in straw, whilst moths, and wormes
> Feed on your sumptuous hangings, and soft beds.
>   I. i. 53-61

No, Volpone is a Magnifico and will not live like a peasant or a middle-class merchant. Lying in straw may suggest a contrast between Volpone and the infant Jesus in the manger, while moths and worms are possibly an ironic echo of Christ's counsel to lay up treasures in heaven where 'neither moth nor rust doth corrupt'.

In this first scene, then, religious imagery, such as saint, adoration, and soul, is used to refer to something irreligious and mean. One effect of this perversion of religious images is to suggest two worlds at the same time. One is that world

75

of Christian and humanistic values which exalts the eternal over the temporal, and the spiritual over the worldly. The other is the debased world in which these values are reversed. The traditional Christian world is suggested in the listener's mind by the various vehicles—saint, shrine, blessed—which have become meaningful after long centuries of use. The debased world of Volpone enters the listener's mind when these vehicles are compared to their tenors, when, for example, saint is equated with gold. By itself the tenor, gold, means little or, rather, it means so much that one does not know exactly what meaning to fix on. The various vehicles —shrine, relic, god, blessed—suggest a system of values, the Christian order, to which the tenor can be referred. When the tenor and the vehicle are related, we find the relation shocking. When the tenor plus the vehicle is measured against the order of things (which the vehicle itself had helped suggest) we see a disproportion, a trans-valuation of values which may be one of the things Jonson is saying here. But, of course, he is saying it in a richer, more memorable way than this prosy version can indicate. The religious imagery helps dramatize the kind of society that is created when the main pursuit of men is the acquisition of riches. Volpone's morning hymn embodies a new meta-physic and a new ethic, almost point for point the reverse of the Christian. Gold is the new god, the world's soul, and its own saint. The visible, the temporal, the material is all. Hell, with riches, is 'worth heauen'. Work is sin. Instead of humility, there is arrogance. Instead of the soul being inviolate, a soul has a price.

Another effect of the use of religious imagery is ironic shock. L. C. Knights has pointed out that 'religion and the riches of the teeming earth' are used in Volpone's hymn 'for the purpose of ironic contrast'.[1] Our feelings are outraged when '*saint*', 'adoration', and 'sacred' are applied not to the

[1] Knights, *Drama and Society in the Age of Jonson* (London, 1937), 202.

divine or even—in that easiest of all metaphoric leaps—to a loved one, but to gold. The outrage is as great as it is because the implications of the religious imagery are at the opposite pole from the implications of gold. In conventional Christian ethics money is a symbol of this world's power; as such it is evil, though unavoidable, and is held in a healthy contempt. At the other extreme from worldly power is that allegiance to an unselfish, unworldly life which is the ideal, distant and at times timidly reached for, but always inspiring, of any true religion. To compare one extreme with the other, as the listener is forced to, is to create a tension between these two worlds. The sudden drop from the Christian implications of '*saint*' and 'soule' to the gross implications of riches and gold helps create that tone of irony which is part of the emotional effect of the play. In order to increase the shock of expecting one set of values and being given another, Jonson has used simple figures in a rhetorical structure which is direct to the point of being violent. As Alexander Sackton has shown recently, the rhetoric of hyperbole in the opening soliloquy creates an attitude of ironic detachment in the listener.[1] This detachment also keeps the tone close to the comic, or as close as it can be in the first scene.

One way to see what effect religious imagery has on this scene is to compare it with a somewhat similar scene which lacks religious imagery—the opening scene of Marlowe's *Jew of Malta*. Barabas in his counting house with heaps of gold before him does not shock our sensibilities as Volpone does kneeling before his idol at his shrine.

III

The first scene dramatized that reversal of values which is at the heart of this play. The second scene has two

[1] Sackton, *Rhetoric as a Dramatic Language in Ben Jonson* (New York, 1948), 121 ff.

functions: one is to prepare for the coming of the birds of prey; the other is to dramatize one of the effects of this perversion of human values. Let us analyse how Jonson accomplished this second function.

Nano, a dwarf, Androgyno, an hermaphrodite, and Castrone, a eunuch, are introduced in an interlude dealing with the Pythagorean transmigration of the soul. Nano, Mr Interlocutor in this scene, says that in Androgyno *'is inclos'd the Soule of* PYTHAGORAS, / *That iuggler diuine'*, and relates some of the transmigrations which this soul has taken. The progress of the soul from Apollo to Androgyno is, I think, symbolic of the way the classical world has spiralled down to the modern world.[1] From classical figures such as Pythagoras, Aspasia, and Crates, the soul has moved into kings, knights, beggars, lords, asses, and goats. But the animal level is not the lowest. From there it moved down into *'one of the reformed'*, that is, a Protestant. Then to a mule. From a mule it descended into a strange beast—*'a precise, pure, illuminate brother'*. In short, a Puritan. From there the soul of Pythagoras finally came to Androgyno, where it is content, not because, as Nano suggests, he can vary *'the delight of each sexe'*, but because the fool is *'The onely one creature, that I can call blessed'*. *'Soule'* and *'blessed'* recall the religious imagery in the first scene. The soul of the classical world finds blessedness in the Volpone world in the form of a fool because fools make themselves and others merry. *'All they speake, or doe, is sterling.'* The pun on *'sterling'* harks back to the worldly implications of gold in the first scene.

What strikes one first about this transmigration is the way it has blurred the distinctions usually kept between man, beast, and god. The soul, though moving generally

---

[1] Jonson may have been influenced by Donne's use of this Pythagorean doctrine in *Metempsychosis* (1601). According to Drummond, Jonson said that Donne's initial intent was to have brought in all the heretics from Cain down to Calvin and Queen Elizabeth. The progress in Donne's poem, like the progress in *Volpone*, would have been downward. Herford and Simpson, I, 136 and 158.

downward, has slithered all around the chain of being, starting as a god and sliding into all conditions of men, then into different animals, back into a special kind of man—a Puritan—and finally into a being set apart from the normal, an hermaphrodite. One result of this fast and loose progress is to suggest that the distinction normally kept between man and beast and man and god has been lost in this world. Though there is a gradual descent from Apollo to Aethalides, one of the Argonauts, and to Euphorbus, a Trojan, once the soul reaches the human level it moves easily from whore to philosopher, from king to beggar, from lord to fool, from a mule into a Puritan.

Note how the great ones of the past are treated. Menelaus is called *'the Cuckold of* Sparta', Pythagoras, a *'iuggler diuine'*. As for Aspasia

> *From* PYTHAGORE, *shee went into a beautifull peece,*
> *Hight* ASPASIA, *the* meretrix; *and the next tosse of her*
> *Was, againe, of a whore, shee became a Philosopher,*
> CRATES *the* Cynick:

The language is nakedly brutal: piece, meretrix, toss, whore. The Golden Age of Pericles has guttered down to this—the golden age of Volpone. And Aspasia, one of the great women of the classical world, has come to be, in the sewer of Nano's world, only a harlot. She, like Pythagoras and Crates and even Apollo (from whom this soul came first), is cheapened by the company she is made to keep—the beggars, knaves, fools, lords, asses, and Puritans she is related to. The soul of Pythagoras deliberately chooses to be in this world in the one creature it can call blessed—an hermaphroditic fool. This deliberate choice indicates how completely values have been reversed. Finally, the verse used in this scene carries the same burden of tawdriness. Nano comments on *'the false pase of the verse'* (I. ii. 4). Falsely paced it is, and lame, suiting the progress it is concerned with. An additional twist is given when one remembers that Androgyno's soul originally came from Apollo, god of poetry. The descent from the god of poetry to a fool is fittingly expressed in this disjointed music.[1]

What these three fools are is as functional as what they say. A eunuch, a dwarf, and an hermaphrodite—all are unnatural beings in whom the equipoise of body and soul has been disturbed. They are the living emblems of the perverted culture of this mean world. The debasing of the real values of life has gone so far in Volpone that he surrounds himself with these abnormal beings, none of whom is capable of a normal relation with the world outside. As symbols, they stand for what goes on in Volpone's soul as much as what Volpone's world is like—if any distinction between the two can be made. We see how close is the relationship between these fools and their master when Mosca later answers Corvino's question about Volpone's children by saying that the dwarf, the fool, and the eunuch are only a few of Volpone's many bastards. Of course, Mosca may be talking loosely, to frighten Corvino into giving more jewels to insure his primacy. So far as the imagery is concerned, whether or not he is telling the truth does not matter, because the connection between Volpone and his 'family' is made in the listener's mind. We see them, then, as symbols of what the Volpone world produces: the misshapen, the degenerate, and the castrated.

We also see them as symbols of what this Magnifico does with his leisure. While waiting for the gulls to come, he

---

[1] This scene is, of course, greatly indebted to Lucian's 'The Dream or the Cock', a sermon in praise of poverty cast in the form of a dialogue between a cobbler and his cock, which claims to be Pythagoras reincarnated. Many of the details are the same, but the differences are more important than the similarities. Lucian's dialogue has the tone and atmosphere of a beast fable; Jonson's scene is far from being a beast fable. Jonson changes the whole point of view by having a man tell the transmigrations which, in Lucian, a cock described. Finally, the specific details and allusions which are stressed here are generally Jonson's. See Lucian, *Works*, trans. A. M. Harmon (New York, 1915), II, 175-213.

calls for his dwarf, eunuch, and fool to make him 'sport'. What do they do—sing madrigals, converse, read poetry? No, Mosca, who acknowledges himself to be the inventor of the piece, presents a parody of a masque in which Nano and Androgyno recite, all apparently dance, and Nano and Castrone sing. Then, later, after gulling Corvino, Volpone calls for music, banquets, all delights, boasting that he will rival the Turk in sensuality (I. v. 87-89). The hell that most men shape for themselves, given the opportunity, is incredibly trite: garish houses, flashy women, rich food, pseudo-culture, and parasites. But the allusion to the Turk marks the Magnifico of Venice, suggesting, as it does, the ancient vice of the Orient, the promiscuity of the harem, and the endless opportunity for pleasure. Edgar in *King Lear* strikes the traditional note when he claims that he 'in woman out-paramoured the Turk' (III. iv. 92).

One purpose of Scene 2 of Act I has been, then, to dramatize the effects of the perversion of human values which in Scene 1 was suggested by the debasing of religious imagery. In Scene 2 classical allusions are used in a parody of a masque. To bring together, indiscriminately, the great and the mean, the fine and the vulgar, as these allusions to Pythagoras, Aspasia, various animals, an hermaphrodite, and a eunuch do, is to debase the great and vulgarize the fine. Finally, Nano, Androgyno, and Castrone appear to be symbols of the world which this perversion of values has created—unbalanced, irrational, emasculated, reduced to entertaining the wealthy in a vulgar show.[1]

A descent comparable to the progress from Apollo to Androgyno later appears in the second scene of Act II in which Volpone tries to sell the powder that made Venus a goddess; he claims that it passed from her to the half-goddess, Helen, and finally reached French ladies who have

---

[1] For a different interpretation of I. ii. see Harry Levin, 'Jonson's Metem-psychosis', *Philological Quarterly*, XXII (July 1943), 231-239.

used it to make their teeth firm. The ambrosia of the gods is debased to the level of a dentifrice capable of curing pyorrhea.

IV

The second function of Scene 2 in Act I is to prepare for the birds of prey. At the end of the song by Nano and Castrone, Mosca recognizes the knock of Signior Voltore and goes to usher him in. At this time Volpone first uses the bird imagery which runs through the rest of the play.

> Now, now, my clients
> Beginne their visitation! vulture, kite,
> Rauen, and gor-crow, all my birds of prey,
> That thinke me turning carcasse, now they come:
> I. ii. 87-90

This together with Volpone's answer to Mosca's description of the plate that Voltore brought:

> Good! and not a foxe
> Stretch'd on the earth, with fine delusiue sleights,
> Mocking a gaping crow? I. ii. 94-96

makes us see this human situation in inhuman terms. It suggests a comparison with a bestiary such as the familiar one from *Physiologus* by Theobaldus, in which the fox pretends to be dead in order to capture birds ready to prey on his flesh.[1] But this similarity to such a medieval bestiary does not make *Volpone*, as is sometimes claimed, a beast fable cast in the form of classical comedy. For beast fables are stories in which lower animals associate with each other as reasonable beings endowed with the virtues and vices of humanity. Do lower animals appear so in *Volpone*? Quite the contrary is true: reasonable beings appear as lower animals with the instincts of lower animals. Or, more exactly, men capable of reason reduce themselves to an

---

[1] See Jessie Weston, *Chief Middle English Poets* (New York, 1914), 329-330.

animal level by selfishness. The whole force of the animal imagery in the scenes with Voltore, Corbaccio, and Corvino comes from the certainty that we are dealing with men, not animals. For a vulture or a raven to hover around a dying fox is, while not a pretty sight, all in the nature of things in this best of all possible worlds. But for a Venetian advocate or a venerable gentleman or a wealthy merchant to lose his rationality and humanity so completely as to act the part of a vulture, a raven, or a crow is not according to the nature of rational human beings. To indicate how unnatural it is Jonson uses imagery in which the men are metaphorically, but not literally, identified with birds of prey. If a literal identification were made, if, that is, Voltore were called Mr Vulture and appeared in the guise of a large black bird, the effect might be comic fantasy and even satire, but it would lack the vigour and the scorn that Jonson achieves by having an advocate compared to a vulture. Probably Voltore was dressed to suggest a vulture (as Daumier's lawyers are), but he would always have been seen as a man. The force of the comparison comes as much from the disparity between the tenor and the vehicle as it does from the similarity. The actions of Voltore make him like a vulture; but his human nature, his possession of a reasoning power which he does not use or which he abuses, and his debasing of a human soul mark his immense difference from a bird of prey. In short, only by imagery could Jonson say dramatically, 'Voltore is a vulture preying on a dying fox, and yet he is not a vulture at all, but a man.' Voltore and all the others live their dramatic lives somewhere between the men they pass for and the birds of prey they are compared to, partaking of the natures of both and never being entirely either.

The names of the characters obviously identify them. In order to avoid turning the play into a beast fable, Jonson refrains from using names that are too close to the English and bases them on Latin derivatives. Voltore refers to the

Latin form of vulture which is *vultur* or *voltur*. Corbaccio and Corvino are confused by Jonson, who refers to the former as a raven and the latter as a crow. Strictly, Corbaccio comes from the Italian *corbo*, a crow, and is the diminutive, used in disparagement. Corvino is derived from the Italian *corvo*, a raven, and is the adjective, meaning raven or jet black. The confusion is understandable because *corvo* = *corbo*. Furthermore, crow refers to any of the large group of birds of the genus *Corvus* which includes ravens, rooks, and jackdaws. Volpone is, of course, from the Latin *vulpinus*, which is from *vulpes*, fox. To choose names with Latin derivations is characteristic of Jonson, and he did so wisely. Imagine the context that would have been created if the visitors had been called Raven, Vulture, and Crow, and Volpone called Reynard.

Furthermore, Jonson makes use of traditional associations in using this imagery. The fox as a symbol of covetousness and craft comes out of ancient oral tradition and appears in the literary tradition at least as early as Aesop. The symbolism was so old by the Middle Ages that in the *Ancrene Riwle* it had become a symbol of one of the seven deadly sins—'the fox of covetousness'.[1] In *King Lear* such traditional symbolism became 'fox in stealth, wolf in greediness . . . lion in prey' (III. iv. 93-95). But though some of the animal symbolism changed, fox invariably symbolized stealth, cunning, and covetousness.

Another traditional association with the fox was Machiavelli. 'When Ralegh was to give evidence at Essex's trial, the prisoner called out, "What boots it to swear the fox?" The name was presumably due to his Machiavellianism.'[2] Such an association was probably based on the passages in *The Prince* in which Machiavelli advocates that the prince should adopt the animals reigning in his nature. Of all

---

[1] *The Nun's Rule*, trans. James Morton (London, 1905), 148.
[2] M. C. Bradbrook, *The School of Night* (Cambridge, 1936), 186 n. 3.

combinations, a compound of the fox and the lion is the best, because then the Prince can both avoid traps and protect himself from wolves. Volpone, the fox, then, would be recognized as a Machiavellian villain who sometimes acted contrary to faith, charity, humanity, and religion to gain his ends. This association of Volpone and Machiavelli explains some of the later uses of Volpone's name. Clarendon was called 'old Volpone' by his enemies, and Dr Sacheverell in the Age of Queen Anne was impeached because he had referred to Godolphin, the Lord Treasurer, as 'Old Fox or Volpone'.[1] Both nicknames apparently alluded to the Machiavellian nature of their politics.[2]

The use of the animal imagery once Volpone has set it in motion is restrained. It appears more as a frame for the scenes than within the scenes themselves. Thus, when Voltore leaves, Volpone says, 'The vulture's gone, and the old rauen's come' (I. ii. 81). Then, when 'the old rauen', Corbaccio, is preparing to go Mosca says, 'Rooke', meaning, as a verb, to cheat, and as a noun, a member of the crow family. But when Corvino comes, no bird image is used to introduce him or to usher him out. Possibly Jonson felt that the comparisons already made for the first two would be applied to the third. Possibly, too, he wanted Corvino to be the least like a bird of prey of the three so that there would be less shock in moving from him to the warm description of his wife.

The order of these visits is interesting: vulture, raven, crow. This probably is the order in which the circling birds would descend on the carrion. First, the vulture comes down, being the largest and the most voracious of the birds of prey. When the birds flutter around the supposedly dead Volpone in Act V, Mosca says: 'It is the vulture: / He has

---

[1] Ward, *History of English Dramatic Literature*, II, 363 n. 1.

[2] In *'Volpone; or, The Fox*—The Evolution of a Nickname', Robert G. Noyes has traced the many uses of Volpone as a pejorative term. *Harvard Studies and Notes in Philology and Literature*, vol. XVI (Cambridge, 1934), 162 ff.

the quickest sent' (V. ii. 108-109). Then comes the raven, which is noted for its loud, harsh, croaking cry; Corbaccio, a deaf man, probably should be played with the loud voice that is characteristic of deaf people. Finally the smallest of the birds, the crow, comes to pick up the scraps that the others leave. Jonson makes additional use of this order when he presents the vulture as a lawyer. Is that perhaps a way of making what seems like an age-old comment on judicial affairs: when a man dies, the lawyer gets the first and biggest share of whatever is left?

The use of animal imagery all but ceases from the end of the first act until the beginning of the fourth. Jonson may have thought that, once he started the comparisons working, he ought not to stress them, lest the emphasis be taken away from the human point of view.

v

Thus far in the first act three kinds of vehicles have been used—religious, classical, and animal. A fourth kind is brought into the context in the last scene of the act. Volpone makes a natural transition from animals to women—natural to him, at least. Lady Would-be calls, but is told to come back later when, as Volpone says, he is 'high with mirth, and wine'. He wonders at the desperate valour of the English, who 'let loose' their wives to all encounters (I. v. 99-102). 'Let loose', apparently an image from the breeding of cows, suggests the exclusively animal interest that Volpone has in meeting women. Mention of her leads naturally to a mention of the wife of Corvino. Mosca's description of her is the first extended use of the fourth kind of imagery that Act I introduces. Her face is

> the wonder,
> The blazing starre of *Italie*! a wench
> O' the first yeere! a beautie, ripe, as haruest!

Whose skin is whiter then a swan, all ouer!
Then siluer, snow, or lillies! a soft lip,
Would tempt you to eternitie of kissing!
And flesh, that melteth, in the touch, to bloud!
Bright as your gold! and louely, as your gold!

I. v. 107-114

Most of these images are, of course, conventional in love
poetry: star, harvest, swan, snow, lilies, melting flesh. But
in the movement of the play this passage is saved from being
another conventional description by several unusual points.
First, some of the normally conventional images are given
a new meaning after the religious imagery in the first scene.
'Wonder', 'blazing starre', 'eternitie'—all have religious
connotations ordinarily submerged in speaking of love or a
loved one. For example, when one calls a woman a goddess,
one rarely has in mind any pious connotations. Goddess is
only a hyperbolic way of saying that she is impossibly
beautiful. That kind of effortless exaggeration is apparently
used by Mosca here, but to the listener who remembers the
use of religious terms in Volpone's hymn to his gold, the
latent religious connotations spring to life. And the effect is
somewhat like that in the earlier scene. 'The blazing starre
of *Italie*' whose lips would tempt one to an 'eternitie of
kissing' is, though sacred, probably going to be debased to
the same kind of use that the religious terms were.

The second unusual point about these images reinforces
the first point. Slipped in among Mosca's other rapturous
images is the one in which Celia's skin is said to be whiter
than 'siluer'. This comparison may be unconscious because
Mosca may find silver so attractive that he instinctively
compares a woman's skin with it. Or it may be deliberately
chosen to touch Volpone at his most vulnerable point.
Certainly the reference to gold at the end of the speech is
deliberate and, after the other images, shocking. The whole
passage is genuinely moving, and the emotion mounts as it

is focused down from the distant 'starre' and generalized 'beautie, ripe, as haruest' to skin, soft lip, 'And flesh, that melteth, in the touch, to bloud!' At this climax of the erotic imagery Mosca reaches still higher to appeal to Volpone. And where does he go for a comparison—to religion, nature, mythology? No, none of these carries the force of 'Bright as your gold! and louely as your gold.' For Volpone that may have been a genuinely climactic image because, as we have heard him say, gold is his saint, his soul, the 'dumbe god'. But to one with a normal sense of values the effect is crashing anticlimax. The bottom of the whole passage drops out, and we come down to the dirty earth. Mosca keeps us there, and keeps the equation, Celia is gold, in our minds when he says that 'Shee's kept as warily, as is your gold:' (I. v. 118). Since we have seen in the scenes immediately before this how Volpone's gold is kept in such a tantalizing way as to get more gold, we have already a hint as to how Corvino's golden lady may be used.

This fourth kind of imagery—erotic imagery—is debased in something like the way religious imagery is debased. That is, the vehicles are used with tenors which are mean or vulgar, or vehicle and tenor are used in a context which degrades them. Both of these misuses appeared early in the first scene when Volpone, addressing his gold, said,

> Thy lookes, when they to Venvs did ascribe,
> They should haue giu'n her twentie thousand
>   Cvpids;
> Such are thy beauties, and our loues!   I. i. 19-21

Gold is thought of as so potent a lover that even his looks, if given to Venus, would have fathered twenty thousand Cupids. The absurd exaggeration of the figure also helps make it ludicrous. But great as the debasement is, it is only a minor intimation of what is to come in the third act.

VI

Imagery from the classical world, religion, and love combine in the scene of the attempted seduction of Celia. In preparation for that scene Bonario and Celia are shown to stand for the traditional Christian values. Their names are suggestive: Bonario means the good one, and Celia the heavenly one.[1] Celia, especially, symbolizes and expresses the Christian attitude. One of the first things we learn of her is that she only goes out to go to church (II. v. 46), but that in itself is not half so meaningful as the Christian imagery she uses in her pleading first with Corvino, then with Volpone. Her apostrophes and exclamations are to the point: 'O heauen!'; 'Lord! what spirit / Is this hath entred him?'; 'O heauen! canst thou suffer such a change?'; 'O god, and his good angels!'; 'O! iust God'. But her language is more thoroughly Christian than these obvious figures indicate.

Her conversation with Corvino before being left alone with Volpone shows how the normal values of marriage have been reversed by this insatiate crow. He counsels Celia,

> if you bee
> Loyall, and mine, be wonne, respect my venture.
> CEL. Before your honour?
> CORV.   Honour? tut, a breath;
> There's no such thing, in nature: a meere terme
> Inuented to awe fooles. What is my gold
> The worse, for touching? clothes, for being look'd on?
> Why, this's no more. An old, decrepit wretch,
> That ha's no sense, no sinew; takes his meate
> With others fingers; onely knowes to gape,
> When you doe scald his gummes; a voice; a shadow;
> III. vii. 36-45

[1] See Otto Hinze, *Studien zu Ben Jonsons Namengebung in seinen Dramen* (Dresden, 1919), 60. In the *Faerie Queene* (I. x. 4) appears this use of the name: 'Dame *Caelia* did her call, as thought / From heaven to come, or thither to arise.' Spenser's '*Caelia*' is the mother of three daughters—Faith, Hope, and Charity.

Hypnotized by greed, Corvino seems unaware of the double meaning that his words might have. He asks her to show her loyalty by consenting to an act equivalent to disloyalty; to be 'mine' by lying with another; to be won by losing her virtue; and to 'respect' (that is, pay attention to) a business venture that is not worthy of respect. He has so completely lost his sense of values that he uses the language of marriage in playing the part of a pimp. His anatomy of honour indicates how fast and loose he can play with principles when his self-interest is concerned. When, earlier, he thought that his reputation had been soiled by the attention Celia had paid to the mountebank, he began his harangue with 'Death of mine honour, with the cities foole?' (II. v. 1). Now, Celia has really become the death of his honour, and he is to become the city's fool. The ambiguity of the syntax in his dissection of honour plays strange tricks on the movement of the thought. Corvino shifts so rapidly from honour to Celia's lying with Volpone, then to Volpone's feeble condition that the listener continues to think of one when Corvino has slipped on to another. Thus Corvino's honour and Celia's virtue are made to seem things that, like clothes, can be put on or taken off or that are, like gold, the mediums of exchange by which one can buy and sell more durable and important things. Celia's being touched by Volpone is like gold being touched: neither is the worse for wear. Her being looked at by Volpone is like clothes being looked at: neither loses its style or value.

Celia's morality is not blurred in this shameless way. When Corvino tells her that no one, except herself, could tell of her compliance, her answer is uncompromising: 'Are heauen, and saints then nothing? / Will they be blinde, or stupide?' (III. vii. 53-54). Corvino, even as Volpone, can pervert religious terms for his own uses. What he is asking her to do is a 'pious worke, mere charity . . . honest politie' (III. vii. 65-66). The climax is revealing; self-interested polity is more important than pious works or charity. Contrast this sophistry with the simple accent of Celia: 'Sir, what you please, you may, I am your martyr' (III. vii. 107).

Celia and Bonario, then, represent the Christian values, while Corvino and Volpone, so ready with Christian terms to justify their actions, represent the debasing of those values. When Celia is alone with Volpone, the two kinds of imagery at last receive their most eloquent expression.

> CEL. O god, and his good angels! whether, whether
>   Is shame fled humane brests? that with such ease,
>   Men dare put off your honours, and their owne?
>   Is that, which euer was a cause of life,
>   Now plac'd beneath the basest circumstance?
>   And modestie an exile made, for money?
> VOLP. I, in CORVINO, and such earth-fed mindes,
>   That neuer tasted the true heau'n of loue.
>   Assure thee, CELIA, he that would sell thee,
>   Onely for hope of gaine, and that vncertaine,
>   He would haue sold his part of paradise
>   For ready money. . . .   III. vii. 133-144

Celia's image of men putting off their honours may be an unconscious echo of Corvino's passage on honour in which honour and clothes were brought very close together. Volpone's 'true heauen of loue', which might not seem so violent a desecration if he were a true lover, is directly contrary to the torment which Lady Would-be's visit caused him:

>   I feare
>   A second hell too, that my loathing this
>   Will quite expell my appetite to the other:
>   III. iii. 27-29

Hell, to this animal, means a loss of sexual appetite; heaven, a gratifying of it. The fine distinction that he makes between Corvino who sells a woman for gain and himself who buys a woman for pleasure marks the true sensualist. Corvino's mind is 'earth-fed'; his own, by implication, is heaven-fed. But even Volpone makes a reservation about selling Celia: note that he says, '*Onely* for hope of gaine'.

Just as Volpone profanes Christian ethics by misusing its terms, so he profanes song and music by the uses he puts them to. In this connection, F. S. Boas believes that '"one word is too often profaned" when the exquisite song,

> *Come, my* CELIA, *let vs proue,*
> *While we can, the sports of loue;*

is framed for so base a use'.[1] But is not the profanation what Jonson wanted us to feel? Love and poetry and song are profaned by the use this evil man puts them to. If the song were less exquisite, the ironic effect would be that much less sharp. Its use as a song seems comparable to the use of religious imagery in the first scene.

The song, though exquisite as a detached piece adapted from Catullus, is more meaningful if it is related to the rest of the play. In a long poem a metaphor accumulates meanings which are not wholly lost, but remain latent in every subsequent use of the metaphor. Part of the richness of poetic language is in this latency and in the cross-references that the mind can make between one use of a metaphor and another. Some of the metaphors in this song have accumulated meanings which enrich its texture by echoing previous passages. In the second line, for instance, '*sports*' may echo the 'sport' which Volpone called for from his dwarf, eunuch, and fool (I. i. 69-70). Having seen already their obscene show, we have a foretaste of what '*the sports of loue*' could mean.

> *Spend not then his gifts, in vaine.*
> *Sunnes, that set, may rise againe:*
> *But if, once, we lose this light,*
> *'Tis with vs perpetuall night.*

Boas, *Stuart Drama,* 108.

Here, the light imagery may be an echo of the sun image in the first scene of the play. Hovering over these lines, because of that scene, is that brighter light from the 'sonne of Sol' that Volpone paid reverence to in his opening hymn. With some show of gallantry, he at first forbears to use the sovereign power of gold, 'the price of soules', and tries to move Celia with the Epicurean argument (or, more properly, a debasing of that argument) that perpetual night will follow this day. But the imagery of light that he uses betrays the sordidness of the intrigue he proposes.

The line '*Fame, and rumor are but toies*' reminds us of the sophistry by which Corvino, pandering for his own wife, had disposed of 'Honour! tut, a breath'. Volpone is the more confirmed villain because he is not concerned with honour until Celia later says, 'If you haue conscience——.' Then Volpone dismisses it as 'the beggers vertue' (III. vii. 210). His opinion of women is so low that he thinks Celia is worried only about reputation and gossip. And even they are only 'toies'—ornaments or trifles. The figure of Corvino also stands ironically behind the next lines:

> *Cannot we delude the eyes*
> *Of a few poore houshold-spies?*
> *Or his easier eares beguile,*
> *Thus remooued, by our wile?*

For it was Corvino who had complacently told Celia, when he claimed that he was no longer jealous:

> Doe not I know, if women haue a will
> They'll doe 'gainst all the watches, o' the world?
> And that the fiercest spies, are tam'd with gold?
>
> II. vii. 8-10

Corvino's words, here as elsewhere, are lightened by the same flashes of irony which illuminate his whole character in the play. It is not Celia's will, but his own that has brought her to this assault. And he is the fiercest spy who has been tamed with gold.

The final lines of the song are characteristic of Volpone, the fox, whose element is stealth and trickery.

> *'Tis no sinne, loues fruits to steale;*
> *But the sweet thefts to reueale:*
> *To be taken, to be seene,*
> *These haue crimes accounted beene.*

As we saw in Act I, Volpone's ethical system is almost point for point the reverse of Christian ethics. Here is another instance. In the Christian code sin is sin in God's eyes, whether or not discovered by men. To Volpone the only sin is in being found out or, what probably seems worse to him, 'to reueale', that is, confess.

'Sensuall baites' is Celia's summation, and a true one, of Volpone's persuasion, because he mingles the sensuousness of romantic places and enticing pleasures with allusions to nature, classical mythology, and past ages, to produce an erotic vision that, in less harrowing circumstances, might have corrupted an anchorite.

> If thou hast wisdome, heare me, CELIA.
> Thy bathes shall be the iuyce of iuly-flowres,
> Spirit of roses, and of violets,
> The milke of vnicornes, and panthers breath
> Gather'd in bagges, and mixt with *cretan* wines.
> Our drinke shall be prepared gold, and amber;
> Which we will take, vntill my roofe whirle round
> With the *vertigo*: and my dwarfe shall dance,
> My eunuch sing, my foole make vp the antique.
> Whil'st, we, in changed shapes, act OVIDS tales,
> Thou, like EVROPA now, and I like IOVE,
> Then I like MARS, and thou like ERYCINE,
> So, of the rest, till we haue quite run through
> And weary'd all the fables of the gods.
> Then will I haue thee in more moderne formes,
> Attired like some sprightly dame of *France*,
> Braue *Tuscan* lady, or proud *Spanish* beauty;
> Sometimes, vnto the *Persian Sophies* wife;

Or the grand-*Signiors* mistresse; and, for change,
To one of our most art-full courtizans,
Or some quick *Negro*, or cold *Russian*;
And I will meet thee, in as many shapes:
Where we may, so, trans-fuse our wandring soules,
Out at our lippes, and score vp summes of pleasures,

III. vii. 212-235

This is a remarkable speech, ransacking the ages and the
world and exploiting the senses as it does, but it is a speech
entirely in keeping with what we already know of Volpone.
His drink, we might have predicted, would be 'prepared
gold, and amber'; he must even swallow his god. The
central action — his changing into various shapes — is
precisely what this master of disguise would do. But the
changes also bring in the sense of sexual perversity which is
increased by the realization that his 'family' will be looking
on: his dwarf, eunuch, and fool will sing and dance while he
and Celia enact the tales of Ovid. Even the shapes he
chooses are characteristic because he chooses to act the part
of gods—Jove and Mars—and 'all the fables of the gods'.
At first the aristocrat will play at being only a god, but his
desire for variety overcomes his taste, and he, like Jove,
descends to mortal ladies of France, Tuscany, Spain, and
Persia, meeting them 'in as many shapes'. Here, again,
classical allusions and erotic imagery are debased by the use
Volpone puts them to. The speech reaches its climax when
he borrows from Petronius and Catullus to make this comic
proposal.

Where we may, so, trans-fuse our wandring soules,
Out at our lippes, and score vp summes of pleasures,

> *That the curious shall not know,*
> *How to tell them, as they flow;*
> *And the enuious, when they find*
> *What their number is, be pind.*

This is unquestionably one of the grossest images that even

Volpone uses. 'Trans-fuse', which is the core of the image, literally means to pour some substance out of one vessel into another. Apply this denotation to the soul, and the soul is changed into a liquid or into blood, or into something that can wander, moving from the body in a kiss. But the most obscene part of the image is that, by the transfusions, they can 'score vp summes of pleasures'. In other words, they can record their orgasms by the number of times their 'fast and loose' souls are transferred. The transference is so intimate that the curious could not be aware of it, but the shamelessness and perversity of Volpone appear in the fact that there would be someone around to be curious. The publicity implied in this, the interest shown in number, and the desire to make the envious pine—all are marks of a man whose taste has been vulgarized and whose concern is more with the quantity of sensations than with their quality.

Even Celia has been so completely revolted by the treatment she has received from her husband and from this sensualist that she has lost her hold on the normal values of life. Beauty has become a crime of nature to her, a crime which ought to be destroyed by flaying, poisoning, or even leprosy. This extreme zeal puts her into the company of martyrs or saints, where she would be quite at home. Her final pious plea, ineffectual as it is, is the only plea she knows how to make.

> And I will kneele to you, pray for you, pay downe
> A thousand hourely vowes, sir, for your health,
> Report, and thinke you vertuous—
> VOLP.   Thinke me cold,
> Frosen, and impotent, and so report me?

She could not have chosen less persuasive language, for Volpone equates virtue with impotence, and lust with virility. Not to do the act as unthinkingly as a beast is to 'degenerate, and abuse my nation'. The time for words is not before, but after the act, when there is no need for them.

Something of the normal equilibrium is restored when Bonario bursts in and adds force to piety:

> thou shouldst, yet,
> Be made the timely sacrifice of vengeance,
> Before this altar, and this drosse, thy idoll.
> Lady, let's quit the place, it is the den
> Of villany;

All the sorcery of Volpone's language, all the illusions that the sensuous imagery has created are dissipated by the simple touch of this Christian imagery. His gold becomes dross; his god, an idol; his gorgeous room, only the den of a fox.

Seeing the moral implications of the imagery here should not blind us to its romantic and comic aspects. Vile as Volpone's room is, it has its appeal. His allusions to nature and mythology, taken alone, give the scene a glow of the sensuous, the dreamt-of, the impossible. Spoken to an unwilling young girl by a lecher, they bring the scene close to pathos. But, however, sensuously romantic and latently pathetic the scene seems to be, it remains comic. Anyone who is as interested as Volpone is in scoring up 'summes of pleasures' must seem, to normal people, ludicrous. And anyone who pursues an object with Volpone's singleness of aim lacks a sense of proportion. Indeed, all of the pursued pursuers in this play are comic because, in their 'humour', they lack a sense of humour—a sense of the multiplicity of experience and of the various other legitimate ways of looking at life. One function of the imagery is to suggest some of these other views of life—the religious, the erotic, the intellectual—and to show how Volpone's perverted reasoning or Corvino's obsessive greed has twisted all of these into one iron discipline.

VII

The second half of the play does not require as detailed a discussion as the first half, partly because it contains less imagery, partly because what imagery it does contain develops the animal, religious, and classical implications along the lines set down. In the court scene in Act IV the animal imagery used by Corbaccio (IV. v. 111 ff.) and by Corvino (IV. v. 118 ff.) plays off against the religious imagery used by Bonario (IV. v. 96 ff.) and by Celia (IV. vi. 17). The light imagery of the first scene appears in Mosca's speeches in V. ii. 1-4 and 23.

The sub-plot of Sir Politic and Lady Would-be may seem, at first, to have little connection with the main plot, but on closer scrutiny it turns out to be an ironic echo of the Celia-Corvino-Volpone plot. Lady Would-be puts herself in the same position that Corvino put Celia, but while Celia was meek and decorous, Lady Pol is strident and parrot-like enough to frighten away even Volpone. As we have already seen, Volpone wondered at the 'desperate valure' of the English who 'dare let loose / Their wiues to all encounters'. Peregrine later commented on this same peculiarity of 'sir POLITIQVE bawd! / To bring me, thus, acquainted with his wife!' (IV. iii. 20-21). Just before this, Lady Would-be had told Peregrine, with a singularly improper choice of words,

'Pray you, sir, vse mee. In faith,
The more you see me, the more I shall conceiue,
You haue forgot our quarrell.   IV. iii. 17-19

The ambiguity of 'vse' and 'conceiue' and the poise of 'conceiue' at the end of the verse open her speech to an unfair interpretation. For, coarse and greedy as she may be, she is not necessarily as loose as Mosca implies when he dismisses her (V. iii. 40-43). Still, loose or not, she stands in ironic contrast to Celia, just as Sir Politic, the bumbling English Machiavellian, is contrasted with Volpone, the natural Machiavellian.[1]

[1] The best analysis of the sub-plot is by Jonas A. Barish, 'The Double Plot in *Volpone*', *Modern Philology*, LI (November 1953), 83-92. My own brief conclusions, arrived at independently of Barish's brilliant article, are substantially the same as his, though his are much more thoroughly and subtly thought out.

In Act V there are several passages which require careful analysis. The most remarkable is in the second scene when Volpone and Mosca talk about the hearing at court from which they have just returned. Mosca says,

> You are not taken with it, enough, me thinkes?
> VOLP. O, more, then if I had enioy'd the wench:
> The pleasure of all woman-kind's not like it.
>
> .   .   .   .   .
>
> Thou'hast playd thy prise, my precious MOSCA.
> MOS.   Nay, sir,
> To gull the court—
> VOLP.   And, quite diuert the torrent,
> Vpon the innocent.
> MOS.   Yes, and to make
> So rare a musique out of discordes—   V. ii. 9-18

Here is the perfect perversion of the sexual instinct. To fool the court and divert the force of justice upon the innocent is to Volpone a greater pleasure than intercourse with women. One might think that, in view of Volpone's behaviour in the seduction scene with Celia, he, like most men, would prefer sexual intercourse, as a pleasure, to anything else. But greed and vanity and a debased intelligence have so far deranged his normal instincts that the joy of life comes not from giving joy to others but from giving pain.

We have been prepared for this perversion of the sexual instinct from the opening scene in which we saw Volpone kiss his gold and claim that, as the best of things, it far transcends 'All stile of ioy' (I. i. 17). Gold has become so eroticized by his greed that it has perverted the normal course of his passion. Hence, seduction and rape are the only sexual expressions he can have, and even the delight in these is increased if a Celia can be gained by gulling the husband. Gold remains his permanent mistress, whom he uses in an erotic way to make the birds of prey 'Contend in gifts, as they would seeme, in loue' (I. i. 84).

The pleasure, greater than if he had 'enioy'd the wench', that Volpone takes in gulling people throws him into an ecstasy which finally leads to his downfall. He sends out Castrone and Nano to give out that he is dead.

> I shall haue, instantly, my vulture, crow,
> Rauen, come flying hither (on the newes)
> To peck for carrion, my shee-wolfe, and all,
> Greedy, and full of expectation—
> MOS. And then to haue it rauish'd from their mouthes?
>
> V. ii. 64-68

'Rauish'd' emphasizes the sexual aspect of the tormenting. The latent sadism (or what popularly passes for sadism) in these images is made more explicit when Volpone tells Mosca to pretend to be his heir, delude the gaping birds and, as a climax, 'thou vse them skiruily' (V. ii. 75). To think of treating people scurvily is a delight second only to one—seeing them treated scurvily.

> I'le get vp,
> Behind the cortine, on a stoole, and harken;
> Sometime, peepe ouer; see, how they doe looke;
> With what degrees, their bloud doth leaue their
> faces!
> O, 'twill afford me a rare meale of laughter.
>
> V. ii. 83-87

This ludicrous picture of a Magnifico of Venice standing on a stool to peep over a curtain suggests something of the sexually curious little boy looking at forbidden scenes. But a perverted little boy, because he is enjoying the pain of others and not their pleasure.

Since Volpone is erotically attached to his gold and finds a perverted sexual pleasure in tormenting fools with the hope of gold, his eroticism at times carries over to his pander, Mosca. Note how he addresses his servant:

> ... my beloued MOSCA.   I. i. 30
> Louing MOSCA,   I. ii. 122

> Excellent, Mosca!
> Come hither, let me kisse thee.   I. iii. 78-79
> . . . good rascall, let me kisse thee: I. iv. 137
>   My diuine Mosca!   I. v. 84
> Thou art mine honor, Mosca, and my pride,
> My ioy, my tickling, my delight!   III. vii. 68-69
>   Exquisite Mosca!   V. ii. 4
> . . . my precious Mosca!   V. ii. 15

These are epithets generally reserved for a loved one, but applied to Mosca, one supposes, both because he is intimately associated with the gold and because he is Volpone's agent in tormenting the gulls. The most explicit image which shows that Mosca, like the gold, has been eroticized appears at the height of Volpone's joy, when, after the gulls have been 'skiruily' dismissed one by one, Volpone comes down from his stool and cries,

>   my wittie *mischiefe*,
> Let me embrace thee. O, that I could now
> Transforme thee to a Venvs—   V. iii. 102-104

The perversity and the complete reversal of values that this treatment involves is summed up in the final image of that scene: 'O, I will be a sharpe disease vnto 'hem' (V. iii. 117).

Erotic imagery and classical allusion unite in a passage in which gold assumes many of the properties of the elixir of life.

>   Why, your gold
> Is such another med'cine, it dries vp
> All those offensiue sauors! It transformes
> The most deformed, and restores 'hem louely,
> As 't were the strange poeticall girdle. Iove
> Could not inuent, t'himselfe, a shroud more subtile,
> To passe Acrisivs guardes. It is the thing
> Makes all the world her grace, her youth, her
>   beauty.   V. ii. 98-105

Gold has the power normally reserved for love in that it has the divine power of giving youth and beauty. Its medicinal properties make it almost a parody of the miraculous power of a saint who can make the lame walk. The two classical images carry out this interpretation. 'The strange poeticall girdle' refers, as Jonson points out in his note, to the cestus of Venus which gave the wearer the power of exciting love. Gold, which has previously been eroticized, has here been given the supreme sexual function: it excites love. At first the allusion to Jove does not seem to widen the range of the imagery because the shroud referred to was the shower of gold in which Jove appeared to Danaë after passing the guards of her father, Acrisius. The figure becomes richer when we remember that, since Jove is on an erotic adventure, the shower of gold takes on a sexual character, which is in keeping with the rest of the passage. Furthermore, the mention of Jove recalls the seduction scene where Volpone compared himself to Jove, and we see that he, like Jove, passed to Celia by means of a shower of gold—or, more correctly, the expectation of gold.

VIII

This exaltation of gold marks the height and the end of both classical allusion and erotic imagery. Animal imagery, which had been hinted at in the Celia scene, reappears when Bonario calls Volpone a 'libidinous swine', an epithet which may allude to the Circean power of lust (III. vii. 267). In the last two acts allusions to the vulture, raven, and crow once more become prominent. Gradually, the animal imagery becomes so marked and, expressed chiefly by the larger figures of personification and simile, so shocking that there is no room for the subtlety of allusions to mythology, to love, or, except for a few images, to religion. The bestial side of man, so voracious for gold, eats up the intellectual side, particularly in the court scenes. Corbaccio then calls his own son, 'Monster of man, swine, goate, wolfe . . . viper'

(IV. v. 111-112), Voltore accuses Celia of being 'the stale' (stalking horse) of Bonario. Corvino, still hasting for his horns, claims that Celia is a whore 'Of most hot exercise, more then a partrich' (IV. v. 118), and that she 'Neighes, like a iennet' (IV. v. 119). Such figures as these, which have one function of suggesting the animal world, have another of supplying the ludicrous and ironic humour of the court scenes. There is such outrageous disparity between the gentle, nun-like Celia and the jennet, a small Spanish horse neighing in heat, that one is forced to laugh, savage as the scene is. That Corvino should now falsely accuse his wife of the harlotry he had previously been enraged at even speculating about is typical of the kind of irony that the court scene brings out.

Gradually, the range of the animal comparisons widens until it goes out of the animal world altogether, either into the insect world or into fantasy.

1. Corbaccio will curl up 'like a hog-louse' (V. ii. 91).

2. Mosca is a 'Basiliske', a mythical beast who could kill with a look (V. viii. 27).

3. Mosca is a 'flesh-flie', a fly whose larvae or maggots feed on flesh (V. ix. 1).

4. Corvino is a '*Chimaera* of wittall, foole, and knaue'; a chimera was a monster composed of the parts of various animals (V. xii. 91).

The suggestion in these images may be that not even the bounds of the animal world can hold men once possessed by greed and vanity. But the final emphasis is on the world of animals. Mosca, after he has been condemned to the galleys, cries to Volpone, 'Bane to thy wooluish nature.' This shift from the fox to the wolf marks the shift in Volpone's own nature from the craft and cunning of the fox to the rapacity and destructiveness of the wolf. Had he remained a fox, he would not have brought himself and his servant to this trap.

The final lines of the play sum up and comment on the meaning of the animal imagery. The First Avocatori, who seems to have more sense than the others, says, 'Mischiefes feed / Like beasts, till they be fat, and then they bleed.' And it is this natural fattening and natural bleeding which restores the order of things. The principal mischiefs, the fox and the fly, fatten themselves on the birds of prey, and, by their own over-reaching, bleed themselves. Volpone 'must be merry, with a mischiefe to me!' (V. xi. 14). Mosca, the 'flesh-flie' who had so long lived off the flesh of another, began 'to grow in loue / With my deare selfe', felt 'a whimsey i' my bloud' and sought to set himself up (III. i. 1-4). The beasts, not the law, restore the order.

The first half of the play tended to revolve around Volpone's bed; the second half around the court. The true function of both has been perverted. Normally, a bed is an age-old symbol of rest, sex, and conception, and secondarily, of birth, death, and sickness. But in *Volpone* it has become symbolic of pretence and falsity. The sickness is false; the death is false; the rest is false. Volpone is more vigorous and active than anyone except Mosca. Even the sex is false, for Volpone finds gulling fools more pleasurable than making love to women. Since the normal function of the bed has been so perverted, Volpone's punishment is symbolically just:

And, since the most was gotten by imposture,
By faining lame, gout, palsey, and such diseases,
Thou art to lie in prison, crampt with irons,
Till thou bee'st sicke, and lame indeed.

V. xii. 121-124

He had fattened himself up to this fate for some time. Early in the play he was wise enough to see what a 'rare punishment' avarice is to itself (I. iv. 142-143). Then, after his first hearing at court, he begins to 'bleed'. His left leg has the cramp, and some power has struck him with a 'dead palsey' (V. i. 5-7). Volpone, who was a 'sharp disease' to others, has become one to himself.

But the power that strikes him with a 'dead palsey' is brought on by himself, not the court. The knot is undone by 'miracle', according to the First Avocatori. Nothing could be less true, because the Fox, refusing to be gulled, uncases himself. Judicial sanity has been so lost by the court that it, like the third Avocatori, is at one time 'turn'd a stone' (IV. v. 154) and, at another, has 'an earthquake in me' (IV. vi. 58). Magnificent in dealing out punishment, the court is inept at finding the guilty. 'Miracle' implies a Christian providence which has as ineffectual a voice in the court as in the bedroom. Thus:

CORV. VOLT.   We beg fauor,
CEL.   And mercy.
AVOC. 1. You hurt your innocence, suing for the
            guilty.   V. xii. 105-106

Celia, the heavenly one, whose first word was 'patience' and whose last word is 'mercy', is unheeded in both pleas.

IX

The final lines of the play—'Mischiefes feed / Like beasts, till they be fat, and then they bleed'—also sum up the imagery of feeding which has cut across the artificial lines drawn in this analysis. Feeding might be said to symbolize the double theme of greed for riches and lust for sensuous pleasures.[1] One might call it the central image of the play because it is the core of many other images. It is at the heart of the animal imagery; the birds of prey are always 'pecking for carrion' or 'gaping'; Volpone constantly thinks in terms of feeding others or himself. He feeds others in

[1] J. D. Rea claims that the theme is not greed, but folly in all its phases. Rea, ed., *Volpone* (New Haven, 1919), XXVII. But that seems to me a misreading of the play, possibly resulting from his discovery that Jonson used Erasmus's *Praise of Folly* as one of the principal sources.

expectation (III. vii. 188-189), but not Celia: she shall have the phoenix and other rare delicacies. Both Volpone and Mosca think of hope as something to eat. Mosca says,

> Your hopes, sir, are like happie blossomes, faire,
> And promise timely fruit, if you will stay
> But the maturing;   III. v. 30-32

Later he says that the gulls could not sense that they were being tricked because each is 'stuft with his owne hopes' (V. ii. 23-24). Hopes are 'milk'd' (I. ii. 127), and hope itself 'Is such a bait, it couers any hooke' (I. iv. 134-135).

How many things in the Volpone world are eaten! Celia is 'a wench / O' the first yeere! a beautie, ripe, as haruest!' (I. v. 108-109). That would make her a lamb or grain. 'All her lookes are sweet, / As the first grapes, or cherries' (I. v. 120-121). Laughter becomes something eaten, as Volpone indicates when he is anticipating the scurvy treatment of the gulls: 'O, 'twill afford me a rare meale of laughter' (V. ii. 87). Or, once eaten, it is something purged. Mosca counsels his master to contain 'Your fluxe of laughter, sir' (I. iv. 134). Flux, in the physiological sense, meant an 'abnormally copious flowing of blood, excrement, etc., from the bowels or other organs' (OED). The scurvy treatment itself is thought of by Volpone as a 'feast' (V. iii. 108-109).

Gold is drink: 'Our drinke', Volpone tells Celia, 'shall be prepared gold, and amber' (III. vii. 217). Characteristically, Jonson builds imaginatively on what was actually so: aurum potabile (drinkable gold) was thought of as a remedy of great efficacy. But Volpone's drinking gold seems like a parody of the Communion: he must drink the blood of his dumb god, riches. Mosca works on this belief in the efficacy of aurum potabile early in the play when he tells Corbaccio that gold he has brought is 'true physick', 'sacred medicine', 'great elixir' (I. iv. 71-72). The medicinal

VOLPONE

qualities of gold were also the subject of another image already analysed (V. ii. 98 ff.). But gold is not simply something to be drunk. Note the extraordinary figure which Mosca uses in asking Voltore to remember him.

> When you doe come to swim, in golden lard,
> Vp to the armes, in honny, that your chin
> Is borne vp stiffe, with fatnesse of the floud,
>
> I. iii. 70-72

Gold becomes both a bath and a meal.

But the ultimate reach of feeding is beyond gold, hope, woman as a sexual object, or laughter. The final food is man. This is implied in more than one place. Early in the play when Volpone says that he will not earn money by usury, Mosca adds,

> No, sir, nor deuoure
> Soft prodigalls. You shall ha' some will swallow
> A melting heire, as glibly, as your *Dutch*
> Will pills of butter, and ne're purge for't;
>
> I. i. 40-43

Volpone will not feed so; but the implication is that someone in his hideous world will. Just before this, as though to foreshadow this last image, Volpone says that he will

> fat no beasts
> To feede the shambles; haue no mills for yron,
> Oyle, corne, or men, to grinde 'hem into poulder;
>
> I. i. 34-36

Volpone will not grind corn or man into a powder; that is the 'common way' to gain. The definition of a Puritan by Androgyno is another glance at the feeding of man on man: '*Of those deuoure flesh, and sometimes one another*' (I. ii. 44). The next statement of this is as casual as the others. Volpone, in congratulating himself on his morning's 'purchase', says,

> Why, this is better then rob churches, yet:
> Or fat, by eating (once a mon'th) a man.
>
> I. v. 91-92

When Volpone, in his last words, refers to his lying in chains as 'mortifying', he apparently thinks of himself as food for others. 'Mortifying', as Percy Simpson points out, probably plays on the cookery term, which means making meat tender by hanging it up after it has been killed. These images of man being ground at a mill, of a prodigal being devoured, of Puritans sometimes eating one another, give the bite to the last lines in which 'Mischiefes feed / Like beasts, till they be fat. . . .' For mischiefs feed on men.

This picture of the world is universalized in one of the most remarkable speeches in the whole play—Mosca's soliloquy in Act III, Scene 1.

> I feare, I shall begin to grow in loue
> With my deare selfe, and my most prosp'rous parts,
> They doe so spring, and burgeon; I can feele
> A whimsey i' my bloud: . . .
>   I could skip
> Out of my skin, now, like a subtill snake,
> I am so limber. O! Your Parasite
> Is a most precious thing, dropt from aboue,
> Not bred 'mong'st clods, and clot-poules, here on
>   earth.
> I muse, the mysterie was not made a science,
> It is so liberally profest! almost
> All the wise world is little else, in nature,
> But Parasites, or Sub-parasites.   III. i. 1-13

Mosca's 'mysterie', that is, his art or profession, has not been made a specialized science, known only to few, because almost everyone is a parasite or a sub-parasite. The literal meaning of parasite—one who eats at the table of another—remains. To that has been added the biological meaning: an animal or plant which lives on or upon another organism. The qualifications to this universal picture—'almost' and 'in nature'—are important because they give enough freedom of choice to save man from being only a beast. There can be more to life than this parasitic feeding of one man on another. But, though 'in nature' implies a way out, it defines even more sharply how natural such feeding is. Thus, Mosca widens the references of this parasitism, even as Volpone did in Act I, by showing what the common parasite is.

> I meane not those, that haue your bare towne-arte,
> To know, who's fit to feede 'hem; . . .
>   . . . or get
> Kitchin-inuention, and some stale receipts
> To please the belly, and the groine; nor those
> With their court-dog-tricks, that can fawne, and
>   fleere,   III. i. 14-20

Mosca, like his master, is an aristocrat among parasites.

> But your fine, elegant rascall, that can rise,
> And stoope (almost together) like an arrow;
> Shoot through the aire, as nimbly as a starre;
> Turne short, as doth a swallow; and be here,
> And there, and here, and yonder, all at once;
> Present to any humour, all occasion;
> And change a visor, swifter, then a thought!
> This is the creature, had the art borne with him;
> Toiles not to learne it, but doth practise it
> Out of most excellent nature: and such sparkes,
> Are the true Parasites, others but their *Zani's*.
>   III. i. 23-33

The images of the arrow, the star, and the swallow show that Mosca, like Volpone, thinks himself above the 'earth-fed' parasites. The true parasite feeds on man continually, not intermittently as the ones with either 'bare towne-arte' or 'court-dog-tricks' do. Such a fine rascal is 'Present to any humour, all occasion', and able to exploit anyone any time: in short, the perfect entrepreneur of human nature. His ability to 'change a visor [an expression of the face which conceals the real feeling], swifter, then a thought' implies that abuse of reason which all his plots and counterplots demonstrate. The last lines reveal the other side of 'nature'. If 'nature' as previously used implies a certain freedom on the part of a man who will conquer his animal nature, here 'nature' seems to mean natural endowment, intellectual as well as animal. The true parasite is one who uses his natural endowment as a man to feed on others. The others are only buffoons who mimic his tricks.

Feeding, then, is the great symbolic act of the play, the one gross act which dramatizes man's insatiable greed. Bird feeds on fox, fox on bird, and fly on both: that is nature. In so far as man plays the part of a bird of prey, a fox, or a fly by living off another man, he abuses the very quality that makes him a man—his reason. And he breaks the fundamental Christian law which Paul, with imagery similar to *Volpone's*, explained in his epistle to the Galatians, v. 14-15: 'For all the law is fulfilled in one word, *even* in this, Thou shalt love thy neighbour as thyself. But if ye bite and devour one another, take heed that ye be not consumed one of another.'

This Volpone world in which man feeds on man, and possessor is pursued with an animal-like ferocity, might be looked on, by a critic willing to do some violence to the play, as a prophetic vision of the society which capitalism, even in Jonson's day, was creating. One can easily interpret the scenes of Volpone worshipping his gold as extravagant caricatures of that idolatry of wealth which, according to R. H. Tawney, is 'the practical religion of capitalist society', and see in the animal and feeding imagery a horrifying picture of an economic system divided into possessors and pursuers.[1] Or one can claim, as L. C. Knights does, that in *Volpone* and *The Alchemist* Jonson is drawing on the anti-acquisitive tradition inherited from the Middle Ages.[2] A reading of *Volpone* based on either of these views makes

---

[1] R. H. Tawney, *Religion and the Rise of Capitalism* (New York, 1947), 234-235.
[2] Knights, *Drama and Society in the Age of Jonson*, 190.

sense. Yet neither one exhausts the meaning of the play, which is large enough to contain both a medieval tradition and a modern criticism of capitalism. It is precisely this universality that seems to me impressive—but its universality as an artistic structure, not simply as an economic tract.

Let me summarize the function of the imagery in the structure of *Volpone*:

1. Christian terms are debased in a worship of gold that is almost a complete inversion of the Christian religion. By suggesting two orders at the same time—the Christian order and the debasement of that order—the religious imagery at once creates and passes a judgment on Volpone's religion of gold.

2. The contrast implicit in the religious imagery helps create that irony which is fundamental to the tone.

3. The abnormal and irrational beings—Nano, Androgyno, and Castrone—are symbolic of the perverted world which results from such a reversal of values.

4. The classical world is debased by the vulgar use of classical allusions.

5. Animal imagery implies that men are turned into beasts by greed. The animal and human levels are either confused or identified.

6. The abuse of erotic imagery indicates a vulgarizing of love and hints at a perversion of the sexual instinct.

7. The debasing of religious, classical, and erotic imagery reaches its lowest point in the seduction scene. The Greek pantheon is called on to seduce a reluctant wife; erotic images become inflated and gross; and the whole scene is likened to the 'true heau'n of loue'.

8. Animal imagery, quiescent in the second and third acts, returns in the fourth act to dominate the last scenes of the play.

9. Feeding—that act which makes men daily, even hourly, seem most like animals—symbolizes greed.

This analysis has not presented all the images in *Volpone* that could be offered to substantiate this interpretation. For instance, note two similar images used by Mosca. In the first he tells Corbaccio that 'The streame of your diuerted loue hath throwne you / Vpon my master' (I. iv. 105-106). Later, in gloating with Volpone over their trickery at court, he says, 'And, quite diuert the torrent, / Vpon the innocent' (V. ii. 16-17). 'Diuert' is as close as Jonson comes to the term used here—perversion. Such nature images make the same point that the other images do. The normal streams of life as diverted by this hunger for wealth and pleasure: the love of father for son, the love of husband for wife, respect for the law, man's honour, woman's virtue, the sexual instinct, justice—all are diverted from their true course. In short, the perversion of classical allusions, erotic and religious imagery implies—it can do no more than imply— a perversion in the lives of the speakers; for, in drama, man is the language he uses.

To misuse images in this way is to violate the principle of decorum which, Rosemond Tuve claims, was 'the most important regulatory principle determining images' in the Renaissance.[1] The images are indecorous in several ways. Frequently, great vehicles are used with mean tenors: Venus's girdle = gold. Occasionally, the vehicle is exaggerated beyond the bounds of subtlety or imaginative truth: if gold could have been the lover of Venus, he would have given her twenty thousand Cupids. This violation of decorum has a radical effect on the tone because it is so bare-faced and direct that it shocks us by its shamelessness. Sometimes the indecorum is ludicrous, as a combination of the great and the low is likely to be. Always it is ironic, because the vehicle appears to give us one thing whereas the vehicle plus the tenor actually give us quite another. Such a compound of the satiric, the ludicrous, and the ironic

[1] Tuve, *Elizabethan and Metaphysical Imagery*, 230.

is comic, but not purely comic. The very violation of decorum which helps create the comic tone is also involved in qualifying that tone, because the indecorous vehicles carry implications—religious or ethical or classical—which so deepen the tone that there is some sense in agreeing with Bonamy Dobrée in his observation about a kind of comedy 'perilously near tragedy, in which the balance is so fine that it seems sometimes as though it would topple over into the other form, as in *Volpone* or *Le Misanthrope*'.[1]

[1] Dobrée, *Restoration Comedy, 1660-1720* (Oxford, 1924), 15.

CHAPTER VI

'THE ALCHEMIST'

I

A POET re-enacts the roles of God and Adam: he creates a world and names the animals. The naming of the animals in Jonson's plays is, as anyone can recognize, particularly important. So are the epithets, the names which the animals give each other. Mammon calls Face,

> [Subtle's] fire-drake,
> His lungs, his *Zephyrus*, he that puffes his coales,
> Till he firke nature vp, in her owne center.
> II. i. 26-28

This immense blower of bellows blows so hard on the coals of the plot that the whole thing explodes in his face. '*Till it* [the stone], *and they, and all in* fume *are gone.*' The explosion of the furnace in the fourth act is an objectification of what happens to the plot. More than one play of Jonson's seems to work on the same principle of an explosion. Jonson's favourite rhetorical device—hyperbole—radiates into all parts of his plays so that the dialogue trembles on the edge of bombast, the situations move close to burlesque or mock-heroic, the characters become grotesques, and the plot explodes.

This inflation and explosion of the plot is apparent in the way epithets are used throughout *The Alchemist*. In the first scene two motifs are developed side by side; both help to establish the atmosphere of the play. One is the motif of abusive epithets which Subtle, Face, and Dol fling at each other. They call each other rogue, slave, cheater, cut-purse, bawd, and witch. That is all very well; at least all of these fine fellows are human beings. But the vehicles have a wider reference. The impostors are compared to mongrels, scarabs, vermin, curs. These, in their several ways, suggest animals which live on a lower plane than men, or insects which prey on other beings. The dog imagery recurs most often. Dol is a bitch, and Face and Subtle are mastiffs. In short, we are among the snarling animals that live on other beings or each other. We are in that world which Jonson creates so authoritatively—that ambiguous world between the animal and the human.

The second motif in the first scene is developed by Dol's euphemistic epithets for her partners. They are 'gentlemen' (Subtle has just said, 'I fart at thee') and 'masters' who, according to her, ought to have more regard for their reputations. Dol addresses Face, who is in a captain's uniform, as 'Generall', and Subtle as 'Soueraigne'. At the end of the quarrel they are 'My noble Soueraigne, and worthy Generall' (I. i. 172). These royal and martial allusions are absurdly high-flown and comically inappropriate when applied to the impostors and their thievery. After Dol advises them to avoid Don Provost, the hangman, Subtle hails her as 'Royall Dol! / Spoken like CLARIDIANA, and thy selfe!' (I. i. 174-175). The quarrel to Dol is a major historical event: 'Will you vn-doe your selues with ciuill warre?' (I. i. 82). And Dol has grandiose ideas about herself: 'Haue yet, some care of me, o' your *republique*—' (I. i. 110). This republic becomes aristocratic again in the hands of Mammon who compares Dol to 'One o' the *Austriack* princes' (IV. i. 56).

After the first scene and until the next to the last scene almost all of the epithets are inflated. The grandeur of their political and martial references works itself into even casual remarks. Subtle says to himself that 'we must keepe FACE in awe' or he will overlook us 'like a tyranne' (IV. iii. 18-19). Which is more pretentious here—that Face could overlook like a tyrant or that Subtle, even using the royal 'we',

could keep anyone in awe? But from the first Subtle has
thought of himself as awful.

> No, you *scarabe*,
> I'll thunder you, in peeces. I will teach you
> How to beware, to tempt a *furie*'againe
> That carries tempest in his hand, and voice.
>
> I. i. 59-62

Subtle oscillates somewhere between 'the father of hunger'
and a Fury, a bawd and a learned doctor, until he and his
'*republique*' escape over the back wall.

Before the whole plot blows up in their faces, this royal
trio have almost convinced themselves and certainly convinced others of their importance. To others Face and
Subtle are 'your worship'. To Subtle, Face is 'so famous,
the precious king / Of present wits' (V. iv. 13-14). Dol, who
has been the 'Queen of Faery' to Dapper, becomes 'Queene
Dol' to Face (V. iv. 65). She is in line for a promotion, too,
because Face has exacted from Mammon a promise that he
will 'make her royall, with the *stone*, / An Empresse' (II. iii.
319-320). When Face plans to marry Dame Pliant, Dol,
with fine perception, notes that "Tis direct / Against our
articles' (V. iv. 71-72). Each of the distinct points of a treaty
was called an 'article'; 'articles' in the plural meant a 'formal
agreement' (*OED*). The word scarcely seems appropriate
for the usual agreement between thieves. Subtle, too, is
righteously indignant because such a marriage was 'Against
the instrument, that was drawne between vs' (V. iv. 81). An
'instrument' was 'a formal legal document whereby a right
is created or confirmed, or a fact recorded; a formal writing
of any kind, as an agreement, deed, charter, or record,
drawn up and executed in technical form so as to be of legal
validity' (*OED*). When the word is defined in these high-
sounding terms, the pretentiousness of Subtle's language is
thrown into relief. Three cozeners agree to rob as many fools

as possible; they call this 'drawing up an instrument'. They are thieves, but they throw a specious air of legality over their activities by euphemistic terms, believing in the common fallacy that, if one refers to low things in high words, one raises them legally and aesthetically. In short, Dol, Subtle, and Face speak as though they had set up a commonwealth ('confederacie' to Surly [V. iii. 23]), with an instrument and articles, a King and a Queen, and a whole world of subjects.

Then, suddenly, the bubble bursts. 'Lungs' has blown so hard that he blows the confederacy and himself right out of existence. Dol, inflated to the 'Queene of Faerie', shrinks to 'my smock-rampant' (V. iv. 126), whom Face will be glad to recommend to 'mistris AMO' or 'madame *Caesarean*', brothel-keepers. Subtle, who thought of Face as 'the precious king / Of present wits' now finds him a 'precious fiend' (V. iv. 138). As for himself, he is no longer a Fury 'That carries tempest in his hand, and voice', but one who will 'hang my selfe' (V. iv. 146). Subtle has already admitted that he has fallen from his majesty. When Face asked him if he heard the disturbance at the door, he answered, 'Yes, and I dwindled with it' (V. iv. 15). This movement from dogs up to kings, queens, and Furies, and back to rogues and whores reminds one of the final lines of *Volpone* where a similar swelling and bursting of the beasts occur. The circular effect of the epithets is completed, not so much by another quarrel between Face and Subtle (neither has time for a quarrel) as by the chorus of fools who thunder on the door of Love-Wit's house.

MAM. Where is this Colliar?
SVR.   And my Captaine FACE?
MAM. These day-Owles.
SVR.   That are birding in mens purses.
MAM. Madame *Suppository*.
KAS.   *Doxey*, my suster.

ANA.   Locusts
    Of the foule pit.
TRI.   Profane as BEL, and the *Dragon*.
ANA. Worse then the Grasse-hoppers, or the Lice of
    Egypt.
    .   .   .   .   .
MAM. The *Chymicall* cousoner.
SVR.   And the Captaine *Pandar*.
KAS. The *Nun*, my suster.
MAM.   Madame *Rabbi*.
ANA.   Scorpions.
                                                           V. v. 11 ff.

If anything, the quack, the rascal, and the whore have
descended even lower than the level of the curs in the
opening scene. Now they have become hawk-owls, locusts,
scorpions, and caterpillars: that is, parasites which live on
higher beings. Furthermore, Ananias's Biblical allusions
make them appear as plagues.

Mammon's language shows the same deflation. Gone are
the classical allusions which had characterized his speech
when he was under the spell of the elixir. Zephyrus, Jove's
shower, the boon of Midas, and all the gods have been blown
up, along with his hopes. Mammon himself, who was to
have been 'King of Bantam', now has humbler plans: he
will mount a turnip-cart and preach the end of the world
(V. v. 81-82). The picture of the gluttonous Mammon, who
wanted shrimps 'In a rare butter, made of dolphins milke'
and his 'beds blowne vp; not stuft', so deflated that he takes
to a turnip-cart is a magnificent absurdity.

In one sense Face alone remains what he was—that is,
nothing in himself, but living only in the disguises or 'faces'
which he assumes: Jeremy, the butler; Captain Face, the
pander; Lungs and Zephyrus, the blower; the Spanish
count; and always the 'king' of a commonwealth of fools.[1]

---

[1] The *OED* defines face as 'command of countenance, especially with reference
to freedom from indication of shame; a bold front; impudence, effrontery,
"cheek" '. There is some hint that Face is really only the clothes he has on. During

His kingdom includes even Love-Wit, who says, 'I will be rul'd by thee in any thing, Ieremie' (V. v. 143) and who, just before, called Face 'my braine'. Surly suggests the variety of Face when, confronted by the smooth Jeremy, he mutters, 'This's a new Face?' (V. iii. 21). But in another sense Face has blown himself out of existence. He too has come down from a Captain to a butler and is aware that his part fell a little in the final scene (V. v. 158).

Actually, of course, these two motifs of abuse and pretension exist side by side throughout the play. Thus at the very time that Mammon addresses Dol as 'Right noble madame', Face in an aside calls her 'my *Guiny*-bird', a slang term for a prostitute (IV. i. 38). But, normally, now one, now the other of these strains is dominant. In the first act and in the last two scenes of the final act the abusive epithets are dominant, while during most of the rest of the play the pretentious epithets are dominant. But at both times the subordinate strain remains as counterpoint to the principal melody, contrasting with it for an ironic effect.

Furthermore, both the abusive and the euphemistic names are perfectly characteristic of the speakers because they are typical of thieves's cant. Such cant was originally a peculiar slang devised for secrecy. For example, a brothel was called variously an Academy, Corinth, school of Venus, vaulting school, smuggling ken, pushing school.[1] The same impulse which caused thieves to invent such slang makes Face refer to Dol as 'my smock-rampant' or Dol call Face 'Soueraigne'. The pretentious epithets, then, as well as the abusive, are not mere rhetorical flourishes, but names which, while serving a poetic purpose, remain true to the impulse behind thieves's cant.

his quarrel with Face, Subtle threatens to mar 'All that the taylor has made' (I. i. 9-10). Note also his remark (I. i. 63). In his dedication to Lady Mary Wroth Jonson commented on '*the ambitious Faces of the time: who, the more they paint are the lesse themselues*'.

[1] Francis Grose, *A Classical Dictionary of the Vulgar Tongue* (London, 1785).

One of the poetic purposes of these epithets is to show Subtle, Face, and Dol on more than one level. On one level we see them as the rogues they are; on another, we see them as the insects or animals they are compared to; on still another, we see them as the higher beings that they and others think they are. The simultaneous existence of multiple levels helps create some of the humour and much of the irony which gather about a whore who thinks of herself as a '*republique*', a quack who will 'thunder' a man in pieces, and a pander who wears a uniform and calls himself 'Captaine'.

II

Both kinds of epithets belong to comic imagery. The basic strategy in such imagery seems to be to violate decorum. A master of the comedy of burlesque and irony like Aristophanes or Jonson or James Joyce must be, first of all, a master of several traditions—religious, literary, cultural. To secure a comic effect, he violates a traditional reaction by bringing together, unexpectedly and indecorously, a tenor and a vehicle which shock us into laughter. In Joyce's *Ulysses*, we are expected to place the whole plan and its separate scenes beside the whole plan and the separate scenes of the *Odyssey*: this continuous interplay is comic, or rather has its comic side. The comparison between Odysseus and Bloom, the Mediterranean world and Dublin, the Sirens and the barmaids, Circe and Bella Cohen, Penelope and Molly Bloom is amusing because of the disparity between the ancient and the modern, the fabulous and the naturalistic. A traditional response is partly satisfied, partly disappointed. Minor examples of the same violation appear throughout *Ulysses*. One of the simplest is Buck Mulligan's misuse of church liturgy in the opening lines.

Even some Americans are aware of the comic spirit which hovers over the names of their cities taken from ancient history. Classical associations (often expurgated and romanticized) and modern realities play off against each other when one recalls that Cicero, Illinois, in the 1920s was one of the headquarters of the Capone gang. George Kaufman was working this same vein when he named one of his comedies, *Helen of Troy, New York*. One of the classic recognitions of such indecorum was written by Matthew Arnold after his visit to America: 'The mere nomenclature of the country acts upon a cultivated person like the incessant pricking of pins. . . . What people in whom the sense for beauty and fitness was quick could have invented, or could tolerate, the hideous names ending in *ville*, the Briggsvilles, Higginsvilles. . . . On a line from Albany to Buffalo, you have, in one part, half the names in the classical dictionary to designate the stations . . . his strange Marcellus or Syracuse is perhaps not much worse than their congenital Briggsville.'[1]

This violation of decorum is evident throughout *The Alchemist*.[2] Thus far we have considered two kinds—the abusive and the pretentious. The indecorum depends on principles which Aristotle noted in his work on rhetoric. To enhance a subject, take the metaphor (that is, the vehicle) from things in the same genus as the subject or from things in a better genus. To disparage a subject, take the vehicle from things in the same or a worse genus. Dol is enhanced by being called 'the *Queene of Faerie*', and disparaged by being called 'Madame *Suppository*'. In both epithets the disparity is so great that the image is comic. It is as ludicrous to think of a whore elevated to the queen of ethereal beings as it is to think of her reduced to the function of a vaginal plug.

[1] M. Arnold, *Civilization in the United States: First and Last Impressions of America* (Boston, 1889), 175.

[2] Scatological allusions also are comic because they violate decorum, but usually they are so obvious that they do not need to be discussed. An example is the echo of Rabelais (I. i. 3-4). See also IV. iii. 21-22; V. iii. 38; V. iv. 57.

Contemporary statements of the principles of decorum stressed particularly the vice of pretension. For example, Puttenham found the high style 'disgraced and made foolish and ridiculous by all wordes affected, counterfait, and puffed vp, as it were a windball carrying more countenance then matter'.[1] The high style of Dol, Face, Subtle, and even Mammon is comic because it is, as we have seen, puffed up and counterfeit. Jonson was particularly sensitive to different kinds of style—the high, the low, the middle, and the vicious. Many of his characters are comic because they speak the 'vitious Language' which is 'vast, and gaping, swelling and irregular'. To him the principal reason for a comic effect in language is an indecorous style. 'And according to their Subject, these stiles vary, and lose their names: For that which is high and lofty, declaring excellent matter, becomes vast and tumorous, speaking of petty and inferiour things.'[2] 'Tumorous', 'swelling', 'windball', 'puffed vp'—all convey the impression of something blown up beyond its just proportion. This same impression is conveyed by the language of *The Alchemist*, in which the characters are inflated and the tone is mock-heroic.

One of Jonson's (and T. S. Eliot's) favourite methods of achieving a comic effect by violating decorum is to bring together, in a tenor and a vehicle, terms from the ancient world and the modern world which clash. Thus he can create that jarring irony of which he is a master. Mammon's speeches, which might at first seem merely sensual dreams rapturous enough to indicate that Jonson himself is taken in by his own creation, are rescued by their irony. Note how this works in one of Mammon's extraordinary speeches.

> I haue a peece of IASONS fleece, too,
> Which was no other, then a booke of *alchemie*,
> Write in large sheepe-skin, a good fat ram-vellam.
> Such was PYTHAGORA's thigh, PANDORA's tub;

[1] Puttenham, 153.   [2] Herford and Simpson, VIII, 625-626.

And, all that fable of MEDEAS charmes,
The manner of our worke: The Bulls, our fornace,
Still breathing fire; our *argent-viue*, the Dragon:
The Dragons teeth, *mercury* sublimate,
That keepes the whitenesse, hardnesse, and the
    biting;
And they are gather'd, into IASON's helme,
(Th'*alembeke*) and then sow'd in MARS his field,
And, thence, sublim'd so often, till they are fix'd.
Both this, th'*Hesperian* garden, CADMVS storie,
IOVE's shower, the boone of MIDAS, ARGVS eyes,
BOCCACE his *Demogorgon*, thousands more.

II. i. 89-103

What is all this rich mythology to Mammon? 'All abstract
riddles of our *stone*.' Mammon is, of course, only repeating
the conventional rhapsodizing of alchemists who ransacked
the ages for any references to gold and found them all
pointing to the philosopher's stone. The stone may once
have meant something fine and noble to those philosophers
who dreamed of a new Golden Age, but, within the universe
of discourse of this play, the stone has drawn to itself all
sorts of ugly and ignoble associations with quacks and fools,
panders and whores. The myths and fables of the classical
world have spoken only one magic phrase to modern man:
'*Be rich*.' Hence, that low tenor, the stone, related to those
loaded allusions at once creates a kind of glamour and shows
it to be meretricious.

A briefer example of this same juxtaposition is Surly's
comment after Mammon describes how the elixir will make
men

Become stout MARSES, and beget young CVPIDS.
SVR. The decay'd *Vestall's* of *Pickt-hatch* would thanke
    you,
That keepe the fire a-liue, there.

II. i. 61-63

This mingling of the cockney and the classical is one of the surliest comments made by anyone on Mammon's dream. The *'Vestall's'* allude to the Vestal virgins, the chaste priestesses who guarded the eternal fire which was the symbol of Vesta. Her shrine was perhaps the most sacred object of Roman religion. But in this context the shrine becomes *'Pickt-hatch'*, a resort of prostitutes and pickpockets in London, and the vestals become whores. The fire, which they guard, refers apparently to both the fire of passion and the fever caused by venereal disease, which 'decay'd' also suggests.

Jonson used vehicles other than those from the ancient world. Subtle shows Kastril 'the *Grammar*, and *Logick*, / And *Rhetorick* of quarreling' by misusing terms taken from scholastic philosophy (IV. ii. 21-28, 64-65). There is a grammar and logic to things other than quarrelling, as one of Face's remarks shows. After Dol has brought peace again, he hails her:

> thou shalt sit in triumph,
> And not be stil'd Dol Common, but Dol Proper,
> Dol Singular: the longest cut, at night,
> Shall draw thee for his Dol Particular.
>
> I. i. 176-179

Face is playing on the grammatical and logical senses in Dol's last name, then moving on to other terms suggested by 'Common'. A common noun is applicable to each of the individuals which make up a class or genus. It belongs equally to more than one, as Dol does. More generally, common means public or free to be used by everyone. 'Proper' and 'Singular' also have both grammatical and more general meanings which contrast wittily, each making the common Dol something more special than she is. There is the same kind of inflation by pretension that is noticeable throughout the play. The height of this is 'Particular', which means 'private, personal, not public' (*OED*). In logic a particular proposition is one in which the subject is undistributed; Dol, we can be sure, is a proposition whose subject has been extensively distributed. But 'Particular' has another meaning here, as we can see from a later use, when Mammon says to Dol,

> Sweet madame, le' me be particular—
> DOL. Particular, sir? I pray you, know your distance.
> MAM. In no ill sense, sweet lady . . .   IV. i. 77-79

Dol is highly offended because 'particular' can mean 'familiar in manner' or 'specially attentive'.[1]

A sense of irony is at the very heart of much comic imagery. Irony and a lack of decorum generally work together because both deal with the disparity between expectation and fulfilment, appearance and reality, words and deeds. There is an ironic gap between the tenor and the vehicle in many of the images we have examined. Vestal virgins normally connote chastity, fidelity, devotion, piety. But 'The *Vestall's* of *Pickt-hatch*' connote quite different things. Furthermore, irony gathers around characters when imagery is used to describe them. Dol Common is a whore, is known as a whore, and knows herself to be a whore. At various times and by various people in the play she is said to be a brach, Royal Dol, Claridiana, a republic, Queen of Faery, smock-rampant, and Madame Suppository. Some of these names come closer to the truth—whatever the truth about Dol is—than others, but in most of them there is an ironic disparity between what she really is and what she is said to be. In modern plays where whores are treated more tenderly than Jonson chose to treat them there might be a certain wistfulness about one who refers to herself as Queen of Faery. But there is none here. Dol is ludicrous and vicious, but not pitiful. And she is ludicrous mostly because of the pretentiousness of the epithets attached to her.

[1] In eighteenth century brothel slang a courtesan's 'particular' was her favoured gallant. This may have applied in the early seventeenth century also. See Eric Partridge, *Dictionary of Slang*.

III

Indecorum and irony, then, characterize the comic imagery of *The Alchemist*. This imagery brings into the context of the play vehicles which are taken from religion, medicine, sex, commerce, and warfare. In part, these vehicles only extend the implications suggested by the fable of a clever servant, a quack, and a whore engaged in cheating fools. In part, too, they help form the immense scene in which this little war against the world is fought. The imagery does what nothing else in the poet's command can do with equal economy and intensity: it brings in those very values by which one can measure the pretensions and desires of the fakers and fools.

The centre of this complex of religion, medicine, sex, and business is alchemy, which, in one way or another, transmutes all of these diverse elements of life. The first extended mention of alchemy comes during the opening quarrel between Face and Subtle. To impress on Face how much has been done for him, Subtle uses alchemic terms.

> Thou vermine, haue I tane thee, out of dung,
> So poore, so wretched, when no liuing thing
> Would keepe thee companie, but a spider, or worse?
> Rais'd thee from broomes, and dust, and watring
>   pots?
> *Sublim'd* thee, and *exalted* thee, and *fix'd* thee
> I' the *third region*, call'd our *state of grace?*
> Wrought thee to *spirit*, to *quintessence*, with paines
> Would twise haue won me the *philosophers worke?*
>
> I. i. 64-71

To use such terms in reference to gold is nonsense—it's alchemy, but it's nonsense. But to use them in reference to man's nature is not merely nonsense, but also impiety. Subtle claims to have alchemized a man. Significantly, the only man that Subtle cannot alchemize is Surly, who says to

Mammon, 'Your *stone* / Cannot transmute me' (II. i. 78-79). Perhaps the sinister significance of the title is in this transmutation of man: Subtle or rather the power of gold can sublime and exalt man. In *Volpone* we found that the final food of man is man; here the final stuff to project on is man. Man himself can be alchemized; money can give a man spirit. In short, the alchemist (Subtle or gold) becomes a parody of the Creator. To sincere alchemists, who were mystical idealists, alchemy was a religion or quasi-religion. To Jonson, a moral idealist and a dogmatic Christian who approached alchemy with no sympathy for the religious impulse in its heart, it seemed only an obscene fraud, and alchemic terms only a parody of the Word.

In order to ridicule alchemy and to show how it seemed to be a caricature of Christianity, Jonson had his knaves use terms which had one meaning for alchemists and another for Christians.[1] The religious references in Subtle's speech are evident enough—'*Sublim'd*', '*exalted*', '*state of grace*', '*spirit*'. This passage is the first suggestion of a religion of gold which is more violently bodied forth in the first scene of *Volpone*. In *The Alchemist* Jonson, wisely, I think, only sketches it in outline lest the impiety neutralize the comic tone as it tends to do in *Volpone*.

The imagery suggests this religion in two ways. First, alchemic terms are exploited for their religious implications, as in the speech of Subtle just quoted. As Herford points out, Subtle later capitalizes on the similarities between religious terminology and alchemic jargon: 'When Ananias introduces himself as "a faithfull Brother", and Subtle affects to understand by this a devotee of alchemy, the two professions at once assume the air of parallel fraternities.'[2]

---

[1] Edgar H. Duncan has shown the relation of *The Alchemist* to the writings on alchemy in 'Jonson's *Alchemist* and the Literature of Alchemy', *PMLA* (September 1946), LXI, 699-710. Note particularly his interesting analysis of the passage under consideration.

[2] Herford and Simpson, II, 104.

Another example of this exploitation is the exchange between Face and Subtle in which they confuse Ananias with their 'heathen Greeke'.

SVB. Sirah, my varlet, stand you forth, and speake to
him,
Like a *Philosopher*: Answere, i'the language.
Name the vexations, and the martyrizations
Of mettalls, in the worke.

FAC.   Sir, *Putrefaction*,
Solution, *Ablution*, *Sublimation*,
Cohobation, *Calcination*, *Ceration*, and
Fixation.

SVB   This is *heathen Greeke*, to you, now?
And when comes *Viuification*?

FAC.   After *Mortification*.

SVB What's *Cohobation*?

FAC.   'Tis the powring on
Your *Aqua Regis*, and them drawing him off,
To the *trine circle* of the *seuen spheares*.

SVB. What's the proper passion of mettalls?

FAC.   *Malleation*.

SVB. What's your *vltimum supplicium auri*?

FAC.   *Antimonium*.

                                    II. v. 18-30

Enough of these questions and answers are given to indicate that this apparently is a parody of a catechism. Subtle is catechizing Face in the doctrines of their religion to impress Ananias with their piety. Although improvised, the terms were orthodox to alchemists like Dee, Kelly, and Forman, and even the question and answer form was used before by Paracelsus in a treatise called *A Short Catechism of Alchemy*.[1] Though neither Subtle nor Face believes this nonsense, their god had his worshippers, and even Face and Subtle, disbelieving the dogmas, practise the creed. Some of the terms they use, such as '*Ablution*' and '*Mortification*', have a

[1] Hathaway gives part of Paracelsus's work in his edition: Charles Hathaway, ed., *The Alchemist. Yale Studies in English*, vol. XVII (New York, 1903), 291.

genuine religious meaning; some, such as '*Cohobation*', only sound as if they had. For the purpose of enticing Ananias, the genuineness of the terms does not matter, because he is easily gulled into thinking that whatever employs such pious language, even in heathen Greek, cannot be entirely the work of the Devil.

But this religion of gold is sketched more bitingly in the second way. Religious terms are applied to impious things—to Subtle, or the stone, or the effects of alchemy. This perversion of religious vehicles, which was more emphatic in *Volpone*, appears usually in the speech of Face and Subtle, though Mammon is as capable of this kind of perversion as of all others. How easily it comes to Face and Subtle! When Mammon asks him where his master is, Face replies,

> At's praiers, sir, he,
> Good man, hee's doing his deuotions,
> For the successe.   II. ii. 29-31

The insincerity of this is pointed up when Face tells Mammon that the covering of churches can be used as stuff to project on (II. ii. 12-15). In this religion, it is evident, no man can serve two masters—God and Mammon. Face has no division in his nature. To make his Mammon-worship more palatable, he only appropriates the terms traditionally used in worship of God. Gradually we see that this religion is a parody of Christianity. It has its Creator and its catechism, its prayers and devotions. There is even a body of religious writings, which Surly questions in a long and suspiciously knowing passage. The terms of alchemy seem to him 'like tricks o' the cards'; besides, none of the writers agrees with the others. Subtle's answers to this heresy have been heard before in ecclesiastical disputes. According to him, the alchemic names are used 'to obscure their art': 'Speake not the *Scriptures*, oft, in *parables*?' (II. iii. 201-207). Subtle proves almost as adept as Mammon in dressing up the nasty fact in a pretty fiction. The same inflation by means of comparisons which was evident in the epithets is at work in Subtle's speech. Alchemic writings are to the Scriptures as Dol is to the Queen of Faery.

This religion has its mystical Trinity, too, which Face explains at the end of the catechism:

> 'Tis a *stone*, and not
> A *stone*; a *spirit*, a *soule*, and a *body*:
> Which, if you doe *dissolue*, it is *dissolu'd*,
> If you *coagulate*, it is *coagulated*,
> If you make it to *flye*, it *flyeth*.   II. v. 40-44

The parallelism of Biblical verse and the antithetical thought of Christ may be parodied here. Face may be adapting 'the speech of the *"holy Consistorie"* itself', as Sackton claims,[1] or, as Percy Simpson implies, he may be only mouthing the gospel of the alchemists.[2] At any rate, here and in the passage where Subtle speaks of the *'triple Soule'* (II. iii. 30), religious terms are perverted to an impious use, and the gross, dark world of the frauds is thrown violently into the bright realm of the spirit. One is tempted to suppose that the three-in-oneness of the stone has a counterpart in the characters, one of whom is the spirit of the *'indenture tripartite'*, the other the soul, and the third all too palpably the body.

The flying of the stone which Face refers to in this passage may allude to the 'flies' which the unholy three have been selling. A 'fly' was a familiar demon supposed to be in association with or under the power of a man. The *OED* traces the word to the notion that devils assumed the form of flies. Other terms used in *The Alchemist* are 'birde' and 'familiar' (a spirit or demon supposed to attend a call).

---

[1] *Rhetoric as a Dramatic Language in Ben Jonson*, 92. Sackton generally emphasizes Jonson's use of jargon as though the words of Face and Subtle had little meaning other than as rhetorical devices. Such an emphasis underestimates the subtlety and wit of Jonson's language.

[2] Herford and Simpson, X, 76-77, 89.

The 'flies', then, constituted a kind of angelic order which was supposed to guard and wait on the men to whom they were attached.[1] Dapper, who is especially interested in them, wants, according to Face, 'a *familiar* / To rifle with, at horses, and winne cups' (I. i. 192-193). That is, a spirit that will help him gamble on the horses. Later, Face makes a distinction between the orders in the hierarchy when he says that Dapper wants a 'rifling *flye*', not a 'great *familiar*' (I. ii. 83-84). But Dapper corrects him; he wants one for all games. A 'rifling *flye*' would be a guardian angel only in gambling, whereas a 'great *familiar*' would attend him at all times. When he is finally given his fly, Dol, as the Queen of Faery, tells him

> Here is your *Fly* in a purse, about your neck, cosen,
> Weare it, and feed it about this day seu'night,
> On your right wrist—
> SVB.   Open a veine, with a pinne,
> And let it suck but once a weeke: V. iv. 35-38

The connection with witchcraft, latent in any mention of 'fly', is most evident here. As in witchcraft, Dapper's guardian angel is to be a parasite and feed on his lifeblood.[2] The ludicrousness as well as the monstrousness of this is completely lost on Dapper, who takes it as Gospel-truth. If it were not lost on him, of course, the situation would lose most of its monstrousness and all of its ludicrousness.

There are also orders on earth. Subtle, we discover, belongs to the priest class of this religion. The true alchemist as Herford points out, 'enjoyed the prestige simultaneously of the sacrosanct priest and the philosophic discoverer. He

---

[1] Such an order had a real counterpart in life, as Herford reports. Dee and Kelly had—or said they had—spirits at their beck and call and even charms to exorcise them. Herford and Simpson, II, 93.

[2] According to Hope Emily Allen, 'The most complete and clear account in literature of the use of the *fly* in the Elizabethan period is to be found in Jonson's *Alchemist*.' She also points out the connection with witchcraft. 'Influence of Superstition on Vocabulary: Two Related Examples', *PMLA*, L, 1035.

was a divine, in his fashion, and the efficacy of his work even depended, like the priest's, upon his moral state.'[1] Subtle is evidently a parody of these aspects of the alchemists. Like all religions, Mammon's faith has its heretics as well as its priests. Surly—the 'heretique' whom Mammon brought along in the hope of converting—represents that unregenerate order (II. iii. 3-4).

Like most religions, this one has great healing power. This connection between medicine and the religion of gold is latent in the double meaning of 'elixir'. In one sense it was the central term in alchemy, that is, a preparation by which alchemists tried to change metals into gold. Chaucer and Reginald Scot identified it with the philosopher's stone, but, according to the *OED*, it perhaps had a wider meaning, including powders, liquids, and vapours. The second sense, which concerns us now, is its medical sense. *Elixir vitae* was a supposed medicine with the property of indefinitely prolonging life. Alchemists generally thought it identical with, or closely related to, the 'elixir' which they used in alchemy.[2] At any rate, it was thought to be a sovereign remedy for disease. Jonson added nothing to these two meanings of the term, but, by deliberately confusing them, he increased their comic range.

The 'great med'cine', as Mammon calls the elixir, is identified with the philosopher's stone: to him they are produced alike, and they act alike. Once that confusion is made, his speeches acquire a double meaning. Ostensibly, he speaks of the medical benefits of the elixir; but we understand that these benefits come from the alchemizing power of the stone.

> He that has once the *flower of the sunne*,
> The perfect *ruby*, which we call *elixir*,
> Not onely can doe that, but by it's *vertue*,

[1] Herford and Simpson, II, 92-93.
[2] Robert Steele, 'Alchemy', *Shakespeare's England* (Oxford, 1950), I, 465-467.

> Can confer honour, loue, respect, long life,
> Giue safety, valure: yea, and victorie,
> To whom he will.   II. i. 47-52

This claim that the stone will confer love and power is also
made by Subtle in speaking with Tribulation Wholesome
and Ananias about the political usefulness of the elixir. He
asks them if they know that even the 'med'cinall vse' shall
make them a faction in the realm because it can win friends
for their cause by its miraculous cures (III. ii. 25 ff.). Palsy,
dropsy, impotence, gout, leprosy, and syphilis can be cured,
and friends won for the Puritan cause, by the healing power
of this cure-all. The elixir, as Subtle describes it, seems to be
something to drink or rub on the body. But moving across
this description and, indeed, across any passage which deals
with the elixir is the other meaning of elixir, that is, the
philosopher's stone or the power of turning metals into gold.
When a word has a double meaning in a play, the meanings
tend to act on each other and even to coalesce. Thus, the
'med'cinall vse' of the elixir becomes its power of creating
gold; the Puritans can make themselves a faction in the realm
because of their financial power. Money can cure the ills of
mankind because the Primum Mobile of this world is gold.
This coalescence of the medicinal and alchemical powers
appears most explicitly in an image used by Tribulation
when he is assuring Ananias that the *'silenc'd Saints'* will be
restored only by the philosopher's stone.

> *Aurum potabile* being
> The onely med'cine, for the ciuill *Magistrate*,
> T'incline him to a feeling of the cause:
> And must be daily vs'd, in the disease.
>   III. i. 41-44

Aurum potabile (drinkable gold), which was long regarded as
a sovereign remedy for physical ills, has a judicial function
to Tribulation. He thinks that bribery can cure the sickness
in the civil body.

The medical and religious aspects of the elixir come together when Mammon rhapsodizes on his life with Dol.

> and then renew
> Our youth, and strength, with drinking the *elixir*,
> And so enioy a perpetuitie
> Of life, and lust.   IV. i. 163-166

Here is the climax of the parody of Christianity. Like a true god, the elixir promises immortality to its worshippers, of the only kind they would understand: a perpetual resurrection, always this life and this lust. The great medicine, which can cure all the ills of the body politic, social, and personal, can also preserve that body throughout eternity.

IV

The elixir has a sexual power as well as religious, medical, and financial powers. Though several of the characters assume this, it is chiefly dramatized in the scenes with Mammon, who claims that the elixir will make men, like the ancient patriarchs, 'Become stout MARSES, and beget yong CVPIDS' (II. i. 61). This equation of the elixir and sexual potency and fertility becomes most ludicrous when Dol says that she is only 'a poore Baron's daughter'. Mammon replies, 'Poore! and gat you? Prophane not' (IV. i. 43). Mammon's god is profaned by Dol's claim that a poor man could conceive such a beautiful daughter. There is such a necessary connection between riches and fertility that, under Mammon's dispensation, the law would be—the poor get poorer and the rich have beautiful children.

The most extravagant claims for the potency of the elixir are not made in reference to anyone so low as a baron. Mammon, like many of Jonson's major characters, thinks of himself only in terms of kings and gods. When a mean

tenor, like Mammon, is related to classical vehicles, there is
that peculiar combination of the sublime and the low, the
glamorous and the sordid which creates the violated
grandeur and the extravagant bathos characteristic of
Jonson's plays.

This combination appears in two of the most extraordinary passages in the whole play. One of them comes
when Mammon announces that, once he has the stone, he
means

> To haue a list of wiues, and concubines,
> Equall with SALOMON; who had the *stone*
> Alike, with me: and I will make me, a back
> With the *elixir*, that shall be as tough
> As HERCVLES, to encounter fiftie a night.
>
> II. ii. 35-39

If this remarkable sexual potency were passed off simply as
the dream of what a sensual man would do if given scope for
his talents, there might be a certain charm about it, as there
is a charm about the sex life of the Greek gods. Jove's
seductions, Venus's love affairs, Hercules's virtuosity—all
seem so innocent and inconsequential that they are morally
disinfected. But in *The Alchemist* we are never allowed to
forget that the sexual potency is a direct result of the elixir:
'I will make me, a back / With the *elixir*'. And the elixir is,
among other things, the power of making gold. That
financial function undermines the whole image, suggesting
that once one has this great power of transmuting base
metals into gold, one has both increased erotic opportunity
and increased sexual potency. The rich get richer, that is,
polygamous. And the rich still have to pay, because, even
in Mammon's golden age, money will have to be used to
buy lust; men will make a back 'with the elixir'. This
suggestion is strengthened by Mammon's mentioning, a
few lines further on, that he will walk 'Naked betweene my

succubae' (II. ii. 48). '*Succubae*' were strumpets.[1]

The other passage is even more explicit and monstrous than this one. Mammon primes himself to meet Dol Common:

> Now, EPICVRE,
> Heighten thy selfe, talke to her, all in gold;
> Raine her as many showers, as IOVE did drops
> Vnto his DANAE: Shew the *God* a miser,
> Compar'd with MAMMON. What? the *stone* will do't.
> Shee shall feele gold, tast gold, heare gold,
>   sleepe gold:
> Nay, we will *concumbere* gold. I will be puissant,
> And mightie in my talke to her!   IV. i. 24-31

'Heighten' should be read as a term in alchemy as well as the conventional 'lift up your hearts' or 'elevate your style'. It refers to the process of transmutation by which the base metals were elevated.[2] In other words, seduction is related to the alchemic process. Mammon wants the true touch of Midas by which everything, even lust, will turn into gold (apparently not solid gold, as for Midas, but potable). Who but Mammon would think of a Greek god as a miser or as needing to be a miser? And who but Mammon would think of Jove's being a miser in sexual matters? Furthermore, it is quite in keeping with Mammon that he should turn that most civilized of man's actions, talking, into a metaphor for sexual intercourse. Face, that coiner of erotic metaphors, may have suggested this by his play on 'conuerse' when he whispered to Mammon that he would 'steale you in, vnto the partie, / That you may see her conuerse' (II. iii. 294-295). 'Converse' then carried the double meaning of talking and sexual intercourse (*OED*). Later we see that 'talke' has

---

[1] '*Succubae*' also meant 'demons in female form' (*OED*). Reginald Scot explained how the devil, in the likeness of a pretty wench, 'lieth prostitute as *Succubus* to the man'. Scot, *The Discoverie of Witchcraft*, intro. Montague Summers (John Rodker, 1930), 43.

[2] The *OED* does not give this as a meaning for the term, but Face says, 'Sir, I'll goe looke / A little, how it heightens' (II. ii. 87-88).

become, in a satisfyingly ironic scene, only talk to Dol. In Act IV, Scene v, Dol marches up and down '*in her fit of talking*' (the stage direction) quoting and garbling Hugh Broughton's *Concent of Scripture*, while Mammon vainly tries to quiet the jabbering and Face says, 'Nay, you must neuer hope to lay her now.' There is, of course, a further irony in Mammon's desire to 'talke to her, all in gold'. That is the only way he succeeds in talking to her since he has spent money liberally to be alone with her only to be frustrated in his conversation.

The allusion of Jove's visit to Danae in a shower of gold is a favourite one with Jonson. It appears in *Volpone* (V. ii. 102-104), and there is an echo of it later in *The Alchemist* when Mammon confides to Dol that, as soon as he has the stone, she should tell him her first wish,

> And it shall raine into thy lap, no shower,
> But flouds of gold, whole cataracts, a deluge,
> To get a nation on thee!   IV. i. 126-128

Poets before Jonson had used this image of the golden shower to mean buying love with gold, but Jonson gave it his characteristic twist of extravagance and irony. Mammon is not content with raining in a shower as Jove did. No, he must rain as many showers as Jove did drops, or, in the second mention of this image, rain floods, cataracts, a deluge. The sexual symbolism in 'raine' and 'lap' seems to be lost on Dol, whose answer to this allusive seduction is as ludicrous in its way as is Mammon's claim that all this gold will 'get a nation on thee'. She answers modestly, 'You are pleas'd, sir, / To worke on the ambition of our sexe' (IV. i. 128-129).

Though other characters lack Mammon's extravagant speech, the same assumption that the elixir has a sexual power underlies much of their language. The best example of this is an extraordinary image which Face uses in persuading Mammon that Dol is a merry and pleasant creature.

> shee'll mount you vp, like *quick-siluer*,
> *Ouer the helme*; and *circulate*, like *oyle*,
> A very *vegetall*: II. iii. 254-256

Face's comparison of Dol to quick-silver is a reverse twist given to an alchemic figure which Subtle has just explained to Mammon. To the alchemists quick-silver or *argent-vive* and sulphur were 'the parents of all other mettalls', sulphur 'supplying the place of male', and quick-silver the place of the female (II. iii. 153 ff.).[1] Since quick-silver is female, Face evidently thinks it quite suitable that a female should be like quick-silver, particularly in her sexual conduct. The point, presumably, is that Dol, like quick-silver, is volatile and quick in movement. Quick-silver also carries with it a suggestion of venereal disease, as Surly indicates when he speaks of the 'danger of the *quick-siluer*' (II. iii. 287); it was used by doctors trying to cure gonorrhoea. '*Ouer the helme*' is an alchemic term which Subtle used shortly before (II. iii. 60) and which Face echoes for its erotic innuendo. Like many such innuendoes, its vividness depends on its suggestive vagueness. The rest of the image also has an alchemic cast, or at least a chemical cast. 'Circulate' apparently did not have its present meaning of 'revolve' or 'turn around' as an intransitive verb (first mentioned in 1672), but meant 'encircle' or 'surround'. It also had a meaning drawn from chemistry: 'to subject a substance to continuous distillation in a closed vessel in which the vapour was caused to condense at the top of the apparatus and to flow back into the original liquid, the whole thus undergoing repeated vaporization and condensation' (*OED*). To think of sexual intercourse in terms of repeated vaporization and condensation is ludicrous, but it has a certain pertinence. Furthermore, both '*oyle*' and '*vegetall*' were used by the alchemists. Surly speaks of 'your

[1] Duncan, 708, has valuable comments on Subtle's whole speech.

oyle of *height*' in listing all of the terms used in alchemy
(II. iii. 187), and Face refers to Subtle's *'vegetalls'* (I. i. 39).
In short, Dol as a sexual being is compared to the alchemic
process.[1] When Dol tells Mammon, 'I studie here the
mathematiques, and distillation' (IV. i. 83-84), presumably we ought to be aware of the play on the erotic and
chemical meanings of 'distillation'. To compare her proposed intercourse with Mammon to the transmutation of
base metals to gold has its aptness, for Dol is a whore whose
action produces gold, whatever else it misses producing.

V

Even as the imagery is instrumental in relating alchemy
to religion, medicine, and sex, so also does it suggest a
relationship between all of these and business. This connection strikes one on hearing in 'The Argument' that *'A
cheater, and his punque;'*

> *Leauing. their narrow practise, were become
> Cos'ners at large: and, onely wanting some
> House to set vp, with him they here contract,
> Each for a share, and all begin to act.
> Much company they draw, and much abuse,
> In casting figures, telling fortunes, newes,
> Selling of flyes, flat bawdry, with the stone:
> Till it, and they, and all in fume are gone.*

The commercial implications, latent in the central situation
of cheating and prostitution, come out in such words as
'practise', *'House to set vp'*, *'contract'*, *'share'*, *'company they
draw'*, *'selling'*. Each of these alone might not attract
attention to its commercial sense, but, when these words are
used together in the same passage, the commercial sense
tends to rise above the other senses. The final impression

---

[1] One might also add that oil has other properties possibly similar to Dol's:
smooth, sticky, inflammable, lighter than water, soluble in alcohol.

is that Subtle, Dol, and Face have gone into business, with a contract, shares, and an expanding practice—all somewhat dubious, perhaps, but still flourishing. The complexity of this business can be noted in one line, '*Selling of flyes, flat bawdry, with the* stone:' where religion, sex, and gold all come together.

Such commercial terms are used throughout the play. Even in the midst of the opening quarrel Face speaks as a business partner who has drawn 'customers' to Subtle for his 'dosen of trades', given him 'credit' for his 'coales' and a 'house to practise in' where he has 'studied the more thriuing skill of bawdrie, since' (I. i. 40-49). Dol reminds them of their business obligations when she breaks up their quarrel by denouncing Subtle for claiming

a primacie, in the diuisions?
You must be chiefe? as if you, onely, had
The poulder to proiect with? and the worke
Were not begun out of equalitie?
The venter *tripartite*? All things in common?
Without prioritie?   I. i. 131-136

From one point of view such a passage is only another example of Dol's pretentious language. But what strikes one about it is that this whore describes their catch-as-catch-can agreement as a 'venter *tripartite*', 'worke', 'begun out of equalitie', 'without prioritie'. 'Venter *tripartite*' is the most interesting phrase in the passage, partly because it is echoed in several places later. In this context 'venter' (or venture) principally means a commercial speculation. Later, just before the partnership breaks up, Face uses this meaning of the word when he calls Subtle and Dol 'venturers'. A 'venturer' in the early seventeenth century meant either an adventurer or 'one who undertakes or shares in a commercial or trading venture, especially by sending goods or ships beyond seas' (*OED*). It was used particularly of the trading companies such as the Merchant Venturers of Bristol. 'All things in common!' Dol cries, damning herself in doing so, for the line, read in one way, means all things in Common: that is, a three-fold commercial speculation in Common stock without priority. Dol really is a republic to these speculators, a 'common-wealth', indeed. But no matter how the passage is read, it seems to imply commercial dealings on a high plane.

The high plane is kept right to the end. Just as they are dissolving the company, Face formally ends the *'indenture tripartite'* (V. iv. 130-132). Figuratively, *'indenture'* meant contract or mutual engagement. Literally, an indenture was 'a deed between two or more parties with mutual covenants, executed in two or more copies' (*OED*). There are legal and aristocratic dimensions to the term, as well as commercial, for kings and king-makers have used it. In *Henry IV, Part I*, for instance, when Hotspur, Worcester, Mortimer, and Glendower are dividing up England, Mortimer says that their 'indentures tripartite' are drawn (III. i. 80-82). Seen through the lens of such a definition and such a use as this, Face's use of the phrase is comic, as he may mean it to be, because he is at that moment able to stand back and laugh at their absurd pretension to legality and high finance.

Between the time Dol calls it a 'venter *tripartite*' and Face, an *'indenture tripartite'*, commercial terms are frequently used to refer to sex or cheating or the religion of the elixir. Dol settles the quarrel between Subtle and Face by making Subtle swear to leave his 'faction' 'And labour, kindly, in the commune worke' (I. i. 156). She really means that they should cheat fools cheerfully and co-operatively. But, since such a naked way of looking at reality offends her pretentious nature, she generally uses martial or commercial terms to disguise what is called, in plain speech, cheating and whoring. The result is that, when she and others use words like 'worke', 'labour', 'venter', and 'venturers' to refer to activities that, for one thing, are generally not thought of as commercial speculations and, for another, are not legal, then the identification of a tenor (such as whoring) and a vehicle (such as 'venter') appears indecorous and ludicrous, yet illuminating. We are asked to consider to what extent prostitution or cheating can be called a business venture (and possibly even to what extent a business venture involves some kind of prostitution or cheating). The degree to which we can equate business and cheating or business and prostitution or business and religion, as well as the degree to which such tenors and vehicles resist identification, provides some of the humour and meaning of the play.

Let us observe how the imagery suggests connections between business and sex. We have already seen that, in Mammon's world, money and sex are assumed to be monstrous twins of the same bitch goddess. Once money and sex are brought as close together as this, many connections between business (whose blood is money) and sex spring up. Some of these only depend on the nature of things in a world in which some people take money in exchange for sexual experience. The Queen of Mammon's world is, after all, a prostitute whose business is sex. Other connections only capitalize on the ambiguity of many words which have one reference to business and pick up another reference to sex. For instance, both 'venter' and 'venturer' mean 'prostitute' as well as, respectively, 'commercial speculation' and 'commercial speculator' (*OED*). But many of the connections are made simply by the force of the imagery in which commercial vehicles are related to tenors dealing with sex.

Note how commercial vehicles are used in referring to Dame Pliant and Dol. Face and Subtle speak of Dame Pliant in these extraordinary terms:

> FAC. A wife, a wife, for one on'vs, my deare SVBTLE:
>   Wee'll eene draw lots, and he, that failes, shall haue
>   The more in goods, the other has in taile.
> SVB. Rather the lesse. For shee may be so light
>   Shee may want graines.   II. vi. 85-89

Drawing lots seems to be their normal way of determining the fate of women, for that, one supposes, is what Face referred to in a previous speech: 'the longest cut, at night, / Shall draw thee for his DOL Particular' (I. i. 178-179). There is a certain gay detachment about Face's method of settling erotic problems; getting a wife and sleeping with a whore can be settled in the same simple way—just draw lots. But the interesting aspect of this passage is the compensation suggested: if you miss the wife, you get the goods. 'In taile' is a play on the legal word 'tail', which referred to limiting the inheritance of an estate to descendants in a particular line, and on the obscene word 'tail' which meant then as now—the posterior, or the female pudend.[1] This witty union of sex and inheritance is extended by the assertion that whatever one gets 'in taile', the other ought to get in goods. Money or property, then, becomes a possible substitution for a wife or rather for the sexual experience of having a wife.

This same substitution is emphasized later in a somewhat different way. When Surly, disguised as a Spaniard, enters, Face and Subtle forget their quarrel over marrying Dame Pliant and decide to put the Dame to more useful work.

> FAC.   'Slid, SVBTLE, he puts me in minde o'the widow.
> What dost thou say to draw her to it? ha?
> And tell her, it is her fortune. All our venter
> Now lies vpon't. It is but one man more,
> Which on's chance to haue her:
>
> . . . . .
>
> The credit of our house too is engag'd.
> SVB. You made me an offer for my share e're while.
> What wilt thou gi' me, i-faith?

[1] Partridge, *Dictionary of Slang*. One of Kastril's several names for his sister is 'Pvs' (Puss) (V. iii. 38) which is a slang term for the female pudend. Dame Pliant has a somewhat restricted function in this play.

FAC.   O, by that light,
   Ile not buy now . . .
   E'en take your lot, obey your chance, sir; winne her,
   And weare her, out for me.
SVB.   'Slight. I'll not worke her then.
FAC. It is the common cause.   IV. iii. 63 ff.

Face has the spirit of the true capitalist—business before pleasure. Or, perhaps, a better way of putting it is to say—pleasure and business together—because Face's chief pleasure is evidently not sex, but alchemizing people; sex is only one of his many ways of doing so. There is a business terminology in this exchange pretentious enough for even Dol: 'The credit of our house too is engag'd'; 'an offer for my share'; 'the common cause'. When the situation is explained in terms as high flown as these, who can blame them for putting that glorious adventure, commerce, before that mean duty, marriage? The burden of the whole passage is, as Face later puts it, that Dame Pliant is to be 'used' (IV. iv. 79) even as Dol is 'emploi'd' (IV. iii. 51). As sexual beings, they both are commodities to be bought, sold, used, worn, and worked.

   One scene especially reveals how Dol is to be used—the third scene in the third act, where Dol's profession and Subtle's fraud are thought of in terms of warfare. Face announces the arrival of 'A noble *Count*, a *Don* of *Spaine*', who has brought his 'munition' with him and is ready

                              to make his battry
   Vpon our DOL, our Castle, our *cinque*-Port,
   Our *Douer* pire, our what thou wilt. Where is shee?
   Shee must prepare perfumes, delicate linnen,
   The bath in chiefe, a banquet and her wit,
   For shee must milke his *Epididimis*.
   Where is the *Doxie*?   III. iii. 17-23

Face's speech might be the type of the whole play: both begin in abuse, inflate by pretension, and sink into obscenity.

The martial imagery, which is quite in keeping with Dol's previous 'Soueraigne' and 'Generall', moves in a kind of graduated expansion from Dol (the tenor) to 'our Castle' (one vehicle); then to '*cinque*-Port' and '*Douer* pire'; and finally, blown apart entirely, to 'what thou wilt'. Face may be making fun of their own tendency (necessary in the profession of passing a whore off as a noble lady) to think of Dol in pretentious terms. Whether he is or not, there is extravagant humour in picturing Dol first as a castle, then as Dover or Sandwich or what you will—'This fortress built by Nature for herself / Against infection and the hand of war' —Dol, ready to receive the battery of that Spanish Armada which has

> brought munition with him, sixe great slopps,
> Bigger then three *Dutch* hoighs, beside round
> trunkes,
> Furnish'd with pistolets, and pieces of eight.
>
> III. iii. 13-15

The munition is money, the danger is infection, England will fall. The ludicrous end of the whole passage is that Dol, the doxy, 'must milke his *Epididimis*'.[1]

Once Face has introduced the theme that sexual aggression is a kind of warfare, he proceeds to vary it in another involved figure, which has a movement similar to the one just analysed. With her customary ceremony Dol asks him (and ludicrously echoes the King's opening question in *The Spanish Tragedy*),

> lord *Generall*, how fares our campe?
> FAC. As, with the few, that had entrench'd themselues
> Safe, by their discipline, against a world, DOL:
> And laugh'd, within those trenches, and grew fat

---

[1] The epididymis is an organ at the back of the testicles. 'Milke', as a vulgar term, also meant extract all possible profit from someone by illicit means. This sense appears later in Face's declaration that the don will be 'Milked' by them (IV. iii. 45).

With thinking on the booties, DOL, brought in
Daily, by their small parties. This deare houre,
A doughtie *Don* is taken, with my DOL;
And thou maist make his ransome, what thou wilt,
My *Dousabell*: He shall be brought here, fetter'd
With thy faire lookes, before he sees thee; and
    throwne
In a downe-bed, as darke as any dungeon;
Where thou shalt keepe him waking, with thy drum;
Thy drum, my DOL; thy drum; till he be tame
As the poore black-birds were i' the great frost,
Or bees are with a bason: and so hiue him
I'the swan-skin couerlid, and cambrick sheets,
Till he worke honey, and waxe, my little
   Gods-guift.   III. iii. 33-49

Here Face extends the martial imagery to include more than
sex. The impostors, it appears, are at war with the world
and have fortified themselves in their castle, from which,
daily, they send out small sorties. Any enemies captured are
held for ransom and possibly tortured into submission by
Dol's drum. This sardonic picture of economic survival of
the fittest which brings together sex, business, and warfare
ends with a figure as outrageous as milking the epididymis.
Dol's bed first becomes a dungeon and then a beehive in
which the 'doughtie *Don*' produces honey. 'Honey' obviously
has a sexual meaning and partly from its colour and partly
from the context acquires the meaning of gold.

Face is undeniably a virtuoso in erotic imagery. Sexual
intercourse has been compared, in succession, to a battery
on a castle and seaports, to milking, to keeping awake with
a drum, and to extracting honey from a bee. His final erotic
image in this passage follows the musical motif suggested
by 'drum'.

         Sweet DOL,
You must goe tune your virginall, no loosing
ˋ O' the least time. And, doe you heare? good action.

Firke, like a flounder; kisse, like a scallop, close:
And tickle him with thy mother-tongue.

III. iii. 66-70

This cluster of violently indecorous images is about as
absurd as any in the play. The name, 'virginall', applied to
a whore, has its ironic humour, which is doubled when she
is advised to keep it in tune lest she waste time.[1] Face, as a
bawd, has a twentieth century sense of efficiency. Though
'firke' has alchemic (see II. i. 28) and financial connotations,
it seems primarily to echo Face's previous remark about
Dol: 'A wench is a rare bait, with which a man / No sooner's
taken, but he straight firkes mad' (II. iv. 4-5). The obvious
erotic allusion in both places may be reinforced by the
pronunciation of 'firke'.[2] 'Tickle him with thy mother-
tongue' is one of the wittiest images in the whole passage.
'Mother' could then mean 'womb'. 'Mother-tongue' means
either one's native language or an original language from
which others spring (*OED*). Besides the obvious erotic
innuendo, Face may be suggesting that sex is that universal
language which even the Spanish don, who knows not a
word of English, can understand. Mammon unconsciously
takes up this image later when he says he will 'talke to
her, all in gold' (IV. i. 25). Poor Mammon had no way of
knowing what an expert conversationalist he was going to
talk to.

Such obscenity is very far from being aphrodisiac because
the ludicrousness and lack of taste both within the images
themselves and in the relationship of the images to each

[1] Perhaps the implication of 'virginall' in this passage may be clarified by an
image of Prospero's from the Quarto *Every Man in his Humor* (II. iii. 183-185):
'I can compare him to nothing more happely, then a Barbers virginals; for euery
one may play vpon him.'

[2] This unmentionable word was first brought into a dictionary by John Florio
in *A World of Wordes* (1598), but it was almost certainly in common speech long
before that. See Allen Walker Read, 'An Obscenity Symbol', *American Speech*
(December 1934), IX, 264 ff.; and Eric Partridge, *Shakespeare's Bawdy* (New York,
1948), 113.

other neutralize any possible pornography. That Dol should 'Firke, like a flounder' and 'kisse, like a scallop' does not make her particularly seductive. Such an indecorous mixture of vehicles applied to the same tenor helps maintain a continuous comic tone so that never for a moment do we feel close to the characters. The distance between the tenor and vehicle tends to keep us at a distance. Seen through the eyes of Mammon or Dapper, Dol is a heroine and, like the prostitutes in Plautus's plays, can seem a heroine—of a sort —even to us. But she is not romanticized. The exaggerated absurdity of Dol as a Dover pier makes her whoredom ludicrous, not erotically attractive, nor even pitiful.

Martial imagery throws a cloak of authority and high matters of state over other scenes than this one. When the furnace explodes and Subtle swoons, Face says, 'Coldnesse and death inuades him' (IV. v. 63). Supposing that Mammon is about to assault her virtue, Dol, with her high sense of honour, says, 'You meane no treason, sir!' (IV. i. 118). Love-Wit's house is a 'fort' to Face (V. ii. 29), a 'Citadell' to Surly (IV. vi. 9), and a 'castle' to Kastril (V. iii. 36). This martial pretentiousness in part explains why Face calls himself 'Captaine' as well as why Dol constantly promotes him to 'Generall'. A Captaine in the seventeenth century was a commander of a body of troops or of a fortress or castle. The exact function of a Captain in this war with the world can be inferred from the dialogue between Subtle, who announces the arrival of Dame Pliant and Kastril, and Face:

> FAC. I must to my Captaine-ship againe, then.
> SVB. Stay, bring 'hem in, first.
> FAC.   So I meant.   IV. ii. 3-4

A captain is one who brings the customers in. Business is a war, and Face is an Intelligence officer in active service.

VI

Mammon's language is, aside from Face's, the best example of how thoroughly the implications of the imagery relate business, religion, and sex. His name is an example of this. According to the *OED*, Mammon, the Aramaic word for 'riches', was taken by medieval writers as the proper name of the devil of covetousness. Even in the Elizabethan Age Thomas Lodge in *Wits Miserie, or the Worlds Madnesse* (1596) used Mammon as the devil incarnate who tempted man by avarice.[1] After the sixteenth century it was current as a term of opprobrium for wealth regarded as an idol or evil influence. Loosely, 'Epicure' meant 'one who disbelieves in the divine government, and in a future life'. More particularly, it came to mean one who gives himself up to sensual pleasure, especially eating. This idea of a refined taste for the pleasures of the table began as early as 1586 (*OED*). Some sense of what Epicure meant by the time of *The Alchemist* can be gained from the *Nosce Teipsum* (1599) of Sir John Davies. In the passage on the immortality of the soul Davies describes those 'light and vicious persons' who claim that the soul is 'but a smoke or airy blast' and who say, 'Come, let us eat and drink' before we die.

> Therefore no heretics desire to spread
> Their light opinions like these Epicures;[2]

In short, Epicure carries with it a sense of atheism and materialism, just as Mammon symbolized covetousness, riches, and worldliness. 'Epicure', which comes from Greek, and 'Mammon', which is exclusively a Christian term, unite to form a name which is at once a humanistic and Christian comment on impious wealth and immorality.

[1] *The Complete Works of Thomas Lodge* (Glasgow, 1883), IV, 2, 26-45.
[2] Hebel and Hudson, ed., *Poetry of the English Renaissance* (New York, 1938), 363.

The geographical allusions of this immense symbol of worldliness and sensuality reveal him to be a more romantic merchant venturer than Face.

> Now, you set your foot on shore
> In *nouo orbe*; Here's the rich *Peru*:
> And there within, sir, are the golden mines,
> Great SALOMON's *Ophir*! He was sayling to't,
> Three yeeres, but we haue reach'd it in ten months.
> II. i. 1-5

Mammon is not merely the explorer setting his foot on the shore of the New World—not even primarily the explorer— but essentially the merchant venturer. His primary interest is in the 'golden mines' within which shall make him rich. Not the least of many ironies in this scene is that Face has been thinking of Mammon himself as a 'vein' to be mined (I. iii. 106). This idea of exploiting distant lands is brought even closer home when Mammon declares that he will purchase Devonshire and Cornwall and make them 'perfect *Indies*' (II. i. 35-36). These counties were noted for tin and copper mines, which Mammon would transmute into 'golden mines'. The commercial note which opens the scene is brought in most emphatically in his lines on Subtle who makes the stone, 'But I buy it. / My venter brings it me' (II. ii. 100-101). The use of the commercial terms—'buy' and 'venter'—in reference to the stone shows how intimate is the connection between religion and business in Mammon's world. Mammon can buy his god, the elixir. Divinity and immortality can be bargained for. There is a certain justice, as Mammon himself admits, in the fate to which this business venture in religion comes. The sensual dreams which had drawn him on and his pursuit of Dol are said by Subtle to be the cause of the bursting of the glass and the failure of all his hopes. He cries, 'O my voluptuous mind! I am iustly punish'd' (IV. v. 74). It is characteristic of Mammon that he should consider the loss of the power of making gold a just punishment for a voluptuous mind.

Mammon's psychic sensuality is its own best criticism. As L. C. Knights says, each of his speeches 'implicitly refers to a traditional conception of the Mean'.[1] The images he uses more than once betray the essential meanness of his vision. Not simply their constant extravagance—though that is one way of indicating hollowness—but also the action within the image itself shows this. For instance:

> My mists
> I'le haue of perfume, vapor'd 'bout the roome,
> To loose our selues in; and my baths, like pits
> To fall into: II. ii. 48-51

Other associations with losing one's self or falling into pits suddenly betray such lines, suggesting that Mammon may have lost himself already and calling up memories of an Inferno where sinners have fallen into pits of fire. Or the dramatic irony implicit in the imagery he uses may reveal him. Thus he explains to Surly that, once his friends are rich, they shall not have to deal with 'the hollow die' or 'the fraile card', nor keep a 'liuery-punke', nor worship 'the golden calfe', nor 'Commit idolatrie with wine, and trumpets' (II. i. 9 ff.). But we know, from the previous act, that the dice are loaded, that Dol is a punk, that Mammon is worshipping a golden calf and committing idolatry with words if not wine. Or when Mammon, to convince Surly of the authenticity of the elixir, alludes to a classical myth, the myth itself betrays him.

> SISIPHVS was damn'd
> To roule the ceaslesse stone, onely, because
> He would haue made ours common.[2]
>   II. iii. 208-210

---

[1] Knights, *Drama and Society in the Age of Jonson*, 190.

[2] The stage direction may be important here: '*Dol is seene*', exactly on the word 'common'. Is this another way to suggest an equation between the stone and Dol Common?

Sisyphus was punished for his fraud and avarice. Mammon, who is avaricious, if not fraudulent, suddenly turns into Sisyphus, rolling the ceaseless stone of alchemy.

VII

The denouement of the play has troubled more than one observer. Subtle and Dol escape over the back wall without their 'purchase', but also without punishment. Face cuts off his beard, changes his clothes, talks Love-Wit into going along with the hoax, and becomes that 'very honest fellow', Jeremy, again. Love-Wit, 'with some small straine / Of his owne candor', accepts a rich wife and a cellar full of Mammon's goods. Where, one might ask, is the justice in such an end? Elisabeth Woodbridge Morris, who held that Jonson's comedy is 'judicial' but not always 'moral' (a distinction that, in a work of art, escapes me), said that 'the moral of *The Alchemist* . . . would be hard to find'.[1] M. Castelain went even further in his criticism of the ending: 'Voilà un dénouement qui n'est pas très conforme à la saine morale, ni aux habitudes de notre poète. C'est le gros défaut, le seul peut-être de la pièce, mais on ne peut ni l'expliquer, ni l'excuser.'[2] According to M. Castelain, Jonson, troubled about ending his intrigue, drew it to whatever end he could. The answer to such criticism is that Face and Love-Wit are convicted by their own words and actions. For example, note how subtly allusions to heat and dogs connect the impostors with the plague then raging. Heat symbolically associates the plague ('*The sicknesse hot*') with the alchemizing process which finally blows up and with the alchemists—Face, the fire-drake, Subtle who has 'heate' (III. i. 31), and Dol who is 'a fire' (III. iv. 139). Furthermore, since dogs were then thought to be especially dangerous as carriers of the plague,

[1] Elisabeth Woodbridge Morris, *Studies in Jonson's Comedy* (New York, 1898), 29.

[2] Maurice Castelain, *Ben Jonson, L'Homme et L'Œuvre* (Paris, 1907), 351.

the recurrent comparisons of the impostors to snarling curs suggest that they bring a black death of their own.[1] In *Every Man out of his Humour* Carlo Buffone tells Sogliardo to shun Macilente 'as you'ld doe the plague' because he's a 'leane mungrell' (I. ii. 207-212). Another hint that the plague and the impostors may be related appears later in the first scene when Face, assuring Subtle that Love-Wit will not return, says,

> If he doe,
> Hee'll send such word, for ayring o' the house
> As you shall haue sufficient time, to quit it:
> I. i. 185-187

Here the syntactical ambiguity of the phrase 'for ayring o' the house' implies that the house needs airing because of that combined plague, Dol and Subtle.

Love-Wit is drawn into intimate association with the fraud by Face who begs for a chance to advance his own fortune:

> I'll helpe you to a widdow,
> In recompence, that you shall gi' me thankes for,
> Will make you seuen yeeres yonger, and a rich one.
> 'Tis but your putting on a *Spanish* cloake.
> V. iii. 84-87

There are several remarkable things about this passage. One of them is that Love-Wit is invited to take the place of Face, who previously had said, concerning Drugger, 'He is gone to borrow me a *Spanish* habite, / Ile be the *Count*, now' (IV. vii. 99-100). Love-Wit, then, takes Face's place, both as the husband of Dame Pliant and as the manipulator of the fools whom he gets rid of in a manner worthy of Face. The other remarkable implication of Face's words concerns Dame Pliant's effect on Love-Wit: it resembles the supposed effect of the elixir. Like that infallible medicine, she will make him

[1] See F. P. Wilson, *The Plague in Shakespeare's London* (Oxford, 1927), 36.

younger and richer. Love-Wit's final lines carry on this same
implication.

> if I haue out-stript
> An old mans grauitie, or strict canon, thinke
> What a yong wife, and a good braine may doe:
> Stretch ages truth sometimes, and crack it too.
>
> V. v. 153-156

Love-Wit has found what Mammon sought—the elixir of
life which will stretch, perhaps even crack, the truth of old
age—found it in a rich young wife and in his 'good braine',
Jeremy. He does not claim that he has found the fountain
of perpetual youth, as Mammon did, but he clearly hopes
that the quick-silver of Dame Pliant and the sulphur of Face
may alchemize away old age for the time being. By such
implications as well as by his actions Love-Wit is drawn
into the orbit of Face and Mammon, both of whose places
he takes in one way or another. Use of the same language
in a play is one way of striking up similarities between
characters. Thus Love-Wit's use of martial images like
Face's or of alchemic allusions like Mammon's suggests
that he is not much different from them.

Face, too, is accused by the words he uses. His final
address to the audience reveals him to be the same Face
that he was when 'Captaine'.

> My part a little fell in this last *Scene*,
> Yet 'twas *decorum*. And though I am cleane
> Got off, from Svbtle, Svrly, Mammon, Dol,
> Hot Ananias, Dapper, Drvgger, all
> With whom I traded; yet I put my selfe
> On you, that are my countrey: and this pelfe,
> Which I haue got, if you doe quit me, rests
> To feast you often, and inuite new ghests.

To the very end he remains the business man, giving the
monthly report of the companies with whom he has 'traded',
and keeping a sharp eye on those with whom he will trade

in the future. His plea that he is putting himself on the audience, which is his 'countrey' has a sinister note. 'Countrey', which he is ostensibly using in its legal sense of 'jury', has a more normal sense of 'land' or 'nation'. The audience may be there to judge his case, but it is also a nation to be exploited. The bait is a 'feast', but when we remember that Epicure's vision of a golden age was largely one of eating and that various things from gold to Dol and Dame Pliant had been proposed as a meal, we discover that Face is suggesting that we become Epicures in our turn. Furthermore, by using the legal phrase, 'putting himself on his country', he is making the insulting suggestion that he and the audience are, after all, fellow citizens of the same native land, since such a jury was summoned from one's own peers in the neighbourhood.

But the term more than any other which reveals Face and Love-Wit and the whole crew of gulls in proper perspective is 'pelfe'. By the end of the sixteenth century 'pelfe' had come to mean wealth in a depreciatory sense and even trumpery and refuse. In the *Faerie Queene* Malebecco is described thus:

> But all his mind is set on mucky pelfe,
> To hoord up heapes of euill gotten masse.
>
> III. ix. 4

Puttenham's comment in *The Arte of English Poesie* is also revealing. 'Pelfe is properly the scrappes or shreds of taylors and of skinners, which are accompted of so vile price as they be commonly cast out of dores, or otherwise bestowed upon base purposes.' And in comparison to health and conscience, 'all the gold or siluer in the world may by a skornefull terme be called pelfe'.[1] Something of this derogatory sense of the word frames in the whole play. If 'pelfe' is properly 'the scrappes and shreds of taylors', Face has fallen all the way down to the 'liuery-three-pound-thrum' (I. i. 16) that Subtle

[1] Puttenham, 274-275.

accused him of being. For 'thrum' according to one editor
of Jonson, meant 'the waste end or roughly fringed edging
of a piece of woven cloth'.[1] All of the 'pelfe' which he got
has made him precisely what he was before—the refuse of
society. Even before he uses the word we are given a sense
of how trashy his booty is by the ludicrous inventory of their
'purchase', when Face dismisses his junior partners. Aside
from the money given by Mammon, Ananias, Drugger, and
Dapper, there are stolen jewels, 'fish-wiues rings', 'ale-wiues
single money', a sailor's whistle, tavern cups, French petti-
coats and girdles, 'bolts of lawne', and tobacco (V. iv. 105
ff.). This miscellany indicates the admirable democracy of
Face and company: they rob anyone of anything. But the
rubbish they get is its own best punishment.

The justice here is scarcely poetic. To some it may not
seem punishment at all, but it is the only justice that many
ironic comedies have. No one repents, no one reforms—not
even, one suspects, Mammon, although, still extravagant,
he claims that he will 'preach / The end o' the world'. The
fools are fooled; the rascals get away. Yet all endure the
most comic of all punishments: they remain themselves—a
deadly retribution if one is a fool like Mammon or a rascal
like Face.

VIII

The imagery of *The Alchemist* is perfectly functional in
several ways. First, it develops, as alchemy develops, beginning with base metals, such as a whore, a pander, and a
quack, which it tries grandiloquently to transmute into finer
beings—a Faery Queen, a precious king of present wits, and
a divine instructor—finally ending, as the dream of the
philosopher's stone ends, in a return to the state of base
metals. The various vehicles which alchemize the base

[1] Brinsley Nicholson, *Notes and Queries*, 76:385 (November 12, 1887).

situation—the inflated epithets, the erotic allusions, the religious and commercial terms—ultimately show how thoroughly mean the situation is by bringing into the context the very standards by which it could be measured: the Christian and humanistic civilization of rational men. Against that immense background the three impostors and their commonwealth of fools play out their mock-heroic life, their violent little actions contrasting sharply with the permanent values suggested by the imagery. When Subtle is compared to a priest, the comparison itself shows how much he disappoints the ideal. When Dol calls herself Queen of Faeries, we see how far she really is from the Faery Queen.

The imagery is functional in another way. The images work on the same principle that the play as a whole and usually each scene work. They are extravagant, inflated, and ludicrous, because the tenors (gold, Dol, Mammon) are related to great vehicles (god, Queen, Jove). The monstrous gap that opens between the tenor that we know to be mean and the vehicle that we assume to be great, and the demand that we find some similarities between them to bridge that gap, outrages our sense of decency and decorum. That outrage, within the imagery, produces part of the comic tone of the play.

A third function of the imagery is to extend and develop the multiple references that alchemy had in actual life—especially the religious, medical, and commercial references. The alchemic process in this play has religious implications because the desire for gold is thought of as a religion; it has medical implications because the elixir is thought of as a sovereign remedy; it has sexual implications because the elixir is thought to have a sexual power; it has commercial implications because business terms are used in reference to the whole fraudulent practice. When gold or the power of producing gold is spoken of as one normally speaks of a deity, we are expected to question whether this has any connections with reality. Do some people make gold their god? What is the sense in saying that man's nature can be alchemized? Is money in any sense the great healing power of the world? Does the great god, gold, have a sexual power? What is the relation of business to this religion of gold? Is sex to some people a business? Is religion? And so on. In other words, the imagery suggests that, in the Alchemist's world, the acquisition of gold is a religion, a cure-all, a sexual experience, and a commercial enterprise. The world that opens before us, once we understand these multiple references of alchemy, is outrageously obscene, crude in metaphysic and vulgar in emotion. Since this world is, in part, a caricature of the real world, one can make numerous connections between its crudity and obscenity and the crudity and obscenity latent in human experience. But as a universe of discourse, it exists in its own right, comic because it is a caricature, solid and substantial because it has a religion, an ethic, a government, and a flourishing business.

The imagery also suggests that the various peoples whose lives are dedicated to the acquisition of gold—whether they be in secular or religious life, in prostitution or other kinds of business—bear some relation to the alchemists of old. Dol Common is metaphorically an alchemist because she, too, is trying to turn base metals into gold. Mammon's cook is an alchemist in the same way; the reward of all his cooking is the accolade—'there's gold, / Goe forth, and be a knight'. Perhaps the true philosopher's stone is not the stone itself, but simply business—that is, selling the public the things it wants. Face's threatening of Subtle is pertinent:

> I will haue
> A booke, but barely reckoning thy impostures,
> Shall proue a true *philosophers stone*, to printers.
>
> I. i. 100-102

The Golden Age comes when you find that you have what

someone else wants—a sensational book or a new medicine, a shiny gadget or an old fraud. The true alchemist may be Face, that 'parcell-broker, and whole-bawd' who always has something someone wants and who perpetually finds the elixir of life in Drugger, Mammon, Dame Pliant, Subtle, Dol, and finally Love-Wit. Face may be the face of the future, the prophetic vision of the super-salesman who can sell anything to anyone. All that he needs to work on is man —man who, himself another Face, will sell even things he needs in order to buy things he wants. With naked impudence he expresses his philosophy early in the game.

> You [Subtle] must haue stuffe, brought home
>   to you, to worke on?
> And, yet, you thinke, I am at no expence,
> In searching out these veines, then following 'hem,
> Then trying 'hem out. 'Fore god, my intelligence
> Costs me more money, then my share oft comes too,
> In these rare workes.   I. iii. 104-109

That little world, man, contains the base metals on which as alchemist can work. The seams or lodes may lie deep, but they can be searched out and followed. The 'golden mines' of Mammon, his *nouo orbe* and 'rich *Peru*' are only new names for this old world of man—new names, ironically, for Sir Epicure Mammon. Though alchemy itself is a fraud, Subtle, Dol, and Face are successful alchemists in that they have found this golden secret. All who discover this secret— all whores like Dol, all quacks like Subtle, all shrewd rascals like Face, all unscrupulous opportunists like Love-Wit— these are the true alchemists.

This conviction that in man's nature lie the base metals of alchemy appears in a different form in an image that Face uses in speaking of his futile search for Surly.

> 'Slight would you haue me stalke like a mill-iade,
> All day, for one, that will not yeeld vs graines?
>   III. iii. 5-6

Man could be harvested as well as transmuted. Once ground down in the mill, he could yield 'graines'. This kind of gain was the 'common way' which Volpone avoided: '[I] haue no mills for yron, / Oyle, corne, or men, to grinde 'hem into poulder' (I. i. 35-36). But the final source of money for Face is the final source of food for Volpone—man.

CHAPTER VII

'EPICOENE'

I

Harry levin claims that Jonson's trick of making his characters say something which frequently has little explicit meaning reaches its logical limit in *Epicoene*, 'where everything spoken has a high nuisance value and the words themselves become sheer filagree'.[1] There is some truth to this claim, though not so much as Levin and Alexander Sackton (who elaborated on it in *Rhetoric as a Dramatic Language in Ben Jonson*) make for it. At first glance the language of *Epicoene* seems remarkably direct and unequivocal; much of it, of course, remains so after repeated glances. But to think that 'everything spoken' has primarily a nuisance value is likely to make one ignore the subtle allusiveness of much that is spoken.

Allusive language is one of the slier ways of throwing discourse into the parallel engagement of metaphorical language. Allusions suggest another area of experience—a series of concepts or a set of emotions—which can be seen juxtaposed, for a moment, to the rest of the discourse. This juxtaposition of the two worlds—the world of the characters in action and the world suggested by the allusions—creates some of the comic effect of Jonson's plays.

We might begin with the allusions to *epicene*. As a substantive, *epicene* means one who partakes of the characteristics of both sexes. As an adjective, it carries this meaning and, by transference, also means 'adapted to both sexes'. An example of this meaning, according to the *OED*, is Fuller's use of the word in his *Worthies*, where he described 'those Epicoene, and Hermaphrodite Convents wherein Monks

[1] Levin, ed., *Ben Jonson: Selected Works* (New York, 1938), 30.

and Nuns lived together'. Furthermore, *epicene* was sometimes used in the seventeenth century to mean 'effeminate',
though its use in Jonson's 'Epigram on the Court Pucell'
does not seem to carry this meaning, as the *OED* claims it
does. The lines are:

> What though with Tribade lust she force a Muse,
> And in an Epicoene fury can write newes
> Equall with that, which for the best newes goes,
> As aërie light, and as like wit as those?[1]

'Epicoene' can not properly mean 'effeminate' here: a
woman does not do things in an 'effeminate' way. It seems
rather to carry the meanings already explained and to imply
something unnatural. This suggestion of the unnatural is
emphasized by both 'Tribade' and 'force', 'Tribade' referring to a woman who practises unnatural vice with other
women, and 'force' suggesting a sexual assault. Thus,
'Epicoene fury' has more a colouring of the masculine or the
hermaphroditic than of the effeminate. In short, the main
point about all seventeenth century uses of *epicene* is that
they suggested the abnormal no man's land (and no woman's
land, too) between the normal male and the normal female.
This meaning is, I think, central to *The Silent Woman*.

The title, *Epicoene*, refers to much more than the central
twist of the plot in which Morose's wife turns out to be a
boy. Nearly everyone in the play is epicene in some way.
Note, for example, Truewit's description of the epicene
women who have lately formed a College: 'A new foundation, sir, here i' the towne, of ladies, that call themselues
the Collegiates, an order betweene courtiers, and country-
madames, that liue from their husbands; and giue entertain-
ment to all the *Wits*, and *Braueries* o' the time, as they call
'hem: crie downe, or vp, what they like, or dislike in a
braine, or a fashion, with most masculine, or rather *herma-*

---

[1] Herford and Simpson, VIII, 222.

phroditicall authoritie:...' (I. i. 73-80). As Truewit describes these Collegiates, they seem to belong to some intermediate sex between courtiers and women. Though 'courtiers' then could be used for both sexes, it is generally used in this play to refer to men. Truewit seems dubious about their exact nature when he tells how they criticize wit and fashion, at first thinking them 'masculine'—that is, too bold to be feminine—then amending it to '*hermaphroditicall*' apparently because they look like women but act like men. Though 'College' was used loosely for 'company', 'Collegiates' might have suggested something unfeminine in an age when only men gathered in colleges and, above all, only men criticized authoritatively. Jonson emphasizes the educational sense of the term by alluding to the learning, grammar, honours, and heraldry of their College.

Lady Centaure seems the most clearly epicene of these Collegiates. Characteristically, Jonson suggests her abnormal nature in her name. In the Elizabethan Age 'centaur' referred not merely to the fabulous creature with the head, trunk, and arms of a man, joined to the body and legs of a horse, but also, by a figurative extension, to an unnatural hybrid creation or to the intimate union of diverse natures (*OED*). Dekker's use of the word in 1606 reveals this second meaning: 'Sixe of these *Centaures* (that are halfe man, halfe beast, and halfe diuell).'[1] In classical literature the centaur is typically goatish, mischievous, and lustful; in so far as it has any single sexual nature, it is male (a female centaur is possible, but extremely rare). A centaur and a satyr may really be the same.[2] In this play Lady Centaure looks like a woman, and in part acts like one, but the masculine side of her nature is implied by Haughty's remark that Centaure 'has immortaliz'd her selfe, with taming of her wilde male'

---

[1] *The Non-Dramatic Works of Thomas Dekker*, ed. A. B. Grosart (1884), II, 79.
[2] See the chapter on centaurs in John C. Lawson, *Modern Greek Folklore and Ancient Greek Religion* (Cambridge, 1910), 192-253.

(IV. iii. 27-28), apparently by forcing her husband to give her the requisites of a fashionable lady.

All of these Ladies appear so far from the feminine—or what is generally considered the feminine—that Morose, on hearing their loud threats to have him blanketed, cries out, 'O, mankind generation!' (V. iv. 22). I take *mankind* to mean *masculine* or *mannish*, thus disagreeing with Percy Simpson who says that it comes from *mankeen* and means infuriated.[1] Possibly Jonson plays with both meanings, but the primary meaning seems to me to be *masculine*. In two plays written about the time of *Epicoene* Shakespeare used *mankind* to mean *masculine*: see *The Winter's Tale*, II. iii. 86, and *Coriolanus*, IV. ii. 24. Johnson's comment on the *Coriolanus* passage managed to combine both ideas: 'A *mankind* woman is a woman with the roughness of a man, and, in an aggravated sense, a woman ferocious, violent, and eager to shed blood.'[2] In Beaumont's *The Woman Hater* (1607), III. ii, the woman hater, running away from a lady who pursues and tries to seduce him, asks, 'Are women grown so mankind? Must they be wooing?' In all of these passages, as well as in Morose's exclamation, *mankind* is best understood, I think, to mean primarily *masculine* or *mannish*. The mannishness of these women is suggested by other remarks. For instance: after being solicited by Haughty, Centaure, and Mavis in turn, Dauphine says, 'I was neuer so assaulted' (V. ii. 52). Assaulting the opposite sex is generally thought to be a male privilege. Again: note the comment of the Ladies on Dauphine's neatness. Though 'iudiciall in his clothes', he is 'not so superlatiuely neat as some. . . . That weare purer linnen then our selues, and professe more neatness then the *french hermaphrodite*!' (IV. vi. 26-31). Neatness is often thought, not always justifiably, to be more characteristic of women than men. The effemin-

---

[1] Herford and Simpson, X, 45.
[2] See the notes in the Shakespeare Variorum edition of these plays.

ate man has long been associated with a too careful attention to his face and dress, just as the woman who is careless about her neatness seems less feminine. The Ladies thus unconsciously reveal both their own deviation from the feminine and the deviation of their suitors from the masculine. Epicoene adds a remark to this conversation which suggests the inverted sexual customs of their epicene lives. These neat men, according to her, 'are the only theeues of our fame: that thinke to take vs with that perfume, or with that lace. . . .' Men have managed sometimes to interest women, sometimes even to 'take' them, but customarily they have used other means than perfume and lace. True, we ought to remember that men in Jacobean London did wear lace and use perfume in a way that modern men do not. Yet excessive attention to dress was continually satirized by the dramatists, because it was both irrational and unmanly. The more normal way of attracting women—and as comic as the epicene way—is dramatized in the physical conquest of La Foole and Daw by Dauphine, who is, as a result, besieged by the Ladies. Finally, the sterility of these women makes them less feminine. They have 'those excellent receits' to keep from bearing children: 'How should we maintayne our youth and beautie, else?' (IV. iii. 57-60).

The 'most masculine, or rather *hermaphroditicall* authoritie' of these Ladies Collegiates is best shown by the only one of them whom we see with her husband—Mistress Otter. Perhaps because she is only a 'pretender' to their learning, she takes their instruction most seriously. Captain Otter is first mentioned as an '*animal amphibium*' because he has had command on land and sea, but we learn from La Foole that his wife 'commands all at home'. Clerimont then concludes that 'she is Captaine OTTER?' (I. iv. 26-30). Just before the third act when we first see the Otters, Truewit prepares us for the comic view of their transposed marital relationship. Captain Otter, Truewit says, 'is his wifes Subiect, he calls her Princesse, and at such times as these, followes her vp and down the house like a page, with his hat off, partly for heate, partly for reuerence' (II. vi. 54-57). Modern listeners might not appreciate the full reversal implied in 'his wifes Subiect', but anyone who lived before women achieved the legal right to own property and the possession of great financial power (which is the power to subjugate man) must have been aware that the usual relation of husband and wife is reversed, so that she is Captain Otter and he is 'like a page'.

The first scene in Act III carries out this reversal. Captain Otter begs to be heard; Mistress Otter rails at him and asks him, 'Do I allow you your halfe-crowne a day, to spend, where you will. . . . Who giues you your maintenance, I pray you? who allowes you your horse-meat and man's meat?' (III. i. 36-40). Clerimont, who witnesses this feminine usurpation of the role of the male, observes, 'Alas, what a tyrannie, is this poore fellow married too' (III. ii. 10-11). The ultimate reversal of roles appears in the fourth act scene when, according to the stage direction, Mistress Otter *'falls vpon him and beates him'*.

But more important than the epicene nature of Mistress Otter is the epicene nature of Epicoene herself (or, rather, himself). When first seen, Epicoene is quiet enough to please even Morose. Then, as soon as the wedding is over, complaining loudly, she turns on Morose, who laments, 'O immodestie! a manifest woman!' Since 'manifest' implies a display so evident that no other proof is needed, Morose seems to be saying that a loud, demanding voice is woman's most characteristic feature. (Morose previously praised Epicoene for not taking pleasure in her tongue 'which is a womans chiefest pleasure' [II. v. 41-42]). A moment later Epicoene tells Mute that she will have none of his 'vnnaturall dumbnesse in my house; in a family where I gouerne'. The marriage is a minute old, and the wife governs. Morose's answer reveals his awareness of their strange marriage and

Epicoene's peculiar nature: 'She is my Regent already! I
haue married a PENTHESILEA, a SEMIRAMIS, sold my liberty
to a distaffe' (III. iv. 54-58). The allusions are revealing.
Penthesilea, the daughter of Ares, was the queen of the
Amazons who fought in the Trojan war. Semiramis, the wife
of Ninus, the mythical founder of the Assyrian empire, ruled
for many years after the death of her husband. Like Penthesilea, she was especially renowned in war. Soon after,
Morose alludes again to the Amazons, those curiously
epicene beings from antiquity, when he cries out, 'O
Amazonian impudence!' (III. v. 41). Her impudence seems
Amazonian to others than Morose. Truewit, for instance,
describes how all the noise and 'her masculine, and lowd
commanding, and vrging the whole family, makes him
thinke he has married a *furie*' (IV. i. 9-11). When Epicoene
is changed from a demure girl to an Amazon, she takes on a
new name. Haughty tells her, 'I'll call you MOROSE still now,
as I call CENTAVRE, and MAVIS' (IV. iii. 14-15). From then
until she is revealed to be a boy, she is called by this masculine name. It is only just that, since she has taken over the
authoritative power of Morose, she should also take over his
name.

Just as Captain Otter becomes epicene as his wife becomes
Captain Otter, so Morose loses or is willing to lose his male
dominance after Epicoene's 'masculine, and lowd commanding'. The first sign of a change in Morose comes after he has
frightened Mistress Otter with a 'huge long naked weapon'.

MOR. Would I could redeeme it with the losse of an
eye (nephew), a hand, or any other member.
DAV. Mary, god forbid, sir, that you should geld your
selfe, to anger your wife.
MOR So. it would rid me of her! (IV. iv. 8-12)

This willingness to become a eunuch so long as it rids him
of his epicene wife prompts him later to plead impotence as a
reason for divorce. 'I am no man,' he tells the Ladies,

'Vtterly vnabled in nature, by reason of *frigidity*, to performe the duties, or any the least office of a husband' (V. iv. 44-47). When this ruse of declaring himself 'no man' fails, he welcomes even that reflection on virility which the Elizabethans thought the most comic—being a cuckold. 'O, let me worship and adore you,' he cries to La Foole and Daw after they swear that they have lain with Epicoene (V. iv. 120). Castration, impotence, and being a wittol—all suggest that Morose would even lose his own maleness to get rid of a wife who at first seemed feminine but proved epicene.

The epicene natures of the women throw the masculine natures of the men out of line. When one sex changes, the other is likely to change. Otter's nature is dislocated by his wife's masculinity, so that the description of him as '*animal amphibium*' alludes to his divided nature as well as to his amphibious command. Jonson was fond of this sort of word play. In the masque, *Neptune's Triumph*, there is '*Amphibion Archy*', who is described as the chief 'o the *Epicoene* gender, Hees, and Shees'.[1] The Broker in *The Staple of Newes* is called '*Amphibion*' because he is a 'creature of two natures' (II. iv. 132). The adjective *amphibion* (or *amphibious*) meant having two modes of existence or being of doubtful nature. Browne's statement—'We are onely that amphibious piece between a corporall and spirituall essence'—is the best known example of this use in the seventeenth century. Otter is an amphibious piece in this play—a being of doubtful nature who looks like a man, but does not act like one.

Another epicene man is La Foole, who is spoken of first as 'a precious mannikin' (I. iii. 25)—that is, a little man or a pygmy. When he speaks, he apparently speaks in an effeminate manner—rapidly and all in one breath. Talking also characterizes Sir John Daw whom Truewit calls, 'The onely talking sir i' the towne!' (I. ii. 66). As we have seen already, to Morose 'womans chiefest pleasure' is her tongue. That

[1] Herford and Simpson, VII, 689.

the audience is apparently expected to associate women and talking can be inferred from the ironic subtitle—*The Silent Woman*. Who ever heard of a silent woman? Daw's barely sensible poem reflects this same assumption:

> *Silence in woman, is like speech in man,*
> *Deny't who can.*
>
> . . . . . .
>
> *Nor, is't a tale,*
> *That female vice should be a vertue male,*
> *Or masculine vice, a female vertue be.*
>
> II. iii. 123-128

There is little sense to this in itself, but from the context we gather that, though Daw means it one way, we should take it another way. Daw seems to mean that speech is a defect ('vice = defect) in a woman just as it is a virtue in a man. '*I know to speake,*' he says in the last line of the poem, '*and shee to hold her peace.*' Silence, which Daw considers woman's crowning virtue, would then be man's great defect. Daw's distinction between the sexes is so extreme and so unsupported by facts that it is comic to most normal people. The normal Elizabethan feeling about silence and women was probably voiced by Zantippa in Peele's *Old Wives' Tale*, ll. 731-732: 'A woman without a tongue is as a soldier without his weapon.' The whole play suggests that both a silent woman and a talkative man are, if anything, inversions of the normal. The tendency of Daw and La Foole to gossip maliciously suggests the inversion of their natures which their actions reveal. Their feminine or at least non-masculine natures are implied also by their lack of courage. One thinks, perhaps erroneously, that men are usually courageous and that women are usually frightened. Helena in *A Midsummer Night's Dream*, III. ii. 302, says, 'I am a right maid for my cowardice.' Sir Andrew Aguecheek's fear makes him ridiculous, but Viola's fear seems only normal to the spectator, though it makes her ridiculous to the other characters who do not know that she is really a woman. Similarly, when Daw and La Foole prove themselves so frightened that they allow themselves to be publicly humiliated rather than act on their valiant words, we think of them as somewhat less than the men they appear to be. The Ladies Collegiate are loud, demanding, and aggressive. All, like Centaure, try to tame their wild males. All, in short, are Amazons. Of the men, only Clerimont, Truewit, and Dauphine are not warped by the Amazonian natures of these epicene women.

Yet even these apparently normal men are somewhat ambiguous, sexually. Truewit's first speech in the play suggests the epicene quality of their sexual experience when he remarks that 'betweene his mistris abroad, and his engle at home, Clerimont can melt away his time'. Since an 'engle' was a young boy kept for erotic purposes, Truewit is explaining how Clerimont enjoys the pleasures of both sexes. There had already been an allusion to the homosexual relationship of the Boy and Clerimont in the latter's fourth speech in this first scene. The sexual ambiguity of the characters in this play is nowhere better suggested than in the Boy's remark that the Lady 'puts a perruke o' my head; and askes me an' I will weare her gowne; and I say, no: and then she hits me a blow o' the eare, and calls me innocent, and lets me goe' (I. i. 16-18). She calls him innocent because he (who is unconsciously feminine in his relationship to Clerimont) refuses to be consciously feminine in his relationship to the aggressive Lady. To be sophisticated (as opposed to innocent) apparently means to be quadri-sexual: a man to both men and women, and a woman to both women and men.

II

This interest in beings who have the characteristics of both sexes suggests that the play is fundamentally concerned with deviations from a norm. Like all of Jonson's major comedies, *Epicoene* explores the question of decorum—here, the decorum of the sexes and the decorum of society. We recognize that most of the characters are epicene because we still have, even in this age of the emancipated woman, a sense of what is normal for the sexes. We may lack Jonson's strong sense of decorum, perhaps because we can not entirely agree with his concept of what is natural. Jonson clearly anticipated that sense of 'nature' which became a central dogma in the neo-classic age: that is, the natural is the normal and the universal. Normally, men are brave and aggressive, and women are passive and reserved—or are supposed to be. A cowardly man and an aggressive woman become, in a comedy, ludicrous. Some of Jonson's rigid sense of the decorum of nature has been lost in an age which, like the present one, looks on deviations from nature as pathological —that is, as pitiful. For example, Morose. To many, the spectacle of indolent men torturing a man highly sensitive to noise is closer to sadism than to pure comedy. The reviewer for *The Times* in 1924 thought that, in the Phoenix Society production of the play, Morose was a 'tragic figure' tormented by 'bounders'.[1] But to previous ages such 'comedy of affliction' was a social rather than a medical matter. Morose is comic, rather than psychopathic, because he is selfish and vain. When he says, 'all discourses, but mine owne, afflict mee, they seeme harsh, impertinent, and irksome' (II. i. 4-5), we hear the voice of a proud, not a sick man. Or, rather, Morose's affliction is a disease, but a ridiculous disease. Note that Truewit asks Clerimont, 'But is the disease so ridiculous in him, as it is made?' (I. i. 148-149). To us no disease seems ridiculous, not even those which are ostensibly the fault of the diseased person— venereal diseases, for instance. But to the seventeenth century many sicknesses were ridiculous. Bedlam was a

---

[1] *The Times,* November 19, 1924, p. 12, col. 3.

comedy, and D'Avenant's diseased nose, the source of countless jibes. The laughter, cruel to us but simply tough-minded to earlier ages, apparently came from a sense of decorum so rigid that even the deviations of sickness became ludicrous. No healthy, rational man—the terms overlapped for Jonson—should be so sensitive to noise as Morose. He should be 'cured', as Truewit suggests in the last line of the play—that is, brought in line with what Truewit thinks is normal. 'Cure' is borrowed from medicine, as the whole theory of the comedy of humours is, and both keep something of their medical sense even when used as Jonson used them; but they are applied to social rather than physical troubles—to hypocrisy, not heart trouble.

One way to observe how Jonson explores the question of what is natural is to note the allusions to deviations from nature—to prodigies and to the strange, the unnatural, and the monstrous. A prodigy to the Elizabethans was something out of the ordinary course of nature, something either abnormal or monstrous. Because Morose is so ridiculously sensitive to noise, Truewit thinks, 'There was never such a prodigie heard of' (I. ii. 3). Morose himself has a contrary view of prodigies. When someone winds a horn outside of his house, he cries out, 'What villaine? what prodigie of mankind is that?' (II. i. 38-39). Just as Morose thinks that anyone (except himself) who makes noise is a prodigy, so Truewit thinks complete silence is unnatural. To him the silent Morose and Mute are 'fishes! *Pythagoreans* all! This is strange' (II. ii. 3). Pythagoreans were noted for their secrecy as well as for their belief in metempsychosis. Speechless men may look human, but they have the souls of fishes: they are 'strange'. 'Strange' and its equivalents are crucial words to everyone in the play. 'Strange sights', according to Truewit, can be seen daily in these times of masques, plays, Puritan preachings, and mad folk (II. ii. 33-36). He then proceeds to tell Morose the 'monstrous hazards' that

Morose shall run with a wife. Among these hazards is the
possibility of marrying a woman who will 'antidate' him
cuckold by conveying her virginity to a friend. 'The like has
beene heard of, in nature. 'Tis no deuis'd, impossible
thing, sir' (II. ii. 145-147).

The relationship between Epicoene and Morose appears
to others and to themselves as strange, even monstrous. At
their first meeting Morose tells her that his behaviour, being
'rare', may appear strange (II. v. 23). Truewit had previously
complimented Epicoene on 'this rare vertue of your silence'
(II. iv. 91). Epicoene has another idea about silence which
appears when she calls Mute down for his 'coacted, vnnaturall
dumbnesse' (III. iv. 54). Speechlessness apparently seems a
deviation from nature to the Ladies Collegiate too because
they come to see Epicoene, thinking her a prodigy, but they
find her normal—that is, loquacious. Her loquacity, so
natural to them, later seems only a 'monstrous' impertinency
to Morose (IV. iv. 36). Just as she seems a monster to him,
so he seems a 'prodigious creature' to Mavis when he pleads
impotence (V. iv. 48). The spectators, who stand outside of
this created world, measure its prodigies against their own
concept of what is normal and natural, and find, presumably,
that most of its strange creatures are comic.

Connected with this question of what is natural is another
question, a favourite in the seventeenth century—what is the
relation of art and nature? This question is brought up early
in the opening scene when Clerimont curses Lady Haughty's
'peec'd beautie'—pieced, apparently, from her washings,
patchings, paintings, and perfumings. Because her artificial
beauty offends him, he writes the famous song, 'Still to be
neat, still to be drest'. In this song Clerimont upholds
simplicity and nature because, so he thinks, the artifices of
powder and perfume may only conceal what is not sweet and
not sound. Such pretences are '*adulteries*'—that is, adultera-
tions or debasings of what should be natural. The natural to

him is simple, careless, and free. To be natural a woman must be unpinned, uncorseted, and unadorned. Truewit declares himself to be 'clearly o' the other side': he loves 'a good dressing, before any beautie o' the world'. 'Beautie', one gathers, is only nature; 'a good dressing' is art. A well-dressed woman is 'like a delicate garden' to Truewit, apparently because nature in her is trimmed, artificially nurtured, and artfully arranged; its delicacy comes deliberately, not naturally. Art, as he uses it, means the technique of revealing what is naturally attractive and of concealing what is naturally ugly; thus, if a woman has 'good legs', she should 'wear short clothes'. Nor should a lover wish to see his lady make herself up any more than one would ask to see gilders overlaying a base metal with a thin covering of gold: one must not discover 'how little serues, with the helpe of art, to adorne a great deale'. A lover should only approach his lady when she is a 'compleat, and finish'd' work of art.

Because clothes are the most common of all artifices by which the natural is concealed, the relation between art and nature is suggested most clearly in allusions to dress. Clerimont seems swayed from his earlier disdain for the artifices of women when he sees Lady Haughty in all her finery. Truewit assures him that 'Women ought to repaire the losses, time and yeeres haue made i' their features, with dressings' (IV. i. 35-37). In the conversation that follows this observation, art takes on an added dimension: it comes to mean social decorum. Truewit repeats his former point that a woman should artfully conceal her natural limitations. Then the talk slips over into what is socially acceptable when Clerimont ridicules some women whose laughter is rude because it is loud, and Truewit ridicules women whose walk is offensive because it is as huge as that of an ostrich. Characteristically, Truewit says, 'I loue measure i' the feet' —'measure' meaning moderation as well as rhythm. Decorous behaviour, then, is to the whole person what careful dressing is to the body: an artistic way of repairing the defects of an offensive nature. Even the uncourtly Morose shares the courtly conviction that art can serve and rival nature. He tells Epicoene that he longs to have his wife be the first in all fashions, have her council of tailors, 'and then come foorth, varied like Nature, or oftner then she, and better, by the helpe of Art, her aemulous seruant' (II. v. 73-75). On a lower social plane Otter reveals that he too is aware of how women can use the artificial to gild or transform the natural. When he is drunk enough to be brave, he begins to curse his wife for being naturally vile. She makes herself endurable only by the most ingenious artifices. 'Euery part o' the towne ownes a peece of her', Otter claims. 'She takes her selfe asunder still when she goes to bed', and the next day, 'is put together againe, like a great *Germane* clocke' (IV. ii. 94-99).

But clothes do not merely artificially conceal nature or repair the losses that the years have made; at times the artistic can take the place of the natural: a person's dress can become the person. Thus, in this play as in other comedies of Jonson, knighthood is thought to be largely a matter of clothes. Clerimont, speaking of Sir John Daw, asks, 'Was there euer such a two yards of knighthood, measur'd out by *Time*, to be sold to laughter?' (II. iv. 151-152). In a bitter arraignment of knighthood Morose implies that the artificial can become the natural when he says that knighthood 'shall want clothes, and by reason of that, wit, to foole to lawyers' (II. v. 125-126). The most striking reference to the way that dress can change man's nature is Truewit's remark about the disguised Otter and Cut-beard. After he fits them out as a divine and a canon lawyer, he tells Dauphine, 'the knaues doe not know themselues, they are so exalted, and alter'd. Preferment changes any man' (V. iii. 3-5). Dress can so alter what a man is thought to be that his own nature is changed accordingly.

Epicoene, then, is a comedy about nature, normality, and decorum. Its various scenes explore comically and searchingly a number of questions to which, since it is a play, it does not offer any final answers. What is natural and normal for the sexes? What does society expect of men and women? Are women normally gossipy and men normally courageous? What is the relation between the natural and the artificial in social intercourse? But, though the play offers no final answers, it suggests throughout that the various answers dramatized in the physical and verbal action of the play are comic in so far as they violate certain standards of what is masculine and what is feminine, as well as what is natural and what is artificial in dress, behaviour, and beauty—standards which, presumably, the spectators bring to the theatre with them.

Comparing Jonson's text with any of the many adaptations of the play may reveal how effective its allusive language is in bringing these standards to the attention of the audience. For instance, George Colman's acting version in 1776. Colman had a good eye for emphasizing the farcical element in the plot, but apparently little feeling for what Jonson's language might suggest. The 1776 acting version is a simpler and, by eighteenth century standards, a more genteel play, but its comedy is thinner and more obvious because Colman (who said in his prologue that Jonson's farce was 'somewhat stale') cut out much of the play's allusive language. Though he kept in the speech about the Collegiates who speak with masculine or hermaphroditical authority and Morose's reference to 'mankind generation', he generally shifted the emphasis away from the comedy of sexual deviations by cutting out the references to the bi-sexual boy, the Collegiates' living away from their husbands, and Morose's castration, impotence, and cuckolding. The result is what is known as a 'cleaner' play, but a tamer and less searching one. In the same way the theme of art versus nature is mangled: the song, 'Still to be neat', is kept, though transferred to an earlier passage in the play, but Truewit's first act remarks are cut out, along with most of the crucial references to clothes. In short, for all its deceptive likeness to the play that Jonson wrote in his unrefined age, Colman's version is a far less suggestive comedy about nature, artifice, and not particularly epicene people.

Colman's treatment of *Epicoene* is typical of most adaptations, and prophetic of many modern readings of it. But unless one is aware of the allusiveness of Jonson's language, which adapters like Colman have mangled and which modern readers often disregard, one can not entirely understand Dryden's comment that there is 'more art and acuteness of fancy in [*Epicoene*] than in any of Ben Jonson's [plays].'[1]

---

[1] *The Works of John Dryden*, ed. Scott and Saintsbury (London, 1892), XV, 351.

CHAPTER VIII

THE LAST PLAYS

I

MOST readers would agree with James Howell's comment that Jonson was not so 'mad' when he wrote *The Magnetick Lady* as he had been when he wrote *The Alchemist*.[1] The divine fury of creation is perceptibly more earthbound in the plays written after Jonson's return to the public theatre in 1626. This is not to say that there are not admirable passages in these last plays or that these passages have not received praise. Herford, for instance, thought *The Staple of Newes* a 'greater and stronger drama' than *The Divell is an Asse* and felt that its greatest scenes fell short of nothing that Jonson ever did.[2] And Swinburne's hyperbolical praise of *The Magnetick Lady* is well known: 'The higher genius of Ben Jonson as a comic poet was yet once more to show itself in one brilliant flash of parting splendour before its approaching sunset.'[3] But few can share this enthusiasm; most readers are inclined to agree with Ward that in *The Magnetick Lady* 'we have in truth nothing more than the remnants of Ben Jonson—dry leaves from a nosegay of brighter days'.[4] As for *The New Inne*—almost no one since its first ill-starred performance has been heard to praise it (except one Ben Jonson), and even friends, like Randolph and Carew, who agreed that the age was loathsome, had little to say of the play as a play. Carew, in his poem 'To Ben Jonson uppon occasion of his Ode to himselfe' coolly tells Jonson that his comic muse has declined

---

[1] Joseph Jacobs, ed., *The Familiar Letters of James Howell* (London, 1892), I, 267.
[2] Herford and Simpson, II, 169-171.
[3] Swinburne, *A Study of Ben Jonson* (New York, 1889), 81.
[4] Ward, *The History of English Dramatic Literature*, II, 377.

from the zenith touched by his *Alchemist*.[1] The decline is evident enough in all of the last three completed plays (not counting *A Tale of a Tub* which was an early play reworked in 1633, and *The Sad Shepherd* which was left unfinished) to warrant considering them as a group.

At least three main charges have been brought or can be brought against these last plays. First, all, in varying degrees, lack unity. Second, all are, in theme, similar to the comedies of Jonson's major period, but weaker in effect. Third, Jonson's dramatic pattern, never remarkably flexible, hardened into allegory or into a form so schematized as to be lifeless. An analysis of the imagery of these plays may reveal to what extent each of these charges is true.

II

The Staple of Newes

Here, as in his previous plays, Jonson shows the follies of men by inverting the world we all live in and projecting that inverted world as the world of his characters. In this society of Peniboys there is the same religion of money and the same sexualizing of the power of money which appeared in *Volpone* and *The Alchemist*. The centre of this religion and the symbol of the sexualizing is Pecunia, Infanta of the Mynes.[2]

Even before Pecunia is mentioned in Act I, Scene 6, a whole theology of money is shadowed forth. We first catch a glimpse of it when Peniboy Jr. forgives Fashioner, 'the Taylor of the times', for being late and says that without forgiveness he would have been condemned to a hell in

[1] George Tennant, ed., *The New Inn. Yale Studies in English*, XXXIV (New York, 1908), 132.

[2] Herford mentions Barnfield's *Encomion to the Lady Pecunia* (1598) to show that Pecunia was not Jonson's own device. Probably she is a very old allegorical figure. For example, Jean de Meun wrote of 'Pecunia, queen-like' in his section of *Roman de la Rose*, l. 5517 ff.

which he could never stitch for any Peniboy (I. ii. 10-12).
Hell consists in not being a tailor for an heir who has, we
later hear, certain powers that common mortals lack. As
Peniboy Jr. expresses it,

> I doe feele
> The powers of *one and twenty*, like a Tide,
> Flow in vpon mee, and perceiue an Heyre,
> Can Coniure vp all spirits in all circles.
> Rogue, Rascall, Slaue, giue tradesmen their true
> names,
> And they appeare to 'hem presently.
>
> LIN.   For profit.
>
> I. ii. 134-139

All that a man with money needs to do to make tradesmen
appear as familiar spirits is to give them their true names,
such as 'Rascall'—and also give, as the Linener implies by
'For profit', a little currency which calls forth all spirits. If
this seems close to black magic, Peniboy Jr. brings it all
back to traditional terms when he tells his barber, concerning
an office in the Staple, 'I'll put thee in possession, my prime
worke! / Gods so' (I. ii. 142-143). And on the first day God
created heaven and earth: the heir installs Tom, the Barber,
as an 'Emissarie' for the Staple. No wonder that, even after
Peniboy had lost his fortune, Tom still called him 'My
Master! Maker!' (V. i. 22).

At the beginning of the scene immediately following
Peniboy's promise to his barber, the Canter comes in
singing a weakened and more jovial version of Volpone's
morning hymn to gold.

> *Good morning to my* Ioy, *My iolly* Peni-boy!
> *The Lord, and the Prince of plenty!*
> *I come to see what riches, Thou bearest in*
> *thy breeches,*
> *The first of thy one and twenty:*   I. iii. 1-4

The jingling rhymes rob the impiety of much of its force,

so that one is likely to skip over the intended play on the 'Prince of Peace' in the second line and read the allusions as monarchic rather than as religious. The impiety of the Canter's lines is further diluted by the military allusions which remind one more of that economic warfare which Face and company waged against the world than of Volpone's Black Mass (or, rather, golden mass).

But, once *Pecunia doe-all* appears, Peniboy's divinity is seen to be borrowed, and all the worshippers of money turn directly to her. The first mention of her contains all of the symbolism which is exploited later.[1] She is 'not of mortall race' though related to the '*King of Ophyr*'. ('Ophir' was that Biblical land famed for gold which Mammon mentioned.) Her names are '*Aurelia Clara Pecunia*', or 'Golden Bright Money'. Almost from the beginning she is sexualized, implicitly, of course, because she is a woman, but explicitly too when we hear that 'All the world are suiters to her. / All sorts of men, and all professions' (I. vi. 65-66). This Infanta of the Mines, then, is at once 'a desirable heiress', 'a great Princesse', and an immortal being—all because she symbolizes money.

Her first appearance brings forth a long speech by Peniboy Sr. which is full of religious vehicles.

> Your *Grace* is sad, me thinks, and melancholy!
> You doe not looke vpon me with that face,
> As you were wont, my Goddesse, bright *Pecunia*:
> Although your *Grace* be falne of, *two i' the hundred*,
> In vulgar estimation; yet am I,
> You⟨r⟩ *Graces* seruant still: and teach this body,
> To bend, and these my aged knees to buckle,
> In adoration, and iust worship of you.

[1] De Winter, in his edition for the *Yale Studies in English, The Staple of News*, 148, sees no point in making Pecunia '*Cornish*'. Cornwall, he correctly observes, 'never produced gold or silver in commercial quantities'. But it did produce tin and copper. I should surmise that her Cornish home may be an allusion to alchemy. Mammon planned to purchase Devonshire and Cornwall in order to 'make them perfect *Indies*' because their copper mines would supply the raw material for alchemy.

Indeed, I doe confesse, I haue no shape
To make a minion of, but I'm your *Martyr*,
Your *Graces Martyr*.   II. i. 1-11

This speech has more of the meretricious grandeur of
Volpone's hymn to gold than the Canter's song has. The
use of the title 'Grace' brings in a fine irony, because 'Grace'
was normally used for dukes, duchesses, archbishops, and,
at one time, royalty. To apply it to a goddess is to suggest
that titled persons have a divine aura about them or,
conversely, that a goddess is about on the level of a duchess.
In answering her Guardian, Pecunia plays on the religious
meaning of 'Grace', as well as the financial.

Cannot my *Grace* be gotten, and held too,
Without your selfe-tormentings, and your watches,
Your macerating of your body thus
With cares, and scantings of your dyet, and rest?
                    II. i. 22-25

To think of a usurer like Peniboy Sr. being a martyr has a
certain relevance once we accept the worship of the great
goddess, money. Services to such a divinity, as he declares,
'Cannot with too much zeale of *rites* be done, / They are so
sacred' (II. i. 27-28). The reason for such devotion is clear
enough: her powers are '*all-mighty*'.

All this *Nether-world*
Is yours, you command it, and doe sway it,
The honour of it, and the honesty,
The reputation, I, and the religion,
(I was about to say, and had not err'd)
Is Queene *Pecunia's*.   II. i. 38-43

The religion is Pecunia's—there is no doubt of that. She
may kiss like a mortal creature, as Peniboy Jr. observes, but
to him and to the others she is '*Almighty Madame*' (II. v. 49).
As an omnipotent being, she rules her heaven with as little
fear of rebellion as she rules her '*Nether-world*'. When the
Broker is explaining their celestial harmony to Pyed-

Mantle, his words seem like a parody of Dante's *Paradiso*.

> We know our places here, wee mingle not
> One in anothers sphere, but all moue orderly,
> In our owne orbes; yet wee are all *Concentricks*.
>
> II. ii. 54-56

This could be the voice of Piccarda explaining why she is content to be in her sphere, and not closer to God. It could be, except for the simple fact that the centre of these concentric spheres is Pecunia. Of course, Pecunia comes by her celestial position naturally: 'by the Fathers side, I come from *Sol*' (IV. iv. 11).

As the symbol of money, Pecunia has a sexual power as well as a religious. Peniboy Sr. calls the Lady that his nephew longs for—'The *Venus* of the time, and state, *Pecunia!*' (II. v. 34). When Peniboy Jr. courts his Princess, he falls into that style, so close to gross rhetoric, yet still comic, that Jonson could call up for passages of love or piety.

> O, how my *Princesse* drawes me, with her lookes,
> And hales me in, as eddies draw in boats,
> Or strong *Charybdis* ships, that saile too neere
> The shelues of *Loue!* The tydes of your two eyes!
> Wind of your breath, are such as sucke in all,
> That doe approach you!
> PEC.　　　　　Who hath chang'd my seruant?
> P. IV.　Your selfe, who drinke my blood vp with your
> 　　　beames;
> As doth the *Sunne*, the *Sea! Pecunia* shines
> More in the world then he: and makes it *Spring*
> Where e'r she fauours! . . .
> 　　　　　her smiles they are *Loue's* fetters!
> Her brests his apples! her teats St⟨r⟩awberries!
> Where *Cupid* (were he present now) would cry,
> Farewell my mothers milke, here's sweeter *Nectar*!
>
> IV. ii. 42-56

Even if Pecunia were only a woman, such praise would be ludicrous. Few women would enjoy having their attractions thought of in such grandiose terms as eddies, Charybdis, tides, wind, the sun. But the praise is monstrous as well as ludicrous because Pecunia is more a symbol of money than a woman. Characteristically, the shock is increased when her charms are compared to the lovely women of mythology —Venus, Juno, Leda, Hermione, Flora, and Helen. Jonson apparently enjoyed this perverse juxtaposition of the contemptible tenor and the beautiful vehicle. The contemptible rarely is without its glamour in Jonson's plays, just as the beautiful is rarely untouched by meanness. Without considering the possible biographical inference that can be drawn from thus glamorizing the contemptible or staining the beautiful, we ought to see that it is an effective satiric device.

This sexualizing of money is reflected throughout the play. Fitton jeers at the usurer by calling him 'old *Money-Bawd*' (II. iv. 1) and, later, 'a meere *Bawd*' (II. iv. 79). When the usurer tells Peniboy Jr. that Pecunia can go anywhere with him, the Canter mutters, 'I see / A *Money-Bawd*, is lightly a *Flesh-Bawd*, too' (II. v. 99-100). Then, once Pecunia is out of his control, the usurer himself calls on these same terms to curse Band and Wax who are 'whores' and 'bawds', and Pecunia who is 'a whore' (IV. iii. 58-82). To the Canter 'the *Prodigall* prostitutes his *Mistresse*!' when he insists that everyone kiss her (IV. ii. 123). During the boy's song the Canter notes

how all their eyes
Dance i'their heads (obserue) scatter'd with lust!
At sight o' their braue *Idoll*! IV. ii. 130-132

The force of such sexual imagery comes from the oblique light which it casts on the way money is sometimes used. A usurer lives off man's greed for money in the same way that a bawd lives off man's desire for sexual experience: both can justifiably be called money-bawds. 'The *Prodigall* prostitutes his *Mistresse*!' is a more suggestive way of saying that the prodigal throws his money away in return for pleasure. Such imagery deepens the tone of the play by suggesting that any foolish use of money—either the parsimony of a usurer or the prodigality of an heir—is not merely vulgar, but immoral and perverse.

The religious and sexual imagery is, as always in Jonson, more thoroughly worked into the verse of the play than this summary shows, but perhaps enough has been analysed to make one fault of the play apparent.[1] The symbolism is too obvious and simplified. If the play were the morality it sometimes seems to be, the allegorical abstraction would seem quite proper. In the 'second Intermeane' Jonson shows that he had the medieval morality in mind when he wrote this play. Mirth explains to her friends that the Vice no longer comes in *'like* HOKOS POKOS, *in a Iuglers ierkin . . . but now they are attir'd like men and women o' the time, the* Vices, *male and female!'* The story of a prodigal son and the triadic grouping of the three Peniboys to illustrate Aristotle's Prodigality, Parsimony, and Liberality might easily involve the abstractions of the morality. Furthermore, Jonson's tendency in many of his early plays and in his masques had been toward the symbolic and, at times, the allegorical. But the difference between the symbolism of *Volpone* and the symbolism of the last plays is one of subtlety. What had been left to implication in his major plays is in *The Staple of Newes* brought out and explicitly insisted upon. Gold in *Volpone* is a concrete thing that is worshipped, to be sure, but the imagery drawn from Christian theology throws much of the worship on to an invisible deity, the god, gold. This moving beyond the concrete to an abstraction increases the shock of *Volpone*. But in *The Staple of Newes* Pecunia is a character constantly before our eyes, and as a symbol of

---

[1] For other tenor-vehicle relationships which substantiate this argument see: I. v. 33-35; I. v. 62; II. iv. 3-13; II. iv. 29; II. iv. 85 ff.; II. iv. 111; II. iv. 120; II. iv. 181; II. v. 23; II. v. 65 ff.; Second Intermeane, ll. 19, 30; III. ii. 270; IV. i. 46; IV. iii. 23; IV. iv. 130; Fourth Intermeane, ll. 40-44; V. vi. 20 ff.

money she keeps our imagination in close check so that we think of her more in terms of a lady than of money. This potential humanity of Pecunia makes any worship of her less profane than Volpone's worship of gold. The shock is less, and the satire is blunted. One possible value in making a woman the symbol of money is that the sexualizing of gold which had been implied in *The Alchemist* and *Volpone* is emphasized; but that is a dubious gain.

Along with the obvious symbolism goes the obtrusive moralizing which is also in keeping with a morality play. This direct admonition, which Jonson writes with his characteristic force, appears throughout the play. By means of the Canter who, as the symbol of the liberal and wise man, is the chief *raissoneur* of the moral, Jonson keeps pressing a point which, in his best plays, was left to the listener's inference. For example, when Cymbal calls Pecunia forth as the '*State*, and wonder' of the times, the Canter bursts out,

> Why, that's the end of wealth! thrust riches
>   outward,
> And remaine beggers within: contemplate nothing
> But the vile sordid things of time, place, money,
> And let the noble, and the precious goe,
> Vertue and honesty; hang 'hem; poore thinne
>   membranes
> Of honour; who respects them? O, the *Fates*!
> How hath all iust, true reputation fall'n,
> Since money, this base money 'gan to haue any!
>
> III. ii. 241-248

This has Jonson's effective trick of so dramatizing the opposite of what he loves that it appears vile. But the point is that Jonson has returned to his unhappy tendency, discarded in his major plays, of making the moral clear. In *Volpone* he casts a whole world into being and lets it revolve there, hideous in its implications. But the objectivity of *The Staple of Newes* is spoiled by passages in which the Canter castigates 'the gallant spirits o' the age!', praises the scholar, defends his satirical thrusts at 'Court-rats' and 'dog-Leachs', and, in the final scene, summarizes the theme of the right use of money. Explicit moralizing in a dramatic work is likely to be ineffective no matter how eloquent it is. It suggests that the dramatist has somehow lost control of his medium, or is uncomfortable in it and has to fall back on the didactic because the implicit and the oblique are not powerful enough for him.

This obvious symbolism and didacticism might be more acceptable in a work which was simply a morality, with the uncomplicated tone and the pious attitude of a morality. But this play is called *The Staple of Newes*, and part of it— perhaps the freshest part—deals with a satire on news-vendors. The Staple plot and the Pecunia-Peniboy plot are joined somewhat loosely by Pecunia herself, whose coming to the Staple office will make it immortal. The power of money to immortalize a news office or deify an heir gives a certain unity to a play which is otherwise loosely ordered. Thematic unity may hold together more than one Eliza-bethan play which seems to fall apart, but, normally, Jonson organized his plays more tightly than he did any of the last three, except perhaps *The Magnetick Lady*. All of them, even the last, seem somewhat off centre.

The thematic unity of *The Staple of Newes* appears when we observe that the news, which seems like a new satiric interest for Jonson, is related to man's greed even as alchemy is in *The Alchemist*, though less thoroughly. We first hear of it as 'A place / Of huge commerce' from which Emissaries are sent abroad 'To fetch in the commodity' . . . 'By way of exchange, or trade' (I. ii. 27-53). The Staple, as its name implies, is another of those Jonsonian businesses whose function is to feed on the lowest desires of men. The venting of news, like everything else in the play, falls within the orbit of that religion of money whose centre is Pecunia.

When she is taken away, the Staple blows up even as the furnace blew up in *The Alchemist*. The Staple, then, is one more variation on Jonson's old theme of greed, but somewhat less effective than the treatment of alchemy in *The Alchemist* or of monopolies in *The Divell is an Asse* because the greed is not entirely reciprocal. In the major plays both the gulls and the impostors feed each other's greed, each living parasitically on the other. But here the impostors are greedy, while the gulls have an unquestioning curiosity, which is only a diluted kind of greed, and not for money but rumours.

A certain unity is given to the play by the characteristically Jonsonian tone which is created, partly, by the imagery. Everything seems to fall into its proper place in that special world which Jonson's characters inhabit when we note that here, as in *Volpone*, eating seems to symbolize that parasitic living on one another which Mosca considered existence to be. Each man, poet or cook, beggar or courtier, must pander to the tastes of the time, or starve. Court-rats gnaw the commonwealth, usurers swallow the improvident, and 'Caniball-Christians' eat one another. This recurrent cannibalism may be Jonson's way of saying that civilized people still feed on each other economically or politically, if not physically. The image of cannibalism rarely fails to follow any use of one man by another. For instance, there is this passage in the *Discoveries*: '*I have* discovered, that a fain'd familiarity in great ones, is a note of certaine usurpation on the lesse. For great and popular men, faine themselves to bee servants to others, to make those slaves to them. So the Fisher provides baits for the Trowte, Roch, Dace, &c. that they may be food to him.'[1] Expressing such exploitation in terms of parasitism and cannibalism arouses the horror and disgust that cruelty ought to arouse.

Even such a cursory survey of the imagery may have

[1] Herford and Simpson, VIII, 597-598.

revealed to what extent the conventional criticisms of the play are justified. Jonson's strategy has been the same here as in his major plays: invert the alleged values of society, and create a world in which these inverted values are the accepted values. Thus, money is worshipped and sexualized. The material is all; the spirit, nothing. People feed on each other, worship the strong, and jeer at the weak. But in *The Staple of Newes* the dramatic effect is weakened when money is personified in the figure of Pecunia. The symbolism becomes too obvious and simplified to be imaginative. And Jonson's intermittent didacticism, forceful as it is, robs the play of much of its remaining subtlety. Finally, even the unity inherent in theme and in tone cannot entirely compensate for a certain looseness of organization.

III

The New Inne

If one could forget all the criticism written about *The New Inne* and read it with a fresh mind, one might discover it to be a good—though not faultless—comedy. But the complete failure of the play in its first and apparently only performance, Jonson's cursing 'the hundred fastidious *impertinents*' who came to the first performance 'to see, and to bee seene' rather than to judge the play fairly, Owen Feltham's slashing attack on Jonson's 'declining witt', and Dryden's dismissing it as one of Jonson's 'dotages' have combined to obscure the real virtues of the play. True, the play has drawn forth some praise. Lamb spoke of its 'poetical fancy and elegance of mind',[1] and Symonds held the uncommon opinion that, even with its preposterous plot, 'in many important respects, [it] is one of Jonson's best comedies'.[2] M. Castelain even thought that '*la Nouvelle Auberge* est peut-être la mieux écrite de ses comédies',

---

[1] Lamb, *Specimens*, 276.   [2] J. A. Symonds, *Ben Jonson* (London, 1886), 177.

though he referred to style rather than dramatic effective-ness.[1] But even this praise is faintly damning, and neither the praise nor the condemnation does justice to the comic virtues of the play.

And its comic virtues seem to me considerable, though less evident than in the major plays. As a matter of fact, one of the principal charges against the play is that it lacks unity because its comic tone and romantic mood jar. G. B. Tennant has come to the conclusion that Jonson meant to write a comedy of humours but unfortunately chose a theme of love and valour which was unfit for such satiric treatment.[2] Herford thinks that the romantic main plot is meant seriously by Jonson, but that his monstrous invention betrayed him into unconscious ludicrousness.[3] F. S. Boas claims that one reason for Jonson's indignation at its failure was that it was 'his unique attempt to give dramatic expression to idealized love', and it was badly received.[4] Now, at first glance, there does seem to be some ambiguity of effect. The preposterous story of the Frampul family sounds like a parody of itself—almost a later *Knight of the Burning Pestle* in places. The gross picture of the lost mother disguised as a drunken Irish nurse and the Host who wears a false beard for so many years are hilarious comments on the absurd situations of romance—if they were meant so. But—so the argument runs—Jonson meant to treat the romantic plot seriously. Lovel, according to Her-ford, is meant to be an ideal gentleman, even an heroic figure, and his speeches in the Court of Love (which are, taken simply as set speeches, finely written) are meant to be genuinely moving. This tender treatment of romance reveals that Jonson was trying to capitalize on the popularity of romantic comedies and the court's interest in courtly love.

---

[1] Castelain, *Ben Jonson, L'Homme et L'Œuvre*, 428.
[2] Tennant, ed., *The New Inn*, XXXII.
[3] Herford and Simpson, II, 194.
[4] Boas, *An Introduction to Stuart Drama*, 127.

And—so the critics conclude—neither such comedy nor such love moves freely in the old Jonsonian world of humorous characters or in the monstrous world of the Frampuls. But, plausible as this criticism is at first glance, it becomes less so at every re-reading of the play. If one can surrender one's self to the movement of the plot and to the quiet hints in the dialogue, one may be surprised at the consistent comic tone of the play.

Jonson maintains this comic tone, of course, by having his characters violate decorum by word or deed. Characteristic of Jonsonian comedy, as we have seen in *The Alchemist*, is the use of indecorous titles. Particularly indecorous in *The New Inne* are the grandiose titles which the lower orders of the Inn give themselves. Fly, for example, gives himself, or is given by others, various titles, such as Deacon, Doctor, Captain, and Quartermaster. Like so many of Jonson's characters, he is shown in a double view—the elevated being he pretends to be, and the creature he actually is. All of the characters below stairs are seen doubly. Tipto, himself a knight, knights Peirce, the drawer: 'Sir *Pierce*, I'le ha' him a Caualier' (III. i. 19). Iordan is named 'the *Don, del Campo* o' the beds', presumably because his name also meant a chamber-pot (III. i. 25). There is a later allusion to this double meaning of Iordan when Barnabe says that the lady he has brought will try Iordan: 'Shee'll finde your gage, your circle, your capacity' (IV. i. 7). Peck, the hostler, becomes '*Maestro del Campo*' (III. i. 27), and Ferret, the servant of Lovel, '*Colonel* o' the *Pyoners*' (III. i. 35). They call each other, with various degrees of pretension: 'yong *Knight*', 'bold professor', 'Caualier', 'great officers', 'man of war'. These are, as the Host says of a speech of Pru, 'Large, ample words, of a braue latitude' (II. vi. 164). The comic tone is always kept by this ridiculous disproportion between tenor and vehicle.

And because the Host's words justifiably apply to Pru

and the Lady, the comic tone extends to the ladies and gentlemen above stairs in the Inn. When 'Queene Prudence', late a chamber-maid, but crowned Queen of the day's sports, orders the Lady to kiss Lovel, the Lady says, 'You'l turne a Tyran'. Pru answers, 'Be not you a Rebell, / It is a name is alike-odious'. The others call Pru—'Excellent Princesse!', 'Iust Queene!', 'Braue Sou'raigne!', 'she *Traian*!' (II. vi. 126 ff.). Later, in speaking of 'Lou⟨e⟩'s Court o' Requests!', Latimer calls her Iudge *Pru*, / The only learned mother of the Law!' (II. vi. 191 ff.). To the Host she is sweet, soft, and amiable, but also 'venerable *Pru*,/*Maiestique Pru*, and *Serenissimous Pru*' (II. vi. 224 ff.). Because all of these titles are part of a game which the guests of the Inn play, they are less ridiculous than the more serious pretentiousness of Tipto, Fly, and the militia below stairs. But the game itself is indecorous as Pru realizes when she discusses being raised above the station of a chamber-maid. 'To be translated thus, 'boue all the bound / Of fitnesse, or *decorum*?' (II. i. 54-55). Such indecorum helps to maintain a comic tone throughout the play and makes it difficult not to read the long scenes on love and valour as comic. The Queene and her Court are so obviously play-acting that to take it seriously seems an affront to the comedy.

At times the latent comedy is pointed up. Below stairs and above stairs come together when Tipto tells Fly that he shall be 'the Bird / To Soueraigne *Pru*, Queene of our sports, her *Fly*' (II. v. 29-30). When Pru is introduced as 'Queene Regent' and Beaufort calls her jocosely 'Translated *Prudence*!', she answers,

> It is not now, as when plaine *Prudence* liu'd,
> And reach'd her Ladiship—

HOST. The Chamber-pot.
PRU. The looking-glasse, mine Host, loose your house
Metaphore! II. vi. 1 ff.

But the Host cannot lose his 'house *Metaphore*' because he

sees Queen Prudence in the same ludicrous light in which Pru sees Fly. Her previous function as a maid, like Fly's as a servant, runs as an undertone whenever their pretentious titles are mentioned. The irony which springs from using pretentious titles for lower things involves the ladies and the gentlemen as well as servants below stairs in one comic atmosphere.

Jonson controls the comic tone, then, by revealing the disparity between the way a character acts and the way he is described. A second, though related, disparity that Jonson works with is the disparity between the ideal and the actual. Note, for example, the Host's scornful description of the life of a page immediately after Lovel's rapturous account of the Centaur's skill and the mystery of Pollux.

> Instead of backing the brave Steed, o' mornings,
> To mount the Chambermaid; and for a leape
> O'the vaulting horse, to ply the vaulting house:
> For exercise of armes, a bale of dice,
> Or two or three packs of cards, to shew the cheat,
> And nimblenesse of hand: mistake a cloake
> From my Lords back, and pawne it. Ease his pockets
> Of a superfluous Watch; or geld a iewell
> Of an odde stone, or so. Twinge three or foure buttons
> From off my Ladyes gowne. These are the arts,
> Or seuen liberall deadly sciences
> Of Pagery, or rather Paganisme,
> As the tides run. To which, if he apply him,
> He may, perhaps, take a degree at *Tiburne*,
> A yeare the earlier: come to read a lecture
> Vpon *Aquinas* at *S. Thomas* a Waterings,
> And so goe forth a Laureat in hempe circle!
>
> I. iii. 72-88

This juxtaposition of the seven liberal arts and the seven 'deadly sciences' is a favourite device of satirists like Jonson who are sensitive to the ironic interplay of the ideal and the actual. Jonson could always see the underside of things, the bathos to which most high things descend in this world, and the height from which they fall.

This same disparity appears in what are usually taken to be the least comic—if comic at all—passages in the play: the scenes in the Court of Love. Usually, these scenes are interpreted as romantic expositions of Platonic love and Aristotelian valour, static and dull, though interesting as rhetorical pieces. But such an interpretation misses the delicate comedy in a chambermaid's pretending to be Queen for a day and tyrannizing over her mistress, or in Lovel's discriminating, with Aristotelian precision, the causes of love while looking at the beautiful Lady Frampul. His exquisite definition is comically counterpointed by Beaufort's more earthy love and by the Nurse's drunken misunderstanding of both Lovel and Beaufort (III. ii. 91-118). The comic—and earthy—touch is also kept by Pru, especially in her remark after Lady Frampul had said that she would give Lovel twenty kisses: 'Beware, you doe not coniure vp a spirit / You cannot lay' (III. ii. 251-252).

As for the Act IV scene in the Court of Love, it too is lightened by a similar comic irony. Lovel delivers an extended analysis of the various kinds of valour, but he is seen as valiant only once: when he scatters the quarrelling braggarts and topers in the inn yard ('His rapier was a *Meteor*, and he wau'd it / Ouer 'hem, like a *Comet*!'). He becomes so nearly a voice, like a younger Don Quixote, that the Lady's comment on his description of the valiant man—

Most manly vtterd all!
As if *Achilles* had the chaire in valour,
And *Hercules* were but a Lecturer!

IV. iv. 138-140

reveals precisely the comic disproportion between the great

mythical heroes who acted and Lovel who lectures. There is fine irony, too, in Lovel's becoming 'angry valiant' immediately after discoursing on how mean it is to have angry valour about anything. If Lovel is taken simply as a straightforward hero, as Herford takes him, he fails, as all of Jonson's 'good' people fail. Jonson could not do at all what Shakespeare could do surpassingly well: make a Viola or a Benedict absurd and attractive and decent and believable. Jonson's absurd people are almost never attractive, and his decent people are rarely believable. But Lovel is meant to be ridiculous, whatever good sense he speaks. He remains comic, in fact, exactly because the good sense he speaks reveals the great disparity between the ideal life he describes and the actual life he lives in the New Inn.

The imagery helps to sustain this comic tone in the Court of Love. For example, the religious imagery in Act III, Scene 3, by which love is idealized. In this scene we are obviously in the midst of what C. S. Lewis called 'the irreligion of the religion of love'. Love is a deity, with a congregation, a church, canons, miracles, 'Fathers', and even a Higher Criticism. One can be an atheist, an infidel, an heretic; one can trespass and blaspheme or be penitent and worship. Such profanation of religious terms is not so shocking as the deification of gold in *Volpone* is, probably because there is a natural tendency to idealize a loved one, whereas it requires an extraordinary and perverted imagination to deify money. Besides, the use of religious vehicles for erotic purposes had been made conventional by the tradition of courtly love. Nevertheless, this imagery, in the context which Jonson has created, remains comic. Lovel's first expression of his fine unspoken Platonic love ends with a characteristic Jonsonian exaggeration: 'though my passion / Burne me to cinders' (I. vi. 158-159). The Host exploits this ludicrous image in a way that brings any high-flown spectator crashing down to earth.

> Be still that rag of loue,
> You are. Burne on, till you turne tinder.
> This Chambermaid may hap to proue the steele,
> To strike a sparke out o' the flint, your mistresse,
> May beget bonfires yet, you doe not know,
> What light may be forc'd out, and from what
> darknes.   I. vi. 163-168

Platonic love, which unbelievers might think extravagant to begin with, is treated hyperbolically throughout the play, and to an artist with Jonson's sense of restraint and decorum, hyperbole inevitably meant ridiculousness. Could Lady Frampul's rhapsodizing after Lovel's ethereal wooing be anything but ludicrous?

>   By what alchimy
> Of loue, or language, am I thus translated!
> His tongue is tip'd with the *Philosophers stone*,
> And that hath touch'd me th⟨o⟩rough euery vaine!
> I feele that transmutation o' my blood,
> As I were quite become another creature,
> And all he speakes, it is proiection!
>   III. ii. 171-177

Even if we do not realize that she is speaking of love as Mammon or Face spoke of it, we can scarcely be unaware of the monstrousness of this whole figure. A metaphor like 'the alchemy of love' (or art or language) is harmless enough in itself, but when it is developed as thoroughly as this one is, it moves into burlesque. The process of transmuting base metals is not allowed to remain quiescent, but is referred to in five different ways. There is even an added pun on 'vaine': veins of blood and veins of ore. The unexpected and, in its context, unfortunate result is that the Lady goes the way of all flesh in Jonson's comedies—to gold. Such indecorous hyperbole prepares the spectator for Lady Frampul's misuse of religious allusions, all conventional in courtly love, but extravagant enough to burlesque her emotionalizing.

Who hath read *Plato*, *Heliodore*, or *Tatius*,
Sydney, *D'Vrfé*, or all Loues *Fathers*, like him?
He'is there the Master of the Sentences,
Their Schoole, their Commentary, Text, and
    Closse,
And breathes the true diuinity of Loue!

. . . . .
Where haue I liu'd, in heresie, so long
Out o' the Congregation of Loue,
And stood irregular, by all his Canons?

. . . . .
What penance shall I doe, to be receiu'd,
And reconciled, to the Church of Loue?
Goe on procession, bare-foot, to his Image,
And say some hundred penitentiall verses,
There, out of *Chaucers Troilus, and Cresside*?
Or to his mothers shrine, vow a Waxe-candle
As large as the Towne May-pole is, and pay it!
Enioyne me any thing this Court thinks fit,
For I haue trespass'd, and blasphemed Loue.
I haue, indeed, despis'd his *Deity*,
Whom (till this miracle wrought on me) I knew not.
                  III. ii. 205 ff.

Surely, no one can fail to sense the ludicrousness of an image as extravagant as that of the May-pole. But some critics of Jonson have had trouble seeing the comedy not only of such speeches but also of an even more ludicrous passage—Lady Frampul's confession of love.

                I burne, and freeze,
My liuer's one great coale, my heart shrunke vp
With all the fiuers, and the masse of blood
Within me, is a standing lake of fire,
Curl'd with the cold wind of my gelid sighs,
That driue a drift of sleete through all my body,
And shoot a *February* through my veines.
                V. ii. 46-52

Carpenter could not decide whether this confession is the

worst of Jonson's dotages or the best of burlesques.[1]
Alexander Sackton concluded that it is 'Jonsonian hyperbole
gone to seed. It has the extravagance of the language of
Volpone without its irony. The audience is expected to accept
this language as an expression of strong, natural feeling.'[2]
But does not extravagant dramatic language always carry its
own irony with it? The spectator measures it against some
standard of decorum, and finds it, in its context, ironically
unfit. And would not an audience, after so much indecorous
language from the Lady, find her expression of love as
comic as her use of religious allusions? Jonson's own feeling
about the profane use of sacred language might be
remembered here. According to Drummond, Jonson called
Donne's 'Anniversaries' on the death of Elizabeth Drury
profane and full of blasphemies because a mortal being was
spoken of in terms suitable only to the Virgin Mary.[3]
Throughout his life, Jonson had a sensitivity to profanity
that bordered on the superstitious. He wrote—and
apparently with sincerity—in the dedicatory epistle to
Volpone that he '*trembled to thinke towards the least prophane-
nesse*'. And, according to George Morley, later Bishop of
Winchester, Jonson was much afflicted in his final days
because he felt he had 'profaned the Scriptures in his plays
and lamented it with horror'.[4] In short, to a writer as
conscious of decorum as Jonson, even the language of the
romantic scenes of this play was meant to be indecorous—
hence comic.

Yet, comic as these scenes are, they do not embody the
central theme of *The New Inne* as dramatically as Jonson
usually embodied his themes in the action and diction of his
plays. The central theme here seems to be the true relation

[1] F. I. Carpenter, *Metaphor and Simile in the Minor Elizabethan Drama* (Chicago, 1895), 134.
[2] Sackton, 158.
[3] Herford and Simpson, I, 133.
[4] *Ibid.*, 115.

of the understanding and the things of sense, or of reality and appearance. The discussions of both love and valour are attempts to distinguish between love or valour as it appears to be or is commonly thought to be and love or valour as it really is. Thus, Lovel praises spiritual love and rational valour, and rejects sensual love and valour for the sake of reputation. The fault of both the scenes in the Court of love is that they tend to be rhetorical without, at the same time, being intensely dramatic; the difference between reality and appearance is talked about without being theatrically embodied. This difference is more vividly dramatized by the use of significant costume and by the allusions to clothes, especially in the episode of Nick Stuffe and his wife, Pinnacia—an episode which more than one critic has thought to be unrelated to the play. Gifford, for example, dismissed the whole episode as 'merely ridiculous',[1] and Mrs Morris considered it an 'incident'.[2] To Ward it was a 'quite useless intermezzo' of 'heavy' and 'tedious' comedy.[3] But these criticisms ignore the relation between that scene and the theme of appearance and reality.

We first hear of Pinnacia Stuffe when Fly brings news of

> A finer, fresher, brauer, bonnier beauty,
> A very *bona-Roba*, and a Bouncer!
> In yeallow, glistering golden Satten. III. ii. 272-274

'*Bona-Roba*' is the kind of faded metaphor that Jonson liked to resurrect and play with. Florio's explanation of the term reveals that some of its metaphorical quality in Italian had been lost: 'As we say good stuffe, that is a good wholesome plum-cheeked wench.'[4] New life is given to the 'good stuffe' by such references to clothes as 'finer', 'brauer', and 'Satten'.

[1] *The Works of Ben Jonson*, ed. by Gifford and Cunningham, V, 413.
[2] Morris, *Studies in Jonson's Comedy*, 95.
[3] Ward, *A History of English Dramatic Literature*, II, 376.
[4] John Florio, *Queen Anna's new World of Words, or Dictionarie of the Italian and English Tongues* (London, 1611).

As soon as she comes in, we understand that she is spoken of as 'stuffe' because she is fascinated with fine clothes, which she unquestioningly takes to indicate fine society. Thus, dressed in the gown which her husband, as Lady Frampul's tailor, had made for Pru, she is offended when he calls her 'wife'.

> Doe you thinke I'le call you husband i' this gowne,
> Or any thing, in that iacket, but *Protection?*
> Here tie my shooe; and shew my vellute petticote,
> And my silke stocking! why doe you make me a
> Lady,
> If I may not doe like a Lady, in fine clothes?
>
> IV. ii. 83-87

Clothes are so powerful that they compel a complete re-organization of a person's life, changing someone as un-fashionable as a husband into a footman called '*Protection*' and re-shaping one's moral code. This moral change appears in Pinnacia's remark that, since 'wild Company are fine Company', in fine company 'A Lady may doe any thing, deny nothing / To a fine party' (IV. ii. 96-97).

The nature of this moral change appears as soon as the Stuffes are revealed to be a middle-class married couple rather than a 'Dutchesse, or a Countesse' and her footman. Once Pinnacia is, as she puts it, 'dis-Ladied', she shamelessly explains the actions of her husband and herself.

> When he makes any fine garment will fit me,
> Or any rich thing that he thinkes of price,
> Then must I put it on, and be his *Countesse,*
> Before he carry it home vnto the owners.
> A coach is hir'd, and foure horse, he runnes
> In his veluet Iackat thus, to *Rumford, Croyden,*
> *Hounslow,* or *Barnet,* the next bawdy road:
> And takes me out, carries me vp, and throw's me
> Vpon a bed.
> LAD.   Peace thou immodest woman:
> She glories in the brauery o' the vice.

LAT. 'Tis a queint one!

BEA.   A fine *species*,

Of fornicating with a mans owne wife.

IV. iii. 66-77

Here is the most extraordinary example in all of the final plays of the way people worship appearances (symbolized by clothes) and find in appearances a reality that the truth itself lacks. Pinnacia, actually a tailor's wife, becomes a Countess to her husband by putting on the dress of a Countess, just as Nick Stuffe becomes a steward in a noble family by putting on the velvet jacket, which was the badge of office of a steward. Clothes have the faculty of conveying reality: the Stuffes think Pinnacia is a fashionable lady because she wears fashionable clothes. The extent to which this pretence is accepted even by the 'fine Company' is apparent in their reaction to this presumption on the part of a mere tailor. The clothes have made the pretence so real that the Lady speaks of 'the brauery o' the vice', as though Pinnacia and Nick were Countess and steward rather than wife and husband. Beaufort more judiciously weighs the trick that Nick Stuffe is trying to play on reality by speaking of the 'fine *species*' of love he has found out—that of fornicating with his own wife. He can have the up-lifting pleasure of fornication with a Countess simply by dressing his wife as a Countess—appearances being so convincing—without committing the sin of either fornication or adultery.

The Lady's remark on 'the brauery o' the vice' may also refer to the viciousness of having one of the lower orders pretend to be higher in the social scale even to the point of sexual intercourse. It is degrading enough that the tailor's wife should try on the gown her husband makes, but to carry on sexual intercourse in it is, the Lady says, 'prophanation' (IV. iii. 86). Such sexual presumption apparently prompts the remarks that follow the passage already quoted.

HOST. The very figure of preoccupation.
In all his customers best clothes.
LAT.   He lies
With his owne *Succuba*, in all your names.
BEA. And all your credits.
HOST.   I, and at all their costs.

IV. iii. 79-82

The people in high life are as convinced as the tailor and
his wife that to put on a person's clothes is to appropriate
his name and his reputation. Jonson was so fond of the pun
on 'preoccupation', that he used it in several plays as well as
in his verse. Most editors of *The New Inne* have followed
Gifford in noting the similarity of a passage in *'An Elegie'*
('Let me be what I am') to the Pinnacia scene.

> It is not likely I should now looke downe
> Upon a Velvet Petticote, or a Gowne,
> Whose like I have knowne the Taylors wife put on
> To doe her Husbands rites in, e're 'twere gone
> Home to the Customer: his Letcherie
> Being, the best clothes still to praeoccupie.[1]

The play on 'praeoccupie' in this poem and in The Argument to *The New Inne* where Pinnacia is said 'to be preoccupied in all his Customers best clothes, by the footman
her husband' depends on a meaning of 'occupy' which has
been lost in modern speech. Allen Walker Read observes
that 'occupy', which Florio had used in 1598 as one of four
synonyms for the verb 'to carry on sexual intercourse', was
once 'one of the most obscene words in the language'.[2] He
cites Dol Tearsheet's comparison—'as odious as the word
occupy, which was an excellent good worde before it was il
sorted'—to show that it was in bad odour in 1597. Since
it remained in bad odour during all of the seventeenth
century, Jonson must have felt something of Dol's regret

---

[1] Herford and Simpson, VIII, 200-201.
[2] Read, 'An Obscenity Symbol', *American Speech*, IX (December 1934), 270-276.

at the loss of a good word when he wrote in the *Discoveries* that 'Many, out of their owne obscene Apprehensions, refuse proper and fit words; as *occupie, nature,* and the like.'[1] But he was not above using such 'obscene Apprehensions' for a piece of wit. For example, in his epigram, 'On Groyne', he exploits this double sense of 'occupy'.

> GROYNE, come of age, his state sold out of hand
>   For'his whore: GROYNE doth still occupy his
>   land.[2]

Thus, 'praeoccupie' in '*An Elegie*' probably carries this erotic sense as well as the more usual sense, and the final quoted lines mean that the tailor's idea of lechery is to carry on sexual intercourse with his wife when she is dressed in 'the best clothes'. The same use of the two meanings of 'occupy' produces the wit in both 'preoccupied' and 'preoccupation' in *The New Inne*.

The Stuffes would seem to belong to abnormal psychology because of their perverted sexual life. But, in other respects, they are not much different from the people who scorn them. All seem to believe that clothes have the mysterious, almost magical power of ennobling or degrading the persons who wear them. The tailor and his wife believe that Pinnacia can be elevated by wearing a gown meant for a Lady; and the Lady and her companions believe that a gown worn by a tailor's wife would be so 'polluted' that it will besmirch any nobler being that wears it (IV. iii. 92). Later it appears that there is reciprocal relation between clothes and persons. If a gown can be polluted by one woman, it can be 'redeem'd' by another (V. i. 34). As soon as Pru puts on the gown which has been taken off by Pinnacia, Lady Frampul observes a change in both Pru and the gown.

---

[1] Herford and Simpson, VIII, 610.

[2] *Ibid.*, 75. Other passages in which Jonson may be playing with the double sense of 'occupy' are *Cynthia's Revels*, V. ii. 52-53, and *The Magnetick Lady*, V. iii. 25-28.

Sweet *Pru*, I, now thou art a Queene indeed!
These robes doe royally! and thou becom'st 'hem!
So they doe thee! rich garments only fit
The partyes they are made for! they shame others.
How did they shew on good'y *Taylors* back!
Like a Caparison for a Sow, God saue vs!
Thy putting 'hem on hath purg'd, and hallow'd
      'hem
From all pollution, meant by the *Mechanicks*.

V. ii. 1-8

The appearance of things seems so much their reality to the fashionable visitors of the inn that they demand an iron decorum in respect to clothes. The Pinnacia scene has shown how they considered that unfit persons shame rich garments; and here the Lady declares the reverse to be true also—rich garments shame unfit persons. Once caught between such constricting premises, one is forced to the materialistic conclusion that whatever appears to be, is. How does one know that a person is unfit for rich garments? By the name she is called. If she is called a Countess, she is fit for rich garments; but if she turns out to be Pinnacia Stuffe, a tailor's wife, strip her of her 'idolatrous vestures' and send her home like a whore, with her husband beating the basin before her (IV. iii. 94 ff.).

In short, like everything else in a Jonson comedy, the influence of clothes is ultimately conceived of as metaphysical. The characters believe not only that, as Carlyle was to say later, 'Society is founded on cloth', but also that the dress one wears affects one's soul. Thus, when Pru tells Lady Frampul that she thought the Lady was dissembling a passion for Lovel, the Lady, angry, cries,

Stay i' thy state of ignorance still, be damn'd,
An idiot Chambermayd! Hath all my care,
My breeding thee in fashion, thy rich clothes,
Honours, and titles wrought no brighter effects
On thy darke soule, then thus?   IV. iv. 312-316

Aside from the implication that being a chambermaid is to be damned to a state of ignorance, the interesting point revealed by these lines is that the Lady thinks of titles, honours, and clothes as agents of light to the dark (and, perhaps, 'damp') soul of a chambermaid. Though Pru has enough spirit to say that she does not want to 'owe my wit to cloathes', that is apparently only a lingering trace of the chambermaid (V. ii. 26). To the others such worldly and fashionable ornaments as a title or a satin gown have much the same ontological function that Subtle thought alchemy had: they can exalt a spirit and fix it in a state of grace.

This use of the imagery of clothes is characteristic of Jonson's method. Once he desired to satirize a certain human folly or vice—greed or lust or idolatry of clothes— he used the very things he wished to ridicule to form the elements of a new imaginative world. To ridicule excessive attention to clothes, for example, Jonson suggested metaphorically that, in the imagined world of his play, clothes are reverenced as though they influenced one's mind and soul. In *The Staple of Newes* Peniboy Jr. discovers that, when he puts his new suit on, he becomes wittier. In *The New Inne* clothes become so completely the reality of life that they mark one's station in life and can either ennoble or degrade one. The folly detested by Jonson becomes the virtue cherished by the characters he creates; and everything follows this initial assumption. The creatures he wants to satirize are turned loose in a world of their own making and create their own hell, usually unaware of the hell of it.

IV

The Magnetick Lady

Jonson's last comedy of humours has the same ironic plot that many of his earlier comedies had: the usurer, Sir Moath Interest, is cozened; the gossiping parasite, Mrs Polish, is outwitted; and each of the deserving men, Compass and Ironside, receives a magnetic lady—with a 'portion'. It is the old Jonsonian method of reconciling the humours by money, but the pattern has been so hardened and the symbolism made so obvious that most of the life has been squeezed out of the play. To make a lady a magnet dehumanizes her more than most previous women in Jonson's plays; only Pecunia, who suffers the same treatment is as inhuman. Herford is quite right in saying that the device of making the plot revolve around a magnetic mistress is 'no radical novelty' among Jonson's plots and that 'his most artful plot-structures might have been described in similar terms'. Volpone and Subtle, as he says, are 'magnetic centres' who hold a number of humorous characters in a kind of hypnotic sway. But he exaggerates the novelty of the intrigue when he claims that it is 'of a kind virtually new in Jonson's art'.[1] Though match-making had not figured largely in Jonson's earlier comedies, the use of women or money as magnets to draw men was always one of Jonson's devices. The only difference is one of subtlety: the method of *Volpone* and *The Alchemist* is made cruder when the heroine is named Lady Loadstone, referred to as the '*Magnetick Mistris*', and married to Captain Ironside. Crude as it is, the symbolism is confused without being made richer when the real magnetic lady turns out to be the niece, and her only magnetic quality, her money. That is an almost absurd simplification of Volpone's legacy or Subtle's stone—which were never especially complex symbols to begin with. The very crudity of the symbolism imposes a certain unity on a plot which, as Harvey W. Peck correctly says, 'lacks the unifying force of a central satiric motive, such as is exhibited in *Volpone* and *The Alchemist*'.[2] The imposed unity

---

[1] *Ibid.*, II, 205.
[2] H. W. Peck, ed., *The Magnetic Lady. Yale Studies in English*, XLVII (New York, 1914), xii.

cannot conceal the fact that Jonson scattered his fire over a number of current abuses—astrology, usury, monopolies, duelling, demoniac possession, the extravagance of court costume, and the worldliness of clergymen—rather than concentrating, with his massive energy, on one or two.

The same hardening which is discernible in the larger pattern of the play is also evident in the recurrent tenor-vehicle relationships. Right to the end of his dramatic career (with the exception of *The Sad Shepherd*) Jonson involved his characters in a religion of the world. In *The Magnetick Lady*, as in the earlier plays, the accepted things to worship are the things which, in an ideal society, it would be impious to worship—food, money, and clothes. The worship of food, which is a power or domination in Jonson's hierarchy, is centred in that 'Prelate of the Parish', Parson Palate, who 'Comforts the widow, and the fatherlesse, / In funerall Sack!' (I. ii. 26-27). The symbolism of money receives its usual thorough development. Money has a monarchic function to Dr Rut (II. iii. 51 ff.), the stature of a god to Sir Moath Interest (II. vi. 39 ff.), and the inevitable Jonsonian connection with sex for all the characters.

The imagery recurrently emphasizes this connection between money and sex. Probably Jonson chose to dramatize the story of a wealthy heiress who is being sold off to the highest bidder because he was—or seems to have been—abnormally concerned with the connection between money and marriage, or money and man's erotic life. Instead of merely observing the connection, as most dramatists are content to do, he kept turning it around to look at it from every angle he could think of. In *The Magnetick Lady* he is chiefly interested in marriage as a financial affair. Compass observes Interest, Bias, and Practise talking about marrying Placentia to Practise, and says, 'twill be a bargaine, and sale' (II. v. 51). Practise confirms this arrangement when he concludes the '*Contract*' with the statement—'A direct bargaine, and sale in open market' (II. vi. 23). Then, since Compass thinks that Practise means to marry Pleasance, he asks her if she is 'to be joyn'd / A Patentee with him' (II. vii. 5-6). A 'Patentee' in the seventeenth century was one to whom letters patent had been granted—that is, a 'licence to manufacture, sell, or deal in an article or commodity, to the exclusion of all other persons' (*OED*). Erotic experience, in the eyes of Compass, would seem to be a commodity, and monogamy, a commercial monopoly signed with a marriage licence. Now, of course, there were marriages in seventeenth century England, just as at times in twentieth century world, in which contracts were used, and money or property was exchanged. That is the real basis on which Jonson built many of his allusions. But he went further within the confines of his plays by assuming that woman *is* money or can be used as money is used. For instance, note how Interest describes the proposed wife of Practise as 'a soft, tender, delicate rib of mans flesh, / That he may worke like waxe, and print upon' (II. vi. 19-20). To a usurer a woman is a piece of gold, and sexual intercourse a kind of minting. But not only to a usurer, because both Practise and Diaphanous make the same assumption. After Placentia is found with child, Practise comments that she has proved 'Of light gold'. And Diaphanous adds, 'And crack't within the Ring' (III. vii. 19-20). These lines refer to gold coins which, because of damage, can no longer be current; a maiden who has known a man can no longer be sold for the same price that she could when she was sound.[1] She is, as Bias says, 'a crack'd commoditie' (IV. iii. 3) or, as the quaint modern phrase goes, 'damaged goods'. The illegitimate baby is therefore 'a bad Commoditie' (IV. vii. 3) which must be disposed of surreptitiously—presumably on what is now called the black market. Diaphanous makes another

[1] See Cunningham's note on this image. *The Works of Ben Jonson*, ed. by Gifford and Cunningham, V, 469; II, 551-552.

monetary allusion to the child-birth when he asserts that he would have been 'Abus'd i' the busines, had the slip slur'd on me, / A Counterfeit' (III. vii. 27-28). While 'Counterfeit' was not restricted to coins, its financial sense is reinforced here by 'slip'. Among other things, 'slip' meant a counterfeit coin made, for example, of brass covered with silver or of gilded copper (*OED*). Since Diaphanous had no part in that particular coining, he would have been only a counterfeit father if he had been accused of being the true one.

The imagery of *The Magnetick Lady* is perhaps the clearest illustration of the major fault of the imagery of the last plays: it is predictable. These plays are characterized by many of the same tenor-vehicle relationships that we observed in the major plays. Gold is raised to the height of a religious object, and, frequently, sexualized. The universe becomes alchemized, with a golden sun, a silvery moon, and jewel-like stars. Mean things are pretentiously elevated. Human beings are devoured by human beings. It is almost all there, the world of Volpone and Mammon, somewhat less powerfully stated, but not much changed for all that. Jonson was forced by his own narrow view of metaphor to concentrate on only a few interactions of tenor and vehicle. The narrowness of this relationship, the fact that, given the tenor, only a few vehicles were likely to be chosen, produced a strong texture, tight, formalized, and symbolic. This strength is its virtue. Its weakness is its lack of imagination—its predictableness. There simply is not enough surprise in Jonson's last plays. We could not write them ourselves, but we can recognize that Jonson would write them in this way.

This charge of predictableness is, in part, unfair. That is, Jonson meant his imagery to be predictable or, at least, not too daring or occult. One coins a new metaphor always with some danger, yet one must adventure. But Jonson's danger was conservatism, not linguistic riotousness. In time he fell back on what he had used before, preferring the tried to the new. Whether he was ever capable of moving out of his pattern we cannot know. If *The Sad Shepherd* is any indication, we can surmise that he could, because, even in its unfinished state, this tender pastoral play reveals a lighter, less congealed touch. But *The Sad Shepherd* belongs to the side of Jonson that could create masques. He was interested principally in comedy which was burlesque and satire and poetry all at once. Given that kind of drama, the imagery he chose was decorous.

One reason that the symbolic pattern of the last plays seems to have hardened may be precisely this emphasis on decorum—an emphasis which Jonson, a little pathetically, makes as late as the first Epilogue to *The New Inne*.

> *for he sent things fit*
> *In all the numbers, both of sense, and wit,*
> *If they ha' not miscarried!*
>
> . . . . .
> *Yet iudgement would the last be, i' the field,*
> *With a true Poet.*

To the end he was concerned with the fitness of things, as a comic poet should be. But, however essential a strong sense of decorum is to a comic poet, a rigid interpretation of decorum narrows the choice of vehicles. The more strictly a poet applies the principle of fitness to his language, the less 'play' there is likely to be in the imagery he uses. If the last plays seem to repeat the earlier plays in theme, situations, characters, and language, one explanation may be that the possible range of decorous vehicles was so narrow that, in time, a certain tenor was almost destined to draw forth a certain vehicle. Why, for instance, is the symbol of money in *The Staple of Newes* a woman and not a man? Why is she deified? Why is the final play called *The Magnetick Lady* and not *The Magnetick Gentleman*? Certainly, one answer to all of these questions is that Jonson had decided early in his career that, in comedies, gold ought to be sexualized and worshipped. In the middle plays his language could imply this worship and this sexualizing, but in the last plays a more economical, but unfortunately less imaginative, device was found which could combine these implications: that is, personify gold as a woman who could be both courted and worshipped. Here, as in so many other ways in his final dramas, Jonson only used more emphatically a device he had used before. Pecunia and Lady Loadstone (or Placentia) are lineal descendants of that metallic Lady Argurion in *Cynthia's Revels* whom Mercury describes briefly as 'Monie, monie' and Cupid somewhat more fully as 'A *Nymph* of a most wandring and giddy disposition . . . shee's more loose and scattering then dust, and will flie from place to place, as shee were rapt with a whirle-winde'. It is characteristic of Jonson's treatment of both love and money that Cupid should describe the symbol of money and that the description should end on this note: 'she's for any coorse imployment you will put vpon her, as to be your procurer, or pandar' (II. iii. 164-185).

This may be only another way of saying that Jonson looked at human life from one point of view and, to the last of his comedies, remained hypnotized by what he saw. He never really developed philosophically; there are no periods in his life as there are in Shakespeare's or Chaucer's. There is, admittedly, some artistic development or at least change. The middle plays do have, to borrow F. P. Wilson's phrase, 'a splendid equilibrium of matter and means'.[1] And this equilibrium is upset in the last plays. But all of Jonson's plays are more like each other than they are like any other plays written; all of them belong to a special kind of world with a special religion and moral code. The last plays, with

[1] Wilson, *Elizabethan and Jacobean* (Oxford, 1945), 95.

the possible exception of *The New Inne*, bring nothing new to the Jonson canon because they are only more rigid, more obvious, and less unified versions of *The Alchemist* and *Volpone*. In them Jonson turned back on himself and kept on varying his old theme—but less effectively.

CHAPTER IX

LANGUAGE SUCH AS MEN DO USE

T HE most common criticism of Jonson (usually
following an extensive comparison with Shakespeare) is that he lacked poetic imagination. Some
even think of him more as a translator than as a genuinely
creative artist. There is a certain justice in such a criticism
if we restrict the imagination to the power of creating ideal
experience out of whole cloth. His *Sejanus*—so goes the
criticism—is only a versifying of Livy and of Roman history.
The *Discoveries* is patently a book of plagiarized excerpts.
In *Catiline* he translated some of Cicero's speeches almost
literally, and in *The Alchemist* whole passages seem lifted
out of manuals of alchemy. *The Staple of Newes* is only a
combination of *The Bloody Brother*, *The London Prodigal*, *The
Contention between Liberality and Prodigality*, and Aristophanes' *Plutus*. And so on. Furthermore, what else can one
make of Jonson's theory of 'imitation'—apparently one of
the most ludicrous theories ever held by a great man of
letters? 'The third requisite in our *Poet*, or Maker, is
Imitation, to bee able to convert the substance, or Riches of
another *Poet*, to his owne use.'[1] Taken in isolation, that
definition would seem to be another instance of how rarely
a poet has even an adequate explanation of the creative
process. Taken along with other remarks, it becomes even
more puzzling. If Jonson believed in such a theory of
imitation, why did he tell Drummond that Du Bartas was
not a poet but a verser 'because he wrote not Fiction?'[2] Or
why did he write in the second prologue to *Epicoene*,

> For he knowes, *Poet* neuer credit gain'd
> By writing truths, but things (like truths) well fain'd.

[1] Herford and Simpson, VIII, 638.　　[2] *Ibid.*, I, 133.

Even in the passage from which this definition of imitation is taken there are some qualifying remarks which take the edge off his extreme statement. The poet, he goes on, should be 'Not, as a Creature, that swallowes, what it takes in, crude, raw, or indigested; but that feedes with an Appetite, and hath a Stomacke to concoct, divide, and turne all into nourishment'. This digestive metaphor suggests something more than servile imitation or literal translation, and the something more is implied when he adds that a poet should 'draw forth out of the best, and choisest flowers, with the Bee, and turne all into Honey, worke it into one relish and savour'.[1] 'Art', he concludes, should be added to all the rest of the poet's requisites, and even if a large part of 'art' is what we now call judgment, the word brings us closer to true creativeness than his definition initially suggested.

One way to make sense of this Horatian theory of imitation and to determine what kind of creative imagination Jonson had is to observe how he made use of contemporary material in the imagery of his plays. Even a cursory reading of both Jonson and the pamphlet literature of the late Elizabethan and the early Jacobean ages reveals some striking parallels in their metaphorical language. In the analysis of *The Alchemist* we noticed how Face and Dol spoke of their thieving and pandering in military terms. Two years before the performance of this play Dekker in *The Bellman of London* described how the trade of a thief and his companion, a whore, 'goes vnder the name of the *Sacking-law*; and rightly may it be called sacking, for as in the sacking of a City, all the villaines in the world are set abroach, so when a Harlot comes to the sacking of a man's wealth and reputation (for she beseigeth both together) she leaves no strategem vnpractised to bring him to confusion'.[2]

---

[1] *Ibid.*, VIII, 638-639.
[2] *The Non-Dramatic Works of Thomas Dekker*, ed. A. B. Grosart (London, 1885), III, 152.

The following year, in *Lanthorne and Candlelight*, when Dekker compared the cheating which was practised in London to hunting, he carried on this basic image. 'Hunting is a noble, a manly & a healthfull exercise; it is a very true picture of war, nay it is a war in it selfe; for engines are brought into the field, stratagems are contrived, ambushes are laide, onsets are giuen . . . the enemy is pursued . . . then are spoiles diuided.'[1] One would be foolish to say categorically that Jonson picked up his military imagery from Dekker's pamphlets, even though he was familiar enough with Dekker or his writing to call him a 'rogue'. More probably both Jonson and Dekker had a common source for such imagery—the colloquial language and the cant terms of the age. According to the writer of *Martin Mark-all* (Samuel Rowlands?), Dekker stole whole sections from Thomas Harman's *Caueat*. Actually, of course, the material was so traditional that it could have been picked up in many places. As early as 1532 Gilbert Walker mentioned that 'sacking law, signifieth whoredom'.

There are other examples of Jonson's use of such imagery. His misuse of religious terms in most of his comedies was not peculiar to him. When Thomas Nashe in *Pierce Penilesse* (1592) declared that Westminster must answer for a 'maydenhead' and added that 'Not a Wench sooner creepes out of the shell, but she is of the Religion', he used only a common play on words, the most famous of which was Hamlet's advice to Ophelia—'Get thee to a nunnery'.[2] Jonson's ironic use of educational terms for some low practice also had a reasonable place in the literature of roguery. In *A Manifest Detection of Dice Play* (1532), Gilbert Walker referred to dicing as a 'good and liberal' science which grew to 'the body of an art' and had peculiar terms applied to it even as had 'grammar, or logic, or any other of

---

[1] *Ibid.*, 228.
[2] *The Works of Thomas Nashe*, ed. R. B. McKerrow (London, 1910), I, 216.

the approved sciences'.[1] Even coney-catching, which Jonson
made so central a symbol or synecdoche for economic
preying, had gathered to it symbolic value by the time he
began writing plays. In *The Defence of Conny-Catching* either
Greene or an anonymous pamphleteer ironically defended
such thieving by the simple expedient of showing how
common it was. Usurers, millers, butchers, drapers, lawyers,
brokers, seducers of women, tailors—all, according to this
defender, were coney-catchers. Even Robert Greene was a
coney-catcher because he sold *Orlando Furioso* to two
different companies. 'What trade can maintaine his traffique?
what science vphold itself? what man liue vnlesse he growe
into the nature of a Cony-catcher?'[2] If coney-catching is so
necessary to the mere existence of man, then one is impelled
either to excuse cheating at cards, as the writer seems to
plead for at the end—'Thus haue I proued to your maships,
how there is no estate, trade, occupation, nor mistery, but
liues by *Conny-catching*, and that our shift at cards compared
to the rest, is the simplest of al'[3]—or to condemn the
respectable types of unfair dealing even more severely than
his 'shift at cards'. Even as a profession like coney-catching
could be symbolic of commercial or legal or sexual cheating,
so places like a bear-garden or a playhouse, the court or a
tavern could be microcosms of the world's vanity and misery.
John Earle's description of Paul's Walk is a good picture
of one such microcosm: 'the land's epitome . . . the whole
world's map. . . . The best sign of a temple in it is that it is
the thieves' sanctuary. . . . It is the ears' brothel and satisfies
their lust and itch.'[4] This implication that Paul's Walk is
'the land's epitome' or 'the whole world's map' runs

---

[1] Gilbert Walker [?], *A Manifest Detection of the Most Vyle and Detestable Use of Dice Play*, ed. J. O. Halliwell, Percy Society, vol. 29 (London, 1850), 16.
[2] *The Life and Complete Works in Prose and Verse of Robert Greene*, ed. A. B. Grosart (London, 1881-1886), XI, 69.
[3] *Ibid.*, 103.
[4] Earle, *Micro-cosmography*, ed. Philip Bliss (London, 1811), 116-118.

throughout Elizabethan and Jacobean literature, especially in Dekker's *Gull's Hornbook* and in comedies of London life.

What does all this suggest about Jonson's imagination? The more one learns about Jonson's use of sources and surmises his dramatic method, the more one moves toward the conclusion that his imagination worked out from the core of a real event (as in *Sejanus* or *Catiline* or *Bartholomew Fair*) which he had observed or read about or, as in the masques, of which he was to be a part. For instance, the Queen of Faeries episode in *The Alchemist* had real parallels in Jacobean London, as C. J. Sisson has discovered.[1] Allan Gilbert is certainly right in emphasizing that Jonson acted as a poet should act in taking from any book what was useful to him.[2] Gilbert might have added—not merely any book, but any source whatsoever. So far as his imagery is concerned, Jonson's imaginative creation typically began with the real ambiguities in the 'language, such as men doe vse'. His diction, like that of every seventeenth century poet, is ambiguous to a certain degree, but his ambiguity is more what might be called a 'found' ambiguity than an invented ambiguity. He was more likely to play with the multiple senses of words already used in the language than to invent new ambiguities. Face and Subtle are masters at juggling the various meanings of such words as 'grace', 'virtue', and 'price' in order to befuddle others. Face confides to Dapper, 'You doe not know / What grace her *Grace* may doe you in cleane linnen' (I. ii. 174-175). In a sense Jonson, like more than one Renaissance poet, let the colloquial language itself 'poeticize' for him.

Jonson's imagery, then, resembles that of a philologist who could also write poetry. He regarded words somewhat as H. B. Fowler regarded them: they were sensitive beings

---

[1] See *J. Q. Adams Memorial Studies* (Washington, 1948), 739-741, and Herford and Simpson, X, 47 and 98.

[2] Gilbert, *The Symbolic Persons in the Masques of Ben Jonson*, 14.

whose chequered past and varied present ought not to keep them from being used courteously; and since 'language most shows the man', they were revealing companions. Like Fowler, he concluded that metaphors are many times deformed and that the accepted figures of speech are better than the new ones. 'All attempts that are new in this kind are dangerous, and somewhat hard, before they be softened with use.' Yet he is quick to add that 'wee must adventure'. According to Arthur H. King, who has made an interesting analysis of the language of *Poetaster*, Jonson 'maintains a constant linguistic attitude and presents all his characters in terms of language rather than action'.[1] This conclusion, with certain reservations, applies to all of Jonson's plays, as Coleridge long ago noted when he said that Jonson 'individualizes' by manners and modes of speech rather than by moral or intellectual differences.[2] In order to understand what such a poet does with metaphors, one has to discover all the various meanings of the words he uses and observe how he capitalizes on their multiple senses. Much as he may have warned against 'paronomasias', he was as expert, though not so liberal, as Shakespeare at creating them. ('One cannot say he wanted wit,' according to Dryden, 'but rather that he was frugal of it.'[3]) When he criticized them, he may have been criticizing only those which were sheer word play rather than those which added to the meaning of the passage.

To say that Jonson's imagination worked out from the core of real events and that his imagery typically began with 'found' ambiguities should not be construed to mean that he remained bound to the real. Jonson was capable of invention, as his plots, the names of his characters, the epithets,

---

[1] King, *The Language of Satirized Characters in Poetaster: a Socio-stylistic Analysis 1597-1602. Lund Studies in English* (London, 1941), XIII.

[2] Coleridge, *The Literary Remains*, ed. H. N. Coleridge (London, 1837), I, 98-100.

[3] *The Best of Dryden*, ed. Louis Bredvold (New York, 1946), 434.

the animal imagery, and the religious allusions throughout the plays reveal. A short example of how he began and where he went is the epithet which Face applies to Dol Common when he sends her packing—'my smock-rampant' (V. iv. 126). 'Smock' was then used as a derogatory term suggesting loose conduct or immorality in women (*OED*). 'Rampant' could have meant several things in 1610. It could be applied to beasts, especially lions, which were sometimes pictured as rearing or standing with fore-paws in the air, and exhibiting fierceness or high spirits by ramping or similar movements. Figuratively, it meant lustful or vicious. This conventional figurative meaning would have been strengthened when the word was combined with 'smock'; and the animal reference might still have been in the listener's mind because Subtle previously called Dol 'the lioness' (IV. iii. 49), and Face, shortly after this, said that Surly (who is preparing to meet Dol) 'lookes already, rampant' (IV. iii. 58). In view of Dol's pretensions to aristocracy, 'smock-rampant' takes on added meaning when one remembers that 'rampant' is a term in heraldry. Dol is her own coat-of-arms—a 'smock-rampant'. Arthur H. Nason, who has shown how much Jonson used heraldic terms, does not mention this use of 'rampant', apparently thinking that it had no overtone of heraldry. But the Scrivener in the Induction to *Bartholomew Fair* uses heraldic and pseudo-heraldic terms in a similar jocose manner: 'A wise *Iustice* of *Peace meditant*, in stead of a *Iugler*, with an *Ape*. A ciuill *Cutpurse searchant*. A sweete *Singer* of new Ballads *allurant*: and as fresh an *Hypocrite*, as euer was broach'd, *rampant.*' Both here and in 'smock-rampant' Jonson may be using his characteristic device of bringing together the mean and the magnificent by using heraldic terms (or what sound like heraldic terms) to describe the contemptible. The effect is ironic. To describe a cutpurse, a singer of ballads, and a whore as though they were heraldic devices temporarily attracts to them an aristocratic atmosphere which is ludicrously unsuited to their professional activities. In addition, to treat them as heraldic devices 'emblazons' them for the moment. So set off, they become detached enough to be laughed at.

The imagery which resulted from building on the real ambiguities in contemporary language is characterized—perhaps inevitably, perhaps simply because of Jonson's mind—by concreteness and consistency, imaginative restraint and even, at times, a crippling narrowness. Early in his career Jonson defined—or his method defined for him—the borders of metaphoric freedom in order to establish the realm of metaphor within which he could safely work. The centrifugal impulse in most images is carefully controlled. The imagery of Jonson's best plays is centripetal. Instead of flying out in all directions as, let us say, Shelley's imagery tends to, his images tend to have the same 'massive and articulated coherence' which Herford has noted in *Volpone* and *The Alchemist*. Douglas Bush's remark that Jonson, even in his plays, remained essentially an epigram writer can be applied to the imagery.[1] He worked best in a small compass, ordering his thought in short, weighty, controlled expressions, working constantly for concentrated force and clarity. The massive harmony of *Volpone* or *The Alchemist* is achieved by the orchestration of many small notes which are unified by a common emotion and a common point of view. When the coherence is lacking, as it seems to be in the last plays, the play falls in pieces, some of which are pleasing, but the total effect of which is disappointing.

The man who thought that '*it is onley the disease of the vnskilfull, to thinke rude thiugs greater then polish'd: or scatter'd more numerous then compos'd*, would strive for the controlled figure and the limited effect.[2] When he

[1] Bush, *English Literature in the Earlier Seventeenth Century, 1600-1660* (Oxford, 1945), 106.
[2] 'To the Reader', *The Alchemist*, Quarto.

revises, as in *Every Man in his Humour*, he works to draw
the images together into the whole pattern of the play.
There is, then, a solidity and a consistency about the verbal
universe which Jonson creates. This solidity and consistency
help give the plays strength and cumulative intensity.

But the tendency to round out and finish off images, to
make them self-consistent and keep them from dissipating
their strength by losing their direction can involve—and
does involve in some of Jonson's plays—a certain loss in
imagination. To be sure, nothing gets out of hand in such
imagery; but there is little, even in the tragedies, to send the
imagination off on such a journey as Perdita's lines on the
winds of March. Of course, this is an unfair comparison
because, in his plays, Jonson never tried for the 'winds of
March' kind of poetry. Still, even in the kind of poetry he
did try for, the vehicles are so inevitable, once the tenor is
given, that a rigidity, a lack of 'play', and a poverty of
imaginativeness seriously limit the appeal of his imagery.
Gold is always sexualized. Women are almost always compared to animals. Everything is eaten. Classical allusions are
ridiculously misapplied, and the ancient gods consort with
a mule, a fox, a fat knight, and the Ladies Collegiate. Like
many kingdoms, Jonson's realm seemed to narrow as he
grew older and more assured. Being a royalist in politics, a
classicist in literature, and an Anglo-Catholic in religion may
have been comfortable in an age of Stuart kings, Renaissance
learning, and High Church lords. But such assurance on
political, literary, and theological questions can become an
artistic liability if it narrows one's sympathies—sympathies
which, in a satirist, are likely to be narrow to begin with.
Jonson became more, not less, sure of the things he had
always known to be true. Philosophic certainty need not kill
art and did not even in Jonson's last plays; but it may give
art a certain rigidity, too close to the rigidity of death. Too
much of the last plays is predictable, and art should some-

times surprise. Even in Jonson's best plays one is rarely surprised into a whole new emotional state, though that again is a limitation inherent in the kind of play Jonson wrote. The consistency close to rigidity, the certainty not far enough from dogmatism, and the predictableness may have been in Coleridge's mind when he spoke of Jonson's 'mechanical' creations which were products of the fancy rather than the imagination.

These limitations of language must have been obvious even to Jonson. Even he seems to have been aware that his verse depended more on wit than imagination and that his plays were somewhat laboured. But he scarcely could have anticipated how later ages would find his lines difficult and even, at times, obscure. Jonson was praised more in the seventeenth century and has been praised less ever since, partly because so much of his dramatic effect is linguistic, and words die. Probably at no time was 'the green and soggy multitude' moved by his too circumscribed flights of wit, even as it has not been moved by many of Milton's complex images. Shakespeare's imagery, which may ultimately be more complex than either, appeals in so many different ways that it may move one even when only partly understood.

Jonson's language is difficult for reasons other than the change in the meanings of words. One of these reasons is the very stylization that gives Jonson's dramatic speech its bite and colour. He thought that characters in plays should speak 'language, such as men doe vse', but his dramatic speech is a unique language never heard off the stage. At its worst, the style degenerates into Jonsonese—a choked and obscure jargon with too few connectives, a twisted syntax, and an un-English idiom. Dryden described Jonsonese in this way, gently: 'If there was any fault in his language, 'twas that he weaved it too closely and laboriously, in his comedies especially: perhaps, too, he did a little too much Romanize

our tongue, leaving the words which he translated almost as much Latin as he found them: wherein, though he learnedly followed their language, he did not enough comply with the idiom of ours.'[1] At its best this stylized language is a dramatic speech of great power and subtle decorousness. But at no time is it the speech of men, although numerous connections can be made between it and the idiom, the imagery, and the rhythm of colloquial speech.

Jonson's learning—or show of learning—also makes his verse difficult. Recent scholarship has shown his erudition to be less formidable than it has long been thought to be, though it still seems enormous.[2] At times, in such plays as *Sejanus* or *Cynthia's Revels*, one could accuse him, with a good deal of reason, of trying to show off how much he knew. But even when he was pedantic, he did not try to be baffling; like all neo-classicists, he wanted his borrowings and allusions to be recognized and enjoyed. He expected that the educated listeners would know what he referred to or would take the trouble to find out before they came to the theatre again or read his works a second time. Perhaps we think Jonson's language laboured and excessively learned because we have become ignorant of the things he knew about—the fine points of Latin history, alchemy, medicine, law, food, London low life, and ancient high life. His alleged laboriousness may be only our real ignorance. Such a characteristic image as the one describing Dol Common's professional actions in alchemic terms can be understood vaguely without special knowledge of alchemy, mostly because even the most innocent of us is quick to understand

---

[1] *The Best of Dryden*, 435.

[2] Ernest W. Talbert, 'New Light on Ben Jonson's Workmanship', *Studies in Philology*, XL (1943), 154-185.

Ernest W. Talbert, 'Current Scholarly Works and the Erudition of Jonson's Masque of Augurs', *Studies in Philology*, XLIV (1947), 605-624.

D. J. Gordon, 'The Imagery of Ben Jonson's *The Masque of Blacknesse* and *The Masque of Beauty*', *Journal of the Warburg and Courtlauld Institutes*, VI (1943), 122-141.

sexual innuendo (II. iii. 254-256). But the wit of the passage is lost unless the alchemic meanings of *'ouer the helme'*, *'circulate'*, and *'quick-siluer'*, with the implications of repeated vaporization and condensation, are understood. Lost, that is, to us, but probably not to the 'learned' playgoers of Jonson's day. And perhaps progressively lost since that day, so that only several generations later Dryden could think that Jonson weaved his language 'too closely and laboriously'. By the time of Coleridge the works of Jonson called forth this somewhat alarming praise: 'The more I study his writings, the more I admire them; and the more the study resembles that of an ancient classic, in the *minutiae* of his rhythm, metre, choice of words, forms of connection, etc., the more numerous have the points of admiration become.'[1] In time perhaps all Elizabethans, even Shakespeare, will become as inaccessible to the ordinary reader as Sophocles is now, but there is a good chance that Jonson will reach that unenviable state long before any of the others. 'Done himself for not being understood would perish.'[2] Alas, though prophetic of Donne's three-hundred-year neglect, Jonson's remark seems now more justly his own epitaph.

[1] *Coleridge's Miscellaneous Criticism*, ed. T. M. Raysor (London, 1936), 49.
[2] Herford and Simpson, I, 138.

CHAPTER X

THE BROKEN COMPASS

I

JONSON, then, characteristically establishes and maintains a comic tone largely, though not solely, by means
of diction. Without the aesthetic distance and the comic
detachment which this diction gives us, the actions in most
Jonsonian plays might well be unbearably sordid or sinister
or pathetic. But, by means of epithets, allusions, metaphors,
and precisely chosen words, Jonson gives us the proper
comic perspective: cold, hard, and merciless, yet clear, free
of cant, and massively controlled.

The actual words we hear constitute one of Jonson's
major ways of revealing characters simultaneously as the
human beings they are supposed to be in the plot and as
the lower (or higher) beings they are associated with by
means of the imagery. Volpone, a Magnifico of Venice,
thinks of himself at one time as a fox and at another time as
Jove. This double vision reveals a comic disproportion: a
Magnifico of Venice is ludicrously unlike either a fox or a
Greek god. Through the use of such startling juxtapositions
Jonson hoped to force us to see Volpone in a new light or
with a new emotion. The contrast of Volpone's actions with
the associations normally expected of a man, a god, and a
fox makes us both laugh at him and judge him morally.

To gain such an ironic perspective, Jonson habitually
used the devices typical of a small and sometimes misunderstood group of writers who celebrate their allegiance
to an ideal world by creating the perversions of the ideal.
Thus, Swift created his Lilliputians and Yahoos; Baudelaire
his Black Mass; and Poe his sick heroes morbidly concerned
with decaying beauty and terror. These men celebrate

beauty by focusing on ugliness, virtue by dramatizing vice, and harmony by revealing a dislocated and distorted world. The classic answer to such distortion and dislocation is that of Whitman, who explained his distaste for Poe's writings by saying that he wanted for poetry 'the clear sun shining, and fresh air blowing—the strength and power of health, not of delirium, even amid the stormiest passions'. Yet Whitman finally recognized that Poe's genius had 'conquer'd a special recognition for itself'. In time, he admitted that 'the service Poe renders is certainly that entire contrast and contradiction which is next best to fully exemplifying it' [the perfect character].[1]

Baudelaire, Swift, and, in part, Jonson are, like Poe, among those artists who dramatize this contrast and contradiction of the ideal. All use inversion, the principal means of creating this contrast. The best example of inversion in *Gulliver's Travels* is in the voyage to the land of the Houyhnhnms where the ideal virtues appear in the horses and the animal nature of man in the loathsome man-like Yahoos. And inversion is used throughout the *Travels*. Gulliver begins as a giant among the Lilliputians and enjoys a proper scorn for their affectation, vanity, and cruelty. Then, suddenly, in the second voyage, he is the Lilliputian, and the accumulated scorn shifts to him. In turn, he feels the same kind of antipathy for the gross bodies of the Brobdingnags which the Lilliputians had felt for his body. In the final voyage he is caught between the force of the contempt which the Houyhnhnms feel for the Yahoos and transfer to him because he looks like a Yahoo and his own desire to be like a Houyhnhnmn. In short, he finds himself in the human predicament. A comparable method of inversion produces the Satanism that appears in much of Baudelaire's poetry. What redeems this Satanism is the realization that it means something else. Some critics (T. S.

[1] Edmund Wilson, ed., *The Shock of Recognition* (New York, 1943), 423-424.

Eliot, for instance) have even turned Baudelaire into an orthodox Catholic whose real concern was sin and redemption.[1] That seems too simple. When Baudelaire used disease and crime in his poems, he may have been literally interested in them as diseases and crime. Why deny it? But he may also have used them as means of expressing, ironically, his vision of a life saner and happier than the one he was living. Frequently Baudelaire inverted the usual opinions of man in order to emphasize a truth not normally expressed. For example, when he said that 'Woman is *natural*, that is to say abominable', he inverted the romantic view that both women and nature are divine in order to show women in what seemed to him a truer and less blasphemous light.[2]

Because these writers use inversion and transposition, they are often misunderstood. Sometimes they are confused with their heroes—a confusion which an incipient Satanist like Byron might foster. Marlowe, who suffered in the Elizabethan Age from such confusion, was frequently accused of the sins of his heroes—blasphemy, black magic, sodomy, atheism, and treason. Since Faustus 'confounds hell in Elysium', Elizabethans too quickly concluded that Marlowe, who was a free thinker and a bold talker, must also confound heaven and hell. Sometimes these creators of contradiction are reproached with the kind of criticism that is often brought against modern poetry: its subject matter is one of blank negation and of dreary rottenness. But this is the voice of the Philistine who wants only goodness and hope in his literature. Eliot's *Wasteland* and Pound's *Cantos* have been condemned for their 'negative' subject matter and obscure technique. Such criticism is faulty in so far as it assumes that there is a simple and inevitable relation between the subject matter and the theme of a poem. Much of the misunderstanding of modern poetry or of the literature

[1] Charles Baudelaire, *Intimate Journals*, intro. by T. S. Eliot (London, 1930), 18.
[2] *Ibid.*, 61.

of contrast could be cleared up if one would realize that the act of creation places the writer on the side of the angels whatever side his characters seem to be on. Swift has been accused of being misanthropic in *Gulliver's Travels*, but the accusation is unjust. If he had been radically misanthropic when writing the *Travels*, he never would have finished it because he would have thought mankind too far gone to bother with. But he did finish it, and it remains a sign not of despair in man (as a murder or complete silence might be), but of hope in man. Any creative act, in short, is really an act of faith.

Not all the misunderstanding which these creators of inversion suffer from is caused by an improper aesthetic attitude in their audience. Sometimes their own satiric habit of inverting the accepted values makes a true understanding difficult. Jonson is a lamentable example of a writer who used reversal so much that it degenerated at times into contrariness. Everyone else thought that Harington's translation of Ariosto was excellent; Jonson thought it the worst of the age. Sir Philip Sidney was generally considered a handsome and gracious courtier; Jonson felt it necessary, thirty years after Sidney's death, to point out that his face was spoiled by pimples. Jonson seems to have bent over backward to be frank and even rude, apparently to prevent anyone from thinking him a toady to money or titles. Some of his remarks to Drummond sound like the opinions of Pope's learned men who want to be singular:

> So much they scorn the crowd, that if the throng
> By chance go right, they purposely go wrong.

Drummond's comment on this contrariness seems justified. After listening to Jonson for several weeks, he concluded that Jonson 'interpreteth best sayings and deeds often to the worst'. There is no excuse for this unpleasant side of Jonson's personality. One can only hope that a knowledge of his contrariness does not cause a misunderstanding of his works.

A subtler kind of misunderstanding may come from an examination of the imagery used by a writer. Kenneth Burke, who has been interested in what he calls the 'strategies' of the Satanic, seems to me guilty of such a misunderstanding when he claims that, if the enemies of a certain cause apparently advocated by the writer are portrayed with greater vividness than its proponents, then the writer is really on the side of the enemies. 'If a man's virtuous characters are dull, and his wicked characters are done vigorously, his *art* has voted for the wicked ones, regardless of his "official front". If a man talks of *glory* but employs the imagery of *desolation*, his *true subject* is desolation.'[1] Burke later adds that 'a man can, on the surface, maintain any insincerity he prefers. But in the depths of his imagery, he cannot lie.'[2] This attractive theory is at least as old as Blake's celebrated statement that 'the reason Milton wrote in fetters when he wrote of Angels & God, and at liberty when of Devils & Hell, is because he was a true Poet and of the Devil's party without knowing it'. There is certainly some truth to this theory if Blake means that the true poet is one who can state the devil's case as well as the devil himself could—or better, perhaps, because he is not the devil. In the same way Shakespeare can be said to have been on Iago's side or Edmund's side. But, if 'without knowing it' implies that Milton made Satan (or Shakespeare, Iago) so memorable because he was unconsciously as impious and destructive as his hero, then the theory becomes a too simple explanation of a complex creative process. A poet's true subject is not necessarily desolation merely because he uses 'the imagery of desolation'. In order to make this clear, we must distinguish the creative acts of an

[1] Burke, *Attitudes toward History* (New York, 1937), II, 77. See also I, 84 n.; II, 155 n.

[2] *Ibid.*, II, 104. Burke seems to qualify, perhaps even to deny this point in *A Rhetoric of Motives* (New York, 1950), 18-19.

artist from his 'practical' acts. If a poet's true subject in life were desolation, he would probably be out desolating something—a city, a woman, a world—rather than creating an imaginary universe. But, as an artist, he would seek an artistic expression for many of his impulses; and in art, paradoxically, a poet's true subject is always beauty, however much his subject matter is desolation. The paradox of creative work is that even when one uses 'the imagery of desolation' in a poem or painting, one creates rather than desolates. The aesthetic act may well begin as the destructive impulse of a desolator (Aristophanes taking revenge on his enemies, let us say), but, because it rescues some intelligible form, some meaningful reality, from the miscellaneous passing of all things into oblivion, it turns the originally destructive into the permanently aesthetic—that is, into an experience that can be enjoyed contemplatively. The use of ugliness or distortion or desolation need not kill off any possibility of beauty in an artistic work because beauty resides not in the raw materials chosen, but in the created work itself. And the contemplative attitude with which we enjoy the work of art rescues even the ugly, the desolate, and the evil from the hideous consequences which attend them in what is called, not without irony, real life.

There is, then, a difference between the morality of an image of desolation in art and the morality of an act of desolation in life. Even Burke, with his fondness for seeing works of art as 'strategies' for encompassing situations, might admit that Cellini's murder of a man was a different act, morally, from the creation of an image of desolation such as the famous statue of Perseus holding the head of the slain Medusa. This is not to deny that there are intimate connections between art and the rest of life. Artistic desolators may purge their minds, by means of a play or painting, of impulses destructive enough to have landed them in jail if expressed otherwise. Cellini may have kept

himself from murdering other men by symbolically killing
Medusa. Even so, practical desolators might have been
changed by artistic success. If Hitler had been able to
produce 'the imagery of desolation' in art, he might never
have produced the images of desolation in history. But however intimate such connections are, the aesthetic act and the
practical act have morally different consequences.

II

To dramatize the contradictions to the ideal inevitably
involves distortion. Jonson thought of himself as a realist
who would present 'men', not 'monsters', but, as a master
of caricature, he created monsters. Instead of representing
men as he had observed them, he exaggerated their dominant
traits or focused on only one or two traits, catching a man
in an oblique light and casting him into an energetic life
merely by making him talk. By means of real details and
allusive language and characters that are little more than
counters he created a special kind of experience which is in
part like the life men live, but which is distorted into an
experience subtly different from anything but a life we can
imagine. The aim of caricature, as Fielding observed in his
preface to *Joseph Andrews*, is 'to exhibit monsters, not men;
and all distortions and exaggerations whatever are within
its proper province'. Fielding added that the only source
of the truly ridiculous is affectation, and that affectation
comes from either vanity or hypocrisy. The ridiculous
'strikes the reader with surprise and pleasure; and that in a
higher and stronger degree when the affectation arises from
hypocrisy, than when from vanity; for to discover any one
to be the exact reverse of what he affects, is more surprizing,
and consequently more ridiculous, than to find him a little
deficient in the quality he desires the reputation of. I might
observe that our Ben Jonson, who of all men understood the

Ridiculous the best, hath chiefly used the hypocritical affectation.'[1]

Jonson's interest in hypocrisy may help explain his attitude toward the Puritans. He hated them partly because they thought his beloved classics were heathen: 'All's *heathen*', says Ananias in *The Alchemist*, 'but the *Hebrew*' (II. v. 17). The Puritan attempt to return to primitive Christianity seemed to Jonson to deny the Greek and Roman heritage in Western culture. Any traditions other than the Biblical were to the rigid Puritans, as they were to Ananias, '*Popish* all' (III. ii. 107). Yet there was another reason for his hatred: he considered them hypocritical. They preached chastity, frugality, and piety, but their practice frequently belied their preaching. One charge brought against them, especially by orthodox Catholics, was that of carnal laxity, though that accusation was made freely by all sides in the ecclesiastical disputes of the sixteenth and seventeenth centuries.[2] A more serious charge was that of avarice. While some Puritans did serve God rather than Mammon, some, for all their protestations of godliness, acquired wealth 'with a good conscience'.[3] The Puritans were certainly no worse than the Anglicans or the Catholics at money-grabbing, but the halo of sanctity that they added to the appeal of expediency made their sharp commercial practices the better material for satire. To Jonson they must have seemed the exact reverse of what they affected.

Jonson's use of the affectation arising from hypocrisy explains why pretence and disguises are so frequent in his plays. Somebody is always pretending to be something he is not—usually something better than he is. Face, Subtle, Dol, Volpone and the birds of prey, gulls like Stephen and

[1] Fielding, *The Works of Henry Fielding*, ed. G. H. Maynadier (New York, 1907), I, xxxv-xxxvi.
[2] See the essay by C. S. Lewis on Donne's love poems in *Seventeenth Century Studies Presented to Sir Herbert Grierson* (Oxford, 1938).
[3] L. C. Knights, *Drama and Society in the Age of Jonson*, 209.

Matthew who pretend to be sophisticated, braggarts like Bobadill who pretend to be brave, hypocrites like Zeal-of-the-land Busy who pretend to be pious and virtuous—all of these are in disguise. The world, to Jonson, was full of impostors. 'I *have* considered, our whole life is like a *Play*: wherein every man, forgetfull of himselfe, is in travaile with expression of another.'[1] Phantaste in *Cynthia's Revels* (IV. i. 171 ff.) wants to be all manner of creatures—empress, duchess, 'miscelany madam', waiting woman, dairy-maid, queen of the fairies. Such moving up and down the social scale is comic because it is indiscriminate and indecorous, and lack of decorum is comic, as are pretence and disguise.

Irony, distortion, exaggeration, pretence, disguise, and indecorum—these are Jonson's comic ways of presenting the contradictions to the ideal. Comedy, as James Feibleman claims, may indirectly affirm a perfect world by ridiculing imperfect worlds. A comic writer such as Shaw or Jonson says what he means by not saying what he means and frequently by saying the opposite of what he means. When Aristophanes ridiculed his absurd Athens and Jonson, his foul London, both were talking about heaven: an ideal Athens and an ideal London.

III

Jonson, of course, was not the only Renaissance writer to create the contradiction to the ideal, though his peculiar view of life now seems unique. His sense of a perverted age appears in the pamphlet literature of both the Elizabethan and Jacobean Ages. Writers as different as Stubbes and Nashe scourged 'these degenerate effeminate days'. Greene and Dekker satirized the life of the London underworld from the perspective of a sweeter, simpler past or of a religious

---

[1] Herford and Simpson, VIII, 597.

ideal. The more intense Puritans yearned for the pastoral life of the primitive church before the Bishops of Rome spoiled it all. And the witch hunters, like the witches they hunted, were fascinated by the most extensive contradiction of the ideal in the Renaissance—witchcraft's obscene parody of Christian piety.

Jonson was unique in his age for his ability to create a distorted world with a trenchancy of comic language and a control of dramatic form that have made his comedies permanently available. We see in his plays the underside of one of the favourite dreams of the Renaissance—the dream of the Golden Age. His treatment of the story of Hero and Leander in *Bartholomew Fair* is characteristic of his method: the romantic and the ideal are turned upside down. And what is scraped off the bottom of the stone? A mean puppet show in which the characters have shrunk to doll size, the actions have been burlesqued, and the language has been debased. Lanterne Leatherhead, the hobby-horse seller, explains that the puppet show is not played according to the printed page because 'that is too learned, and poeticall for our audience; what doe they know what *Hellespont* is?' Therefore, he has asked Littlewit to 'reduce it to a more familiar straine for our people'. Littlewit's explanation of how he only made it 'a little easie, and *moderne* for the times' shows to what extent the ancient story has been debased: 'for the *Hellespont* I imagine our *Thames* here; and then *Leander*, I make a Diers sonne, about *Puddle-wharfe*: and *Hero* a wench o' the *Banke-side*, who going ouer one morning to old fish-street; *Leander* spies her land at *Trigsstayers*, and falls in loue with her: Now do I introduce *Cupid*, hauing *Metamorphos'd* himselfe into a Drawer, and hee strikes *Hero* in loue with a pint of *Sherry*' (V. iii. 120-128). Confused with this ludicrous story is the trial of friendship between Damon and Pythias, 'two faithfull friends o' the Bankside'. The first meeting of the lovers has a homely touch.

Now, as he [Leander] *is beating, to make the*
   Dye take the fuller,
Who chances to come by, but faire Hero, *in a*
   Sculler;
And seeing Leanders *naked legge, and goodly calfe,*
Cast at him, from the boat, a Sheepes eye, and a
   halfe.   V. iv. 122-125

After this auspicious beginning and a few flattering scatological allusions, Hero finally declares her love in the
deathless accents of

O, Leander, Leander, *my deare, my deare* Leander,
I'le for euer be thy goose, so thou'lt be my gander.
                         V. iv. 295-296

The climactic love scene is broken up when Damon and
Pythias, hearing their cue—'*Kisse the whore o' the arse*'—fall
to. Hero, attacked, screams, '*O my hanches*'; Leander defends
her; and Cupid, the drawer, dismisses them all as '*Whore-
masters*'. All this clamour raises the ghost of Dionysius, and
the scene comes to an absurd close when Busy rushes in to
dispute with the puppet Dionysius about his lawful calling.
But the final debasement has not been mentioned yet. Even
before the puppet show starts, Cokes calls Hero his 'fairing'
(that is, a piece of gingerbread) and presumably while
watching and commenting on the puppet show crams into
his mouth a gingerbread fiddle, which represents Hero, a
fiddle-stick (Leander), a drum (Damon), a pipe (Pythias),
and a hobby-horse (the ghost of Dionysius). Thus, the great
of the ancient world, the lovers and friends of mythology
and poetry all go one narrow way into the belly of the
modern vulgarian.

The comparison with Marlowe's *Hero and Leander* is
devastating, but probably hoped for. Jonson might well be
thought of as the Marlowe of low life. His major comedies
seem now like antimasques to the Renaissance masque of
the Golden Age—grotesque violations of the exalted vision.

Even as Marlowe dramatized the glamour, the aspirations, and some of the dangers of the Elizabethan Age, so Jonson dramatized the aftermath of the aspirations that were never realized and the glamour that could never be more than ideal. He saw the obscene and ludicrous underside of the great heroes of the past, and thought of Tamburlaine, the world conqueror, as a Sejanus or a Volpone whose kingdom was a bed chamber or a council table. Faustus, who even in Marlowe's hands withered under the burden of his own pride, was never larger to Jonson than a Subtle. Mephistopheles shrank to Face, and Helen of Troy to Dol Common. The vast world of Tamburlaine or Faustus was narrowed down to a London house during the plague or to Smithfield during the Fair. Part of this sense of a falling off from the Golden Age may have come from the seventeenth century belief, shared at times by Jonson, that the age itself had fallen off. His remark in the *Discoveries* about the decay of times after Bacon is a prose statement of one of his favourite themes: 'Now things daily fall: wits grow downe-ward, and *Eloquence* growes back-ward.'[1]

So long as greed and lust remain human vices, *Volpone* and *The Alchemist* will continue to be contemporary. They seem particularly relevant in an age, like the present one, in which life has been turned into what Brooks Adams called 'something resembling a usurer's paradise'.[2] The obtaining of money, always a necessary task, has become, for many, an obsessive pursuit which perverts some of the finer things of life in ways curiously reminiscent of Jonson's legacy hunters and alchemists. Just as Volpone called on the Greek pantheon to seduce a reluctant wife, so modern advertisers indecorously exploit classical mythology in order to sell their products. The great god Mercury has become the

[1] Herford and Simpson, VIII, 591-592.
[2] Henry Adams, *The Degradation of the Democratic Dogma*, intro. by Brook Adams (New York, 1920), VII-VIII.

name of an automobile. Adonis and Atlas have degenerated into trade-names for men with large muscles. Venus, who did not give much thought to garments, is now used to sell brassieres; and Medusa (with more appropriateness) to sell cement. Of course, since we do not think of Venus and Mercury as religious or even as poetic figures, there is less profanation and indecorum in their use by modern advertisers than in their use in Jonson's plays. More serious than such minor indecorum is the perversion of the erotic impulse which can be seen in advertisements where sex is used to increase sales. Immemorially, the sexual attractiveness of a woman has promised companionship, the satisfying of desire, and the creation of children; now it is used in advertisements to titillate sexual desire, apparently in the hope that some transference will be made from the lovely girl to the Packard car. Money and sexual experience, which Jonson brought so close together that money is sexualized and sex commercialized, remain close even in a country like the United States, which supposedly believes in marriage for love. The most attractive heroine, in the mythology of modern society, has long been the heiress; lately she seems to have become the movie star, the modern fairy princess. But always there remains the promise of an extraordinary bliss—love in a mansion with the rich beauty or the boss's daughter. Still more serious is the echo of Face in those manuals of salesmanship which screech—'CAN YOU SELL YOURSELF?' Before you can sell your product, you have to sell yourself. To such modern Faces man no longer has character but 'personality', which can be used to promote sales. The grace of life is no longer unbought: one is courteous and kind because it pays. Most serious of all, perhaps, is the degree to which religion and business have been equated by business men who speak of selling and manufacturing as though they were rituals. If Christ were to be reincarnated today, according to Bruce Barton who professed to know

The Man Nobody Knows, He would be an ad-man, presumably because His parables were the most powerful advertisements of all time. But to Henry Ford the new Messiah is the machine, not the ad-writer. To use religious terms in commercial affairs or commercial terms in religious affairs may be quite innocent, but it makes one suspect that the religion is worldly and business, hypocritical. To all these modern debasements of value Jonson's best plays seem peculiarly related. Like all powerful dramatic symbols, they remain alive or gain new life once they are experienced aesthetically. For this reason, when Sir Herbert J. C. Grierson claims that Jonson 'flew at comparatively small game' in *The Alchemist* and in all his plays wasted his powers on 'pigmies whom at the distance of three centuries we can hardly descry', he seems to ignore the universality of Jonson's comedies.[1] *The Alchemist* is fundamentally concerned with the nature of man; alchemy is only its subject matter. It does not lose meaning now that the atomic scientists have brought about one dream of the alchemists by transmuting non-fissionable 238 into plutonium. It never will lose meaning, even in a golden atomic age, as long as men ludicrously try to get something for nothing.

Jonson's unique vision of life is not a pretty one. His 'transchang'd world' is not one that men would like to live in, although many men do live in a world not much different. The dramatic creation of Volpones and Faces does not answer the yearnings of the human heart as profoundly as the creation of a life of romance and sentiment. It may be just as well that the human heart prefers sentiment. But, as imaginative structures, the worlds of Volpone and Face have as much validity and as much excuse for being as any other literary work. We can image living in those worlds, just as we can imagine living in the worlds of Aristophanes or Swift. None of them is fully satisfying—none of them was

[1] Grierson, *The First Half of the Seventeenth Century* (New York, 1906), 102.

meant to be—but none can be dismissed merely because what it contains horrifies us on metaphysical grounds.

One symbol of Jonson's sense of perverted values in an age that was a lamentable falling off from the Golden Age was his own imprese. It represented a compass, which Jonson in *The Masque of Beautie* called one of the 'known ensignes of *perfection*'. In this masque the allegorical figure 'Perfectio' is described as having 'In her hand a *Compasse* of golde, drawing a *circle*'.[1] But in the imprese—and this is the revealing part—the compass is broken, so that the circle is incapable of completion. The motto '*Deest quod duceret orbem*' was adapted from a passage in Ovid's *Metamorphoses* which goes '*altera pars staret, pars altera duceret orbem*'.[2] For Jonson (and perhaps for any comic writer) one part might stand fixed, but the other part could not describe a circle, for the compass was broken, the circle could never be complete, and perfection was eternally marred here below the moon.

---

[1] *The Masque of Beautie*, 221 n. Herford and Simpson, VII, 188.
[2] *Metamorphoses*, VIII, 249. See Allan Gilbert, *The Symbolic Persons in the Masques of Ben Jonson*, 190, and Herford and Simpson, I, 148.

BIBLIOGRAPHY

Adams, Henry. *The Degradation of the Democratic Dogma*, intro. Brooks Adams. New York: Macmillan and Company, 1920.

Addison, Joseph, and Richard Steele. *The Spectator*, ed. G. G. Smith. New York: E. P. Dutton and Company, 1907.

Allen, Hope Emily. 'Influence of Superstition on Vocabulary: Two Related Examples', *PMLA*, L (1935), 1037 ff.

Aristotle. *The Poetics of Aristotle*, trans. S. H. Butcher. London: Macmillan and Company, 1911.

—— *The Rhetoric of Aristotle*, trans. J. E. C. Welldon. New York: Macmillan and Company, 1886.

Arnold, Matthew. *Civilization in the United States: First and Last Impressions of America*. Boston: Cupples and Hurd, 1889.

Barish, Jonas A. 'The Double Plot in *Volpone*', *Modern Philology*, LI (November 1953), 83-92.

Baudelaire, Charles. *Intimate Journals*, trans. C. Isherwood; intro. T. S. Eliot. London: The Blackmore Press, 1930.

Blackmur, R. P. 'Notes on Four Categories in Criticism', *Sewanee Review*, LIV (Autumn 1946), 576-589.

Boas, Frederick S. *An Introduction to Stuart Drama*. New York: Oxford University Press, 1946.

Bodkin, Maud. *Archetypal Patterns in Poetry: Psychological Studies of Imagination*. London, 1934.

Bradbrook, Muriel C. *The School of Night*. Cambridge: University Press, 1936.

Brinkmann, Friedrich. *Die Metaphern: Studien über den Geist der modernen Sprachen*. Bonn, 1878.

Brooks, Cleanth. *Modern Poetry and the Tradition*. Chapel Hill: University of North Carolina, 1939.

Brown, Stephen J. *The World of Imagery; Metaphor and Kindred Imagery*. London: K. Paul, Trench, Trubner and Co., 1927.

Burke, Kenneth. *Attitudes toward History*. New York: The New Republic, 1937.

—— *A Grammar of Motives*. New York: Prentice Hall, 1945.

—— *The Philosophy of Literary Form*. Baton Rouge: Louisiana State University Press, 1941.

—— *A Rhetoric of Motives*. New York: Prentice Hall, 1950.

Bush, Douglas. *English Literature in the Earlier Seventeenth Century, 1600-1660*. Oxford: Clarendon Press, 1945.

Carpenter, Frederic I. *Metaphor and Simile in the Minor Elizabethan Drama*. Chicago, 1895.

Cassirer, Ernst. *Language and Myth*, trans. Susanne Langer. New York: Harpers, 1946.

Castelain, Maurice. *Ben Jonson, L'Homme et L'Œuvre*. Paris: Librarie Hachette, 1907.

Chew, Samuel C. *The Virtues Reconciled: an Iconographical Study*. Toronto: University of Toronto Press, 1947.

Coffman, George R., ed. *Studies in Language and Literature*. Chapel Hill, North Carolina: University of North Carolina Press, 1945.

Coleridge, S. T. *Biographia Literaria*, ed. J. Shawcross. New York: Oxford University Press, 1907.

—— *Coleridge's Miscellaneous Criticism*, ed. T. M. Raysor. London, 1936.

—— *Coleridge's Shakespearean Criticism*, ed. T. M. Raysor. Cambridge: Harvard University Press, 1930.

—— *The Literary Remains of Samuel Taylor Coleridge*, ed. H. N. Coleridge, London, 1837.

Crane, R. S., ed. *Critics and Criticism*. Chicago: University of Chicago Press, 1952.

Dante. *Dante's Convivio*, trans. W. W. Jackson. Oxford: Clarendon Press, 1909.

Day-Lewis, Cecil. *The Poetic Image*. London: J. Cape, 1947.

Dekker, Thomas. *The Non-Dramatic Works of Thomas Dekker*, ed. A. B. Grosart. London: The Huth Library, 1885.

Dobrée, Bonamy. *Restoration Comedy, 1660-1720*. Oxford: Clarendon Press, 1924.

Dryden, John. *The Best of Dryden*, ed. Louis Bredvold. New York: Ronald Press, 1946.

—— *The Essays of John Dryden*, ed. W. P. Ker. Oxford: Clarendon Press, 1900.

—— *The Works of John Dryden*, ed. Scott and Saintsbury. Edinburgh, 1884.

Duncan, Edgar H. 'Jonson's *Alchemist* and the Literature of Alchemy', *PMLA*, LXI (September 1946), 699-710.

Earle, John. *Micro-cosmography*, ed. Philip Bliss. London, 1811.

Eliot, T. S. *Selected Essays, 1917-1932*. New York, 1932.
—— *The Use of Poetry and the Use of Criticism*. Cambridge: Harvard University Press, 1933.

Ellis-Fermor, Una. *The Frontiers of Drama*. London: Methuen and Company, 1946.

Fielding, Henry. *The Works of Henry Fielding*, ed. G. H. Maynadier. New York: The Jenson Society, 1907.

Florio, John. *Queen Anna's new World of Words, or Dictionarie of the Italian and English Tongues*. London, 1611.

Gay, John. *The Poetical Works of John Gay*, ed. G. C. Faber. London: Oxford University Press, 1926.

Gibbon, Edward. *The History of the Decline and Fall of the Roman Empire*, ed. J. B. Bury. London: Methuen and Company, 1902.

Gilbert, Allan H. *The Symbolic Persons in the Masques of Ben Jonson*. Durham, North Carolina: Duke University Press, 1948.

Gordon, D. J. 'The Imagery of Ben Jonson's *The Masque of Blacknesse* and *The Masque of Beauty*', *Journal of the Warburg and Courtlauld Institutes*, VI (1943), 122-141.

Greene, Robert. *The Life and Complete Works in Prose and Verse of Robert Greene*, ed. A. B. Grosart. London: The Huth Library, 1881-1886.

Grierson, Sir Herbert J. C. *The First Half of the Seventeenth Century*. New York: Charles Scribner's Sons, 1906.

Grose, Francis. *A Classical Dictionary of the Vulgar Tongue*. London, 1785.

Hebel, J. W., and Hoyt H. Hudson, ed. *Poetry of the English Renaissance, 1509-1660*. New York: F. S. Crofts and Company, 1938.

Hinze, Otto. *Studien zu Ben Jonsons Namengebung in seinen Dramen*. Dresden, 1919.

Hornstein, Lillian H. 'Analysis of Imagery: a Critique of Literary Method', *PMLA*, LVII (1942), 638-653.

Howell, James. *The Familiar Letters of James Howell*, ed. Joseph Jacobs. London, 1892.

Huguet, Edmond. *Le Langage Figuré an Seizième Siècle*. Paris: 1933.

Hyman, Stanley Edgar. *The Armed Vision*. New York: Alfred A. Knopf, 1948.

Johnston, George Burke. *Ben Jonson: Poet*. New York: Columbia University Press, 1945.

Jonson, Ben. *The Alchemist*, ed. Charles Hathaway. Yale Studies in English, XVII. New York: Henry Holt, 1903.

—— *Ben Jonson*, ed. C. H. Herford and Percy and Evelyn Simpson. Oxford: Clarendon Press, 1925-1952.

—— *Ben Jonson: Selected Works*. New York: Random House, 1938.

—— *The Magnetic Lady*, ed. Harvey W. Peck. Yale Studies in English, XLVII. New York: Henry Holt, 1914.

—— *The New Inn*, ed. George Tennant. Yale Studies in English, XXIV. New York: Henry Holt, 1908.

—— *The Staple of News*, ed. De Winter. Yale Studies in English, XXVIII. New York: Henry Holt, 1905.

—— *Volpone*, ed. J. D. Rea. Yale Studies in English, LIX. New Haven: Yale University Press, 1919.

—— *The Works of Ben Jonson*, ed. Gifford and Cunningham. London: Bickers and Son, 1875.

King, Arthur H. *The Language of Satirized Characters in Poetaster: a Socio-stylistic Analysis, 1597-1602*. Lund Studies in English. London: Williams and Norgate, 1941.

Knights, L. C. *Drama and Society in the Age of Jonson*. London: Chatto and Windus, 1937.

Konrad, Hedwig. *Étude sur la metaphore*. Paris, 1939.

Lamb, Charles. *The Works of Charles and Mary Lamb*, ed. E. V. Lucas. New York: G. P. Putnam's Sons, 1904.

Lawson, John C. *Modern Greek Folklore and Ancient Greek Religion*. Cambridge: Cambridge University Press, 1910.

Leavis, F. R. 'Imagery and Movement: Notes in the Analysis of Poetry', *Scrutiny*, XIII (September 1945), 118 ff.

Lectures in Criticism, the John Hopkins University. Bollingen Series, XVI. New York: Pantheon Books, 1949.

Levin, Harry. 'Jonson's Metempsychosis', *Philological Quarterly*, XXII (July 1943), 231-239.

Lodge, Thomas. *The Complete Works of Thomas Lodge*. Glasgow: for the Hunterian Club, 1883.

[Longinus]. *On the Sublime*, ed. W. Rhys Roberts. Cambridge: Cambridge University Press, 1935.

Lucian. *The Works of Lucian*, trans. A. M. Harmon. New York: Macmillan and Company, 1915.

Lucretius. *De Rerum Natura*, ed. Cyril Bailey. Oxford: Clarendon Press, 1941.

McManaway, J. G., Giles E. Dawson, and E. E. Willoughby. *J. Q. Adams Memorial Studies*. Washington: The Folger Shakespeare Library, 1948.

Morris, Corbyn. *An Essay towards Fixing the True Standards of Wit, Humour, Raillery, Satire, and Ridicule* (1744). Augustan Reprint Society, Ser. 1: Essays on Wit, no. 4. Los Angeles, 1947.

Morris, Elisabeth Woodbridge. *Studies in Jonson's Comedy*. New York: Lamson Wolffe and Company, 1898.

Müller, Max. *Lectures on the Science of Language*. Second Series. New York: 1875.

Munson, Gorham B. *Robert Frost: a Study of Sensibility and Good Sense*. New York: George H. Doran Company, 1927.

Murray, Gilbert. *A History of Ancient Greek Literature*. New York: D. Appleton and Company, 1912.

Murry, J. M. *Countries of the Mind, Second Series*. London: Oxford University Press, 1931.

Nashe, Thomas. *The Works of Thomas Nashe*, ed. R. B. McKerrow. London, 1910.

Nason, Arthur H. *Heralds and Heraldry in Ben Jonson's Plays, Masques, and Entertainments*. New York, 1907.

New English Dictionary on Historical Principles, A, ed. James A. H. Murray, Henry Bradley, William Craigie, and C. T. Onions. Oxford: Clarendon Press, 1888-1933.

Nicholson, Brinsley. *Notes and Queries*, 76:385 (November 12, 1887).

Noyes, Robert G. '*Volpone or, The Fox*—The Evolution of a Nickname', *Harvard Studies and Notes in Philology and Literature*, vol. XVI. Cambridge: Harvard University Press, 1934.

Nun's Rule, The, trans. James Morton. London, 1905.

Parker, M. Hope. *Language and Reality: a Course in Contemporary Criticism*. London: Frederick Muller, 1949.

Partridge, Eric. *A Dictionary of Slang and Unconventional English*. London: Routledge and Kegan Paul Ltd., 1949.

—— *Shakespeare's Bawdy*. New York: E. P. Dutton and Company, 1948.

Pepys, Samuel. *Diary and Correspondence of Samuel Pepys*, ed. Lord Braybrooke. Philadelphia: David McKay, 1889.

Puttenham, George. *The Arte of English Poesie*, ed. Gladys Willcock and Alice Walker. Cambridge: University Press, 1936.

Quintilian. *Institutio Oratoria*, with a translation by H. E. Butler. New York: G. P. Putnam's Sons, 1921.

Read, Allen Walker. 'An Obscenity Symbol', *American Speech*, IX (December 1934), 264 ff.

Richards, I. A. *Coleridge on Imagination*. New York: Harcourt Brace, 1935.

—— *The Philosophy of Rhetoric*. New York: Oxford University Press, 1936.

—— *Practical Criticism*. New York: Harcourt Brace, 1939.

—— *The Principles of Literary Criticism*. New York: Harcourt Brace, 1938.

Sackton, Alexander. *Rhetoric as a Dramatic Language in Ben Jonson*. New York: Columbia University Press, 1948.

Shakespeare's England. Oxford: Clarendon Press, 1950.

Spurgeon, Caroline. *Shakespeare's Imagery and What It Tells Us*. Cambridge, 1935.

Stern, Gustaf. *Meaning and Change of Meaning*. Goteborge Hogskolas Arsekrift, vol. XXXVIII, 1932.

Stevens, Wallace. *Three Academic Pieces*. Cummington, Massachusetts, 1947.

Stubbes, Phillip. *Anatomy of the Abuses in England in Shakespeare's Youth*, ed. F. J. Furnivall. New Shakespeare Society, Series VI, no. 6. London, 1879.

Swinburne, A. C. *A Study of Ben Jonson*. New York, 1889.

Symonds, J. A. *Ben Jonson*. London, 1886.

Talbert, Ernest W. 'Current Scholarly Works and the Erudition of Jonson's *Masque of Augurs*', *Studies in Philology*, XLIV (1947), 605-624.

—— 'New Light on Ben Jonson's Workmanship', *Studies in Philology*, XL (1943), 154-185.

Tate, Allen, ed. *The Language of Poetry*. Princeton: Princeton University Press, 1942.

Tawney, R. H. *Religion and the Rise of Capitalism*. New York: Penguin Books, 1947.

Tillyard, E. M. W. *Poetry Direct and Oblique*. London: Chatto and Windus, 1934.

The Times, November 19, 1924.

Tuve, Rosemond. *Elizabethan and Metaphysical Imagery: Renaissance Poetic and Twentieth Century Critics.* Chicago: University of Chicago Press, 1947.

—— 'Imagery and Logic: Ramus and Metaphysical Poetics', *Journal of the History of Ideas*, III (1942), 365-400.

Vico, Giambattista. *The New Science*, trans. T. G. Bergin and M. H. Fisch. Ithaca, New York: Cornell University Press, 1948.

Ward, A. W. *A History of English Dramatic Literature.* New York: Macmillan and Company, 1899.

Wells, Henry W. *Poetic Imagery.* New York: Columbia University Press, 1924.

—— 'Ben Jonson: Patriarch of Speech Study', *Shakespeare Association Bulletin*, XIII (January 1938), 54 ff.

Weston, Jessie. *Chief Middle English Poets.* New York: Houghton Mifflin, 1914.

Wheelwright, Philip. *The Burning Fountain: a Study in the Language of Symbolism.* Bloomington, Indiana: Indiana University Press, 1954.

Wilson, Edmund, ed. *The Shock of Recognition.* New York: Doubleday Doran and Company, 1943.

—— *The Triple Thinkers.* New York: Oxford University Press, 1948.

Wilson, F. P. *Elizabethan and Jacobean.* Oxford: Clarendon Press, 1945.

—— *The Plague in Shakespeare's London.* Oxford: Clarendon Press, 1927.

INDEX

249

INDEX

Ogden, C. K., 34
Old Wives' Tale, The, 169
Olson, Elder, 10, 22, 29, 37
On the Sublime [Longinus], 25, 41
Ovid, 95, 239

Paracelsus, 128
Parker, M. Hope, 23
Partridge, Eric, 125 n., 143 n., 147 n.
Paul, Saint, 110
Paul's Walk, 216
Peck, Harvey W., 206
Perspective, comic, 225
Petronius, 95
Philosophy of Literary Criticism, The, 46
Philosophy of Rhetoric, The, 31, 39, 43-4
Physiologus, 82
Pierce Penilesse, 215
Poe, Edgar Allan, 225-6
Poetic Image, The, 14, 24, 39
Poetic Imagery, 32
Pongs, Hermann, 30
Pope, Alexander, 228
Pound, Ezra, 227
Practical Criticism, 31-2
Praz, Mario, 15 n.
Predicaments, Aristotelian, 27, 33
Puttenham, George, 20, 28, 52-4, 122, 155
Pythagoras, 78-9

Quintilian, 19, 29, 50 n., 58, 62

Randolph, Thomas, 178

Rea, J. D., 105 n.
Read, Allen Walker, 147 n., 202
Religion and the Rise of Capitalism, 110
Rhetorica ad C. Herennium, 21 n.
Richards, I. A., 20, 22, 29, 31-5, 37, 39, 41, 43-6, 48
Roman de la Rose, 179 n.

Sackton, Alexander, 77, 130, 161, 198
Scot, Reginald, 136 n.
Semanticists, 12
Seneca, Marcus, 56
Sexual deviation, comedy of, 162-70, 202-4
Sexual instinct, perversion of, 99-102
Sexualizing of money, 99-102, 134-48, 179-89
Shakespeare, 10, 15, 16, 17, 30, 58, 60, 213, 218, 222, 224; *Coriolanus*, 164; *Hamlet*, 10, 33, 39-40, 215; *Henry IV, Part I*, 141; *Henry IV, Part II*, 22, 202-3; *King Lear*, 17, 33, 44, 47, 71, 81, 84, 229; *Macbeth*, 10, 12; *A Midsummer Night's Dream*, 169; *Othello*, 229; *Timon of Athens*, 11; *Twelfth Night*, 47, 169; *The Winter's Tale*, 43, 46-47, 164, 221
Shaw, G. B., 233
Sidney, Sir Philip, 228
Simpson, Percy, 10, 57, 108, 130, 164
Sisson, C. J., 217

253